Between Rhetoric and Reality: The State and Use of Indigenous Knowledge in Post-Colonial Africa

Edited by

Munyaradzi Mawere

& Samuel Awuah-Nyamekye

Langaa Research & Publishing CIG
Mankon, Bamenda

Publisher

Langaa RPCIG

Langaa Research & Publishing Common Initiative Group
P.O. Box 902 Mankon
Bamenda
North West Region
Cameroon
Langaagrp@gmail.com
www.langaa-rpcig.net

Distributed in and outside N. America by African Books Collective
orders@africanbookscollective.com
www.africanbookscollective.com

ISBN: *9956-792-69-1*

Dedication

This book is dedicated to the spirit of Walter Rodney, the author of an infamous book: "How Europe underdeveloped Africa," who was an Afrocentric scholar whose life was devoted to the total liberation and holistic development of Africa and the African people

List of Contributors

Munyaradzi Mawere holds a PhD in Social Anthropology from the University of Cape Town in South Africa. Dr Mawere also holds a Master's Degree in Philosophy and B.A (Hons) Degree in Philosophy from the University of Zimbabwe. He is currently an Associate Professor in the Department of Social Anthropology at Universidade Pedagogica-Gaza, Mozambique where he has also worked in different capacities as a Senior lecturer, Assistant Research Director, and Postgraduate Co-ordinator. Before joining this University, Dr Mawere was Philosophy lecturer at the University of Zimbabwe. He has an outstanding publishing record of more than eighty publications which include more than twenty books and over sixty book chapters and papers in internationally accredited scholarly journals. His research interests include, but not limited to, knowledge studies, environmental conservation, African studies, post-coloniality, culture and heritage studies.

Samuel Awuah-Nyamekye is a Senior Lecturer in the Department of Religion and Human Values at the University of Cape Coast in Ghana, where he also received his MPhil, BA, and Diploma of Education. Awuah-Nyamekye holds a PhD from the School of Philosophy, Religion and the History of Science of the University of Leeds in the United Kingdom. Awuah-Nyamekye also has a certificate in HIV/AIDS Counselling and Care Giving from the University of Ghana. He is a member of the Association for the Study of Literature and Environment (ASLE) and the International Society for Environmental Ethics (ISEE) Representative for Ghana. His current research interests are focussed on religion and the environment, environmental ethics, religion and development, religion and politics, and women and religion. Awuah-Nyamekye has written and published two books, and has authored several articles in internationally esteemed scholarly journals. Awuah-Nyamekye has presented papers at several international conferences.

Kwame Osei Kwarteng holds a PhD in African Studies (History) from the University of Birmingham, and an M.Phil. (History), Bachelor of Arts (Hons) and Diploma in Education from the University of Cape Coast, Ghana. He is also an Associate Professor and the Head of the Department of History, University of Cape Coast. He has published 5 books, three of which were co–authored with other colleagues. Dr Kwarteng has published several articles in refereed journals. His research interests include: Ahafo, Institutional History, Environmental Studies, African Elephant, Colonial and Post–Independent History. Currently, he is working on Kwame Nkrumah and Political Opposition in Ghana from 1947 to 1957.

Hezekiah Olufemi Adeosun holds a Ph.D. in Yoruba Literature from the University of Ilorin, Ilorin, Nigeria. He is Senior Lecturer in the Department of Linguistics and Nigerian Languages, University of Ilorin. Dr. Adeosun has many article publications to his credit both locally and internationally. He is the author of "Socio-semiotic Theory and Practice in Yoruba Written Poetry" and "Gender Discourse in Yoruba Written Poetry: A Socio-semiotic Analysis" published by Lambert publishers. Adeosun's research interests include Yoruba Literature, Cultural Studies and Socio-semiotics.

Artwell Nhemachena holds a Ph.D. from the University of Cape Town, South Africa. He also holds an MSc and BSc Honours Degree from the University of Zimbabwe where he lectured briefly before joining the University of Cape Town for Doctoral studies. Artwell Nhemachena is a Laureate of the Democratic Governance Institute of the Council for the Development of Social Science research in Africa (CODESRIA) in which he has been participating since 2010. His research interests include Politics and governance, environment, indigenous knowledge and science, human security and food security, anthropological jurisprudence, personhood, land issues, human rights. He has published a number of papers including in the areas of governance, knowledge/epistemology and environment.

Pius Oyeniran Abioje holds a PhD in Theology from the University of Calabar, Nigeria. He is Senior Lecturer in the Department of Religions, University of Ilorin, Nigeria. Before joining this University, Dr Abioje was lecturer at the SS Peter and Paul Catholic Major Seminary, Bodija, Ibadan. He has more than twenty journal articles; ten chapters in books, and author of a book. His research interests include, but not limited to, Afro-Christian studies.

Elias Asiama is currently at the School of Performing Arts, University of Ghana, Legon and lectures in Theatre for Development, Popular Theatre Laboratory, Popular Theatre Workshop, Drama in African Societies to mention a few. Elias served as a Research Assistant at the School of Performing Arts, University of Ghana, Legon, from 1984- 1986. Elias holds a Diploma in Theatre Arts, Diploma in Theology, B.A. (Hons) in Drama and Religion and M.Phil. /Ph.D. in Theatre for Development from Southampton University (King Alfred's College) in the United Kingdom. He is married to Francisca Sika-Asiama, with three children: Ernest, William and Lilian Asiama. Elias has served on International Research Organizations in various capacities including: being one of the principal investigators on Climate Change for Penn State University, Dar Es Saalam University, Tanzania etc. Elias Asiama's main focus has over the years been the recovery of African cultural heritage for the promotion of development on the continent and beyond. Theatre in Evangelism and Christian Mission is an area of interest within which the researcher has carefully devised plays and sketches for the Presbyterian Church of Ghana.

Blessing Makunike holds a PhD in Africa Studies from the University of the Free State in South Africa. He is the Director for Quality Assurance at the University of Zimbabwe. He has also worked as a part-time lecturer in the Department of Political and Administrative Studies at the University of Zimbabwe. His research interests include land reform, poverty alleviation, rural development, and indigenous knowledge systems.

Liveson Tatira holds a PhD from the University of Zimbabwe and another PhD from Atlantic International University. He is a Senior lecturer in the Department of Curriculum and Arts Education, University of Zimbabwe and is the current chairperson of the Department. He has taught in the same department for eighteen years and has extensively published in books and international journals.

Martin Quephie Amlor, a senior lecturer at the Centre for African and International Studies, University of Cape Coast, holds a PhD in Music (Ethnomusicology) from the University of Cape Coast, Ghana and an M.Phil. (African Studies) Degree from the University of Ghana, Legon. He has to his credit, many published articles in International referred journals. Besides being a composer, his research interests include music in African cultures as well as liturgical music of African Christian and Syncretic Churches in Ghana.

Andile Mayekiso is currently completing his PhD in Social Anthropology at the University of Cape Town (UCT). His interest is on fatherhood and children, particularly the nature of these relationships in post-apartheid South Africa. He has conducted ethnographic research on children born to HIV positive parents in South Africa, has worked with Masibambane NGO and was at one time appointed as a mentor to first year students and a research assistant in Sociology Department at Rhodes University. He has published a number of papers in scholarly journal.

Christopher M. Mabeza is completing his PhD in the Department of Social Anthropology at the University of Cape Town, South Africa. He has published on adaptation to climate by rural communities in Zimbabwe and also co – authored the book – *Memoirs of an Unsung Legend, Nemeso.* He has done consultancy work on climate change awareness for the Government of Zimbabwe that was funded by the United Nations Environment Programme.

Table of Contents

Chapter 1

Rethinking African Indigenous Knowledges and World Civilisations: Pasts, presents and the Futures

Munyaradzi Mawere

Introduction

Traditionally, the people of Africa used a plethora of traditional 'scientific' knowledges and 'technologies' to sustain their respective societies and promote political, socio-economic development. With the advent of colonialism and its enlightenment science (heretofore referred to as modern science), African traditional scientific knowledges and technologies (heretofore referred to as indigenous knowledge) bequeathed from their forefathers were despised, labelled as irrational, void of logical thought, unscientific and anti-development such that their users were either discouraged or forbidden from using them. Instead, modern science and technologies were either encouraged or imposed on the indigenous peoples of Africa. This stance of not even accepting African science and technology with questions by the colonial governments in many parts of Africa had far-reaching consequences and lasting impact on the socio-economic development of the African continent. As Nancy Jacobs (2006: 564) aptly puts it: "We now recognise that colonial science was a highly political enterprise ... It has been observed that the failure of *colonial* science to heed indigenous knowledge led to a 'misreading' of the landscape and inappropriate intervention" (cf. Fairhead and Leach 1996). This introductory chapter introduces the reader to the inexorably complex issues around world civilisations and different African knowledges and technologies as they were traditionally used (and some still used) in many parts of the continent. The chapter goes further to discuss works by different contributors in this impeccable volume, who generally agree that the advent of colonialism and modern science which rubbished African science derailed the scientific and socio-economic development of the African continent and, in many ways, distorted the nature and direction to which the continent's scientific and technological developments were meant to take.

Background to Africa, world civilisations, and knowledge development

There is phenomenal growth in scholarship that examines the concept of indigenous knowledge. However, this has not resolved the current impasse in the methodological praxis of the concept at the global policy arena that has been in existence for the past three decades or so. Moreover, little has been done to measure-up efforts by previously colonised governments especially those in Africa to determine their efforts to universalise or at least to have their indigenous knowledges acknowledged and accorded the same status as Western science. This is in spite of the fact that indigenous knowledge and technology (or what I loosely call African science) has always been pervasive in the African milieu with their basic function and purpose hijacked in the 15th century with the advent of European settlers whose influence reached its climax in the early 20th century. By indigenous knowledge, I mean that knowledge form which, unlike Western science, is rooted in particular long-settled cultures or communities that are geographically traceable and with strong gen and relationships with their physical environments. Under the influence of slavery, the forerunner of the most pernicious process of colonialism and enlightenment science, indigenous knowledges and technologies in the so-called 'primitive societies' (at least in the eyes and language of the Western imperialists) were aggressively despised, labelled as irrational, primitive, unscientific and illegitimate. This pejorative labelling, discrediting and determination to eradicate African science and technology [as well as all other such values] were done both due to lack of understanding of the African science, technologies and cosmologies by Eurocentric 'all-knowing academics' and the envious Westerners [in general] who feared competition from the local practitioners. Unfortunately, the dominance of Western science continues to grow against the backdrop that the intergovernmental policy arena faces substantial impasse on what

2

constitutes acceptable knowledge and why one form of knowledge [Western science] is used as a yardstick to measure the validity of other knowledge forms such as African science. As Semali and Kincheloe (1999: 21) aptly note, "the process of Europeanisation with its colonialistic perspectives toward indigenous knowledge *especially those from Africa* continues to operate despite both insightful and misguided attempts to thwart it". I should, therefore, underline that the disadvantaging of indigenous knowledge forms and technologies in Africa did not end with the demise of colonial administration on the continent. Even today, in the face of a virtually explosion of interest and increasing attention, at global level, in the deployment of indigenous knowledge forms, practices, and technologies (see for example, World Bank Report, 1992) over the past three decades or so, the African science and technology remain in the back seat position, either unrecognised or despised, in many societies across the world. This has always had far-reaching effects on the African societies where indeed "curricular reforms based on the analysis of indigenous knowledge require that educators become hermeneutists (scholars and teachers who structure their work and teaching around an effort to help students and individuals to make sense of the world around them) and epistemologists (scholars and teachers who seek to expose how accepted knowledge came to be validated)" (Semali and Kincheloe 1999: 37).

The radical change of the African curricular by Euro-centric scholars who never dared to promote the idea that educators become hermeneutists and epistemologists on their own rights, instilled in the minds of many Africans falsehoods that Africa was void of any scientific and technological advancement. This has been thought so, especially by many Euro-centric scholars on the continent and elsewhere, despite the notable outstanding achievements of the African ancestors which include but not limited to the welfarist nature of the extended family system across the African continent (Bernheims 1968:13-14), the checks and balance system of African governance (Fadipe 1991:198-242), advanced environmental conservation epistemologies (Mawere 2014a), economic integration and governance in Africa (Olopoenia 1994:81-83), and what George James (1954) and later Iwara (1994) refer to as the "stolen legacy" – critical philosophies – of and from the African continent. In his book: *Stolen legacy: The Greeks were not the authors of Greek philosophy, but the people of North Africa* (1954), James, for example, argued that Greek philosophy originated in ancient Egypt as Greek philosophy was mainly based on ideas and concepts that were borrowed without acknowledgement, or indeed stolen from the ancient Egyptians and other people of Africa. It is reported that James died shortly after the publication of his *Stolen legacy*, which makes his death suspicious. James rightfully notes:

The teachings of the Egyptian mysteries reached other lands many centuries before it reached Athens. According to history, Pythagoras after receiving his training in Egypt, returned to his native island, Samos, where he established his order for a short time, after which he migrated to Croton (540 B.C.) in Southern Italy, where his order grew to enormous proportions, until his final expulsion from that country. We are also told that Thales (640 B.C) received his education in Egypt, and his associates: Anaximander, and Anaximenes, were natives of Ionia in Asia Minor, which was a stronghold of the Egyptian Mystery Schools, which they carried on ... Similarly, we are told that Xenophanes (576 B.C.), Parmenides, Zeno and Melissus were also natives of Ionia and that they migrated to Elea in Italy and established themselves and spread the teachings of Mysteries ... In like manner we are informed that Heraclitus (530 B.C.), Empedocles, Anaxagoras and Democritus were also natives of Ionia who were interested in physics. Hence in tracing the course of the so-called Greek philosophy, we find that Ionian students after obtaining their education from the Egyptian priests returned to their native land, while some migrated to different parts of Italy, where they established themselves (p. 10).

Iwara (1994: 51), following George James avers: "the history of Africa is full of examples of deliberate falsification and plundering of the continent's works of art in their various forms, such as bronze, wooden and stone images". This revelation is germane to The Bernheims (1968. 51) who note with concern that:

Metal, stone, and terracotta objects have been found, the oldest being terracotta heads of the Nok culture, estimated to date from 900 B.C. to 200 A.D. Bronze, ivory, and terracotta pieces belonging to the Ife and Benin cultures of Southern Nigeria and dating back to the thirteenth century A.D., are among the most precious in African art. The first pieces were brought to England in 1897 and bought up by German and British museums ... Today the great African collections are at the Musée de l'Homme in Paris, the British Museum in London, the Museum of Primitive Art in New York City, and the University Museum in Philadelphia (cf. Abioje, this volume).

The point of interest to note here is that Africa contributed immensely and in original terms to the Western and indeed the world civilisations. However, given the colonial nature of education imposed on Africa especially during the colonial era (and which continue being fostered in many parts of the continent), there is need to decolonise the minds of many of the African people and foster deep-seated cultural democracy and critical and independent thinking. As Donaldo Macedo (1999: xv) aptly puts it:

> It is only through the decolonisation of our minds, if not our hearts, that we can begin to develop the necessary political clarity to reject the enslavement of a colonial discourse that creates a false dichotomy between Western and indigenous knowledge. It is through the decolonisation of our minds and development of political clarity that we cease to embrace the notion of Western versus indigenous knowledge, so as to begin to speak of human knowledge.

What Macedo argues here, should not be taken lightly as it emphasises the fact that Western science remains an instrument of colonialism (Levine 1996; Sponsel 1992) and a perpetuation of the colonial vestige of subjugation. Also, Macedo's argument weighs most given that many other forms of knowledge (as is the case of African science) have been subjugated by the Western science to the extent that the former are rarely recognised at least formally. This realisation necessitates full understanding of our colonial legacy, as Africans, to enable us to reconnect with our historical past and illuminate our precarious present historical moment as Renato Constantino (1978: 1) aptly suggests:

We see our present with as little understanding as we view our past because aspects of the past which could illuminate the present have been concealed from us. The concealment has been effected by a systematic process of miseducation characterised by a thoroughgoing inculcation of colonial values and attitudes – a process which could not have been so effective had we not been denied access to the truth and to be part of our written history. We accept the present as given, bereft of history. Because we have so little comprehension of our past, we have no appreciation of its meaningful interrelation with the present.

On the part of Africa as a continent, I underscore that the true history of the continent, particularly in relation to indigenous knowledge, has been concealed for too long from the world and in particular sons and daughters of Africa. Yet, the advancement of architecture, iron smelting, ecological/environmental conservation knowledge, political, and "African art" and other such ways of knowing is widely known and cannot be underestimated; neither should they be dissociated from African science and technology. This is because, as Hawthorne (1986: 15) notes, there is a thin line between the two fields of human knowledge namely science and technology. In fact Hawthorne (Ibid) convincingly explains that "the word 'science' comes from the Latin word for knowledge", even though "nowadays it means the study of nature, natural science", with a method which "relies on observation and experiment." Furthermore, Hawthorne (Ibid, emphasis original) explains that more often than not, "something akin to the inspiration of an artist *namely technological knowledge* may help the scientist to make sense of his/her observations." Basing on this understanding, Hawthorne warns us to remember that it is inappropriate to try to separate, methodically, African "metal, stone, terracotta, bronze, and ivory objects" from scientific observation and manipulation of nature given the flow, continuity and thin line that exist between them.

From the foregoing discussion, there is no doubt, as history tells us, that Greek civilisations and indeed Western civilisations in general, are a stolen legacy from the people of Africa. Stolen in the sense that the West have used and even developed the African sciences and technologies for their own benefit without even acknowledging their sources where they really originated. No wonder, as James argues, in 399 B.C. Socrates was sentenced to death and subsequently caused Plato and Aristotle to flee for their lives from Athens: It was in fact because philosophy was something foreign and unknown to the Greek world, a unique phenomenon from Africa that had found entrance in Greece. For this same reason, we would definitely expect either the Ionians or the Italians exerting their prior claim to philosophy, since it made contact with the Athenians, who were always its greatest enemies and persecutors (and persistently treated it as a foreign innovation) until Alexander the Great's conquest of Egypt which provided for Aristotle free and total access to the Royal Library of Alexander and Museum together with the Temples and other libraries. Most if not all of the philosophical ideas accredited to Aristotle, thus, were looted during the invasion, and were written or presented without acknowledgement of their sources. On the same note, operating on the pretext that philosophy or an idea understood to be alien to the Western milieus, was considered during the time to be a potential threat to human existence, societal peace and harmony, we expect many other subsequent philosophers (or revolutionaries rather) claiming even those ideas they would have heard elsewhere to be originally theirs as long as they were not known to have been recorded. As further argued by James (1954: 11), the Ionians and Italians made no attempt to claim the authorship of philosophy because they were well aware that the Egyptians were the true authors. On the other hand, argues James, after the death of Aristotle, his Athenian pupils, without the authority of the state, undertook to compile a history of philosophy recognised at the time as the Sophia or Wisdom of the Egyptians, which had become current and traditional in the ancient world, which compilation, because it was produced by pupils who had belonged to Aristotle's (who himself was Greek) school, later history has erroneously called Greek philosophy. It should be underlined that this deliberate and false naming of the African works was Aristotle's plan executed by his school to divert the African legacy from its real people and as a way to honour himself (Aristotle) and his country of origin

(Greece). James pushes his argument further to ask us to remember that at this remote period of the Greek history (i.e. Thales to Aristotle 640 B.C. – 322 B.C.) the Ionians were not Greek citizens, but Egyptian subjects and later Persian subjects. In fact when the Persians, through Cambyses, conquered the Egyptians in 525 B.C., they set immigration restrictions against the Greeks and threw Egypt open to Greek research (see James, 1954: 41; cf. Herodotus Book 11: 113).

Although it is a well-known fact even among the Western societies, that Africa is richly endowed with various knowledge forms that span across the realms of health, environment, philosophy, education, ecology, agriculture, business and medicine, among others, the value of such knowledges is only beginning to be widely recognised by European and American peoples now in the twenty-first century. Yet, I should emphasise that the European and American valuing of African indigenous knowledges emerge not from their value per se but first, from the indubitable recognition of their monetary value in the global market. This is true given the fact that only a few centuries ago, before this realisation was made, European scholars entered into a great movement of discrediting, rubbishing and even eradicating African indigenous knowledges from the scene. Second, the recognition of African indigenous knowledge comes to the fore out of necessary epistemological contingency which challenge the universality of Western science. As Semali and Kincheloe (1999: 17) argue:

> Universality cannot escape unscathed in its encounter with socio-cultural, epistemological particularity, just as Newtonian physics could not survive the Einsternian understanding of the power of different frames of reference. In these anti-foundational (a rejection of a transcultural referent for truth such as the Western scientific method) dynamics the hell of relativism is avoided by an understanding of culturally-specific discursive practices.

A guide through the book

As has already been alluded to, this book examines the state and deployment of indigenous knowledge in post-colonial Africa, but with special reference given to four countries namely Ghana, Nigeria, South Africa, and Zimbabwe. While the different chapters that constitute this volume were researched and developed under specific and unique contexts, they rally with determination behind the same point and advance a subtly quasi-similar argument, that which pertains to the need for deployment in the main stream and recognition of [African] indigenous knowledge forms and pluralism in knowledge production. The world today is increasing becoming vulnerable to uncertainties and natural disasters prompted by changing climatic environment. Chapter 2 by Munyaradzi Mawere, for example, explores different ways through which indigenous knowledge was in the past used (and continue to be used today) by some communities in Zimbabwe to predict early warning indicators of impending disaster that is life and environmentally threatening, and prepare for circumstances ahead of time. He notes that 'the knowledge that Africans possessed, and is still possessed by some, served to facilitate the communities in Zimbabwe to sustainably manage their environments, establish early warning indicators, predict and prepare for oncoming disaster(s), respond to disaster(s) and mitigate in a way that make the disaster(s) less severe, that is, for disaster risk management'. Mawere's chapter is not only theoretical but also practical. It does not only make an argument for indigenous knowledge for disaster risk management, but goes further to enumerate some of the *concrete* showcases, based on his findings from fieldwork.

While Mawere explores indigenous knowledge for disaster risk management, it is noted in this book that Western science's research endeavours often emphasised the experimental adventures of their practitioners, their cogitative capacity including the deployment of the scientists' perceptions on how they viewed other knowledge forms, especially those from contexts such as Africa. Mindful of this observation, Pius Oyeniran Abioje's chapter 3 raises the critical but provocative question on whether traditional Africans had scientific and technological knowledge or not, a question that has engaged the attention of many scholars since the colonial era in Africa. Critically following episodes of interactions between African Traditional Religion (ATR), Christianity, and Islam in Nigeria, Abioje records the historic ascendance of Islam and Christianity over African Traditional Religion and culture. He notes that 'the three foreign religious forces: Islam, colonialism, and Christianity have been out, for the most part, to upstage traditional African civilisation, through both subtle and violent means'. He aptly notes that the subtle means deployed by Islamic and Christian fundamentalists, purveyors of colonialism and merchants, included trade interactions with ancient Africans while the violent means featured in the form of Muslim *jihad* such as by Usman Dan Fodio in northern Nigeria in 1804 and other such sadisms currently being deployed against some adherents of ATR by some Christians and Muslims in Nigeria. For Abioje, all these tactics were (and are) meant to eradicate traditional African civilisation as was always the case since the colonial era in Africa. In view of all these realisations, Abioje calls for tolerance in diversity in all spheres of life including religion, culture, and knowledge generation and advancement.

Drawing on his wealth of data gathered during fieldwork in Zimbabwe, chapter 4 by Artwell Nhemachena methodically grapples with matters of indigenous knowledge, translation and sublation as they relate to his ethnographic findings. Motivated by contemporary debates on knowledge translation and in post-colonial literature, Nhemachema makes a courageous move to examine how the resilience of colonial epistemologies across Africa's diverse fields of human endeavours could be destabilised. He is concerned with how, since the dawn of European exploration, imperialism, scholarship on Africa, knowledge was erroneously translated and deliberately vilified. Nhemachena, thus, argues that 'indigenous knowledge systems were systematically sublated in the guise of colonial translation *such that* various aspects of African modes of existence were erroneously conflated in ways that effaced the important distinctions between African ancestors and the devil, Africans and animals'. For Nhemachena, it is unfortunate for Africa and all people of African descent that 'the exploitation and appropriation of African indigenous knowledge continues, in the postcolonies, with very little acknowledgement of

10

African indigenous intellectual property rights'. The exploitation and appropriation continues unjustifiably and even without comprehensive data to substantiate such engagements. Nhemachena concludes his chapter by challenging Euro-centric and African scholarship alike, to rethink some aspects of animism and all translation associated with scholarship on or about Africa.

The issue of exploitation and appropriation of African indigenous knowledge is further pursued in chapter 5 by Andile Mayekiso and Munyaradzi Mawere. In this chapter, it is noted that since the dawn of colonialism in Africa, traditional medicine as indigenous knowledge systems in general have always had serious challenges to be recognised by national laws across the continent. While this is generally the trend on the continent, Mayekiso and Mawere focus on the issue of the state of traditional medicine in South Africa. They note with concern that 'the advent of European imperialists in Africa and in South Africa specifically, gave supremacy not only to the imperialists' ideologies on how Africans should live but also to their health care system'. Under normal circumstances, this scenario was expected to be overturned with the marshalling and ushering in of national independence in South Africa. Unfortunately for majority of the 'indigenous' South Africans and pro-African medical practices, African traditional medicine has been side-lined and continue to suffer prejudices of the Apartheid era even today. This is in spite of incessant calls by Traditional Health Practitioners' support groups to legalise the status of traditional medicine; that it at least enjoys the same privileges mainstream health care system is currently enjoying. It is on this realisation that Mayekiso and Mawere interrogate the current status and prospects of traditional medicine in South Africa, and conclude their chapter by urging the South African government and humanitarian groups to push for recognition of diversity of epistemic and health care systems that appeal to all.

In chapter 6, Kwame Osei Kwarteng traces the history of pre-colonial and colonial wildlife conservation practices in Ghana. While historical in thrust, Kwarteng's chapter makes a milestone in comprehending concepts and practices relating to conservation of the natural heritage of Ghana, particularly national parks, game reserves, and forest reserves, which many a people, due to the influence of Euro-centric scholarship, erroneously think were introduced to Ghanaians by Europeans. Based on his studies of the Akan and other ethnic groups in Ghana, Kwarteng argues that practices related to conservation predate British colonialism in Ghana. To substantiate this claim, Kwarteng explore 'some of the traditional or indigenous conservation practices among the Akan and other peoples of Ghanaland' and juxtapose them with those introduced to Ghana by the European colonialists.

While Kwarteng makes an attempt to set the record on conservation in Africa and in particular Ghana straight, Munyaradzi Mawere and Christopher Mabeza's chapter 7 similarly wrestle hard with the volatile question on the interventions and engagements between non-state actors (NSAs) and local communities in the so-called Third World Countries. The duo courageously and scrupulously 'explores pathways to coping mechanisms to a changing climatic environment at the smallholder – non state – actor nexus in rural Zimbabwe'. Drawing on their rich findings in south-eastern Zimbabwe, Mawere and Mabeza, assert that 'in as much as interventions by external development agents have made inroads in building resilience among rural communities, at times the approach is fraught with contradictions and epistemic pitfalls as more often than not the interventions fail to recognise the indigenous ways of knowing and survival strategies' of the communities in question. For them, rural communities, 'like sheep being taken to the altar' are often enticed to join projects by non-state actors and other such external development agents, only to find themselves 'dumped' along the way as the agents create no exist strategy for communities to fall back on. Even as Mawere and Mabeza make this important observation and analysis, they are quick to acknowledge efforts by some external development agents in building resilience amongst communities in changing climatic environments. Mawere and Mabeza, however, conclude their chapter by urging external development agents to value and respect local communities' ways of knowing and survival strategies if their interventions are to make a positive change in the lives of the community members they are meant to serve.

Equally, chapter 8 by Samuel Awuah-Nyamekye tussles head on with the intellectually delicate but critical question on the relationship between religion and the restoration of health among the Akan people of Ghana. For Awuah-Nyamekye 'sound health, no doubt, is the soul of every human society, for no human society can thrive if her people are afflicted with ill-health'. It is out of this understanding that the Akan prioritise matters of health. Following Parrinder (1961), Mbiti (1969), and Opoku (1978), Awuah-Nyamekye observes that the line between the Akan secular and religious activities is indistinguishable such that the latter's explanation of almost all diseases has supernatural underpinnings or connections. Yet for Awuah-Nyamekye, this is not to argue that the Akan people are non-scientific as they also acknowledge and believe in the 'Germ Theory' or the 'naturalistic' causes of illnesses, though such belief normally depends on the nature of the disease or illness that one is suffering from. Noting this reality, which indeed appears paradoxical especially to many non-African people, the chapter by Awuah-Nyamekye advances the argument that 'among the traditional Akan, religion and medicine are inseparable realities' such that this worldview should be seriously considered in national policy decision making.

Elias Asiama's chapter 9 meticulously examines the use and efficacy of indigenous knowledge in resource utilisation and ecological management in Ghana. His quest to examine the use and efficacy of indigenous knowledge in Ghana comes on the pretext that many nations across the African continent and beyond 'have developed to levels where *they* begin to realise the detrimental effects' of their anthropogenic activities they once thought would make their lives better. In view of this scenario, Asiama advocates the need for 'alternative approaches to promoting development that is much more nature - friendly'. For Asiama, such approaches should emanate from indigenous knowledges of the once marginalised communities as Western scientific solutions have proven futile in their attempt to ease the tapestry of environmental problems the world-over. Asiama, thus, concludes that 'the future of the African continent lies much more in our ability, *as Africans,* to transform the numerous resources it possesses into tangible and intangible products'.

For a long time, particularly since the dawn of colonialism in Africa until recently, the discourse on environmental conservation

13

was believed to be a game of Western-trained environmental scientists with indigenous communities made to assume a back-seat position. To correct this long-time error in environmental science, Liveson Tatira in his chapter 10, deliberately tackles head on the issue of environmental conservation among the traditional Shona people of Zimbabwe. Drawing on his wealth of experience of research and conversant with the Shona culture, Tatira examines the often taken for granted indigenous Shona cultural beliefs and practices such as taboos, among others, which through their supernatural underpinnings, play a double-role as propagators of peace between humans and 'other beings' (Mawere 2014) and drivers of environmental conservation. From his findings, Tatira notes the centrality of such cultural beliefs thereby advancing the important argument that 'the Shona beliefs and practices help to enforce environmentally friendly behaviour' that in no doubt fosters peace, harmony and togetherness between humans and other beings that share the same environment. Tatira, thus, observes that 'there are a wide range of taboos, among other things, which are meant to conserve trees, animals, both domestic and wild, land, bodies of water and birds,' such that through those taboos wanton ecosystemic destruction is prohibited.

In a somewhat similar thrust as that of Tatira, Hezekiah Olufemi Adeosun's luminary chapter 11, targets an often neglected niche of the nexus between indigenous knowledge and conflict resolution. He examines how the Yoruba people use their indigenous knowledge systems in resolving conflicts and promoting peace. Using the Yoruba proverbs selected on the basis of the thematic framework of Nativist Model of Postcolonial theory, Adeosun demonstrates the potency of indigenous knowledge systems particularly proverbs in the resolvement of socio-political differences and in conflict resolution amongst societal members in Nigeria. Based on his study, Adeosun encourages that 'the people and race that had been colonised by the West, at a time in history, should dig deep into their culture and tradition, and make use of their indigenous languages for their literary discourse'. His study, thus, reveals and concludes that indigenous knowledge systems serve as a potent tool in conflict resolution such that they [IKSs] are fountains and advocates of peace and sanity to human society.

14

Chapter 12 by Blessing Makunike and Munyaradzi Mawere conscientiously discusses the controversial issue of the land reform programme in Zimbabwe, particularly the role of indigenous knowledge of the beneficiaries in fostering equity and sustainable development. Contrary to the popular thinking that land reform programme in Zimbabwe flopped due to lack of expertise by the indigenous farmers, basing on their findings, Makunike and Mawere argue that from an epistemological perspective, the programme was a success. Their argument is premised on the observation that the programme, which accommodated people from different locations around the country, proffered the grand opportunity for epistemological showcasing and interpolation of ideas and farming practices among the beneficiaries. Makunike and Mawere's chapter, should however, not be mistaken to be romanticising indigenous farming epistemologies, as it goes beyond to argue for the integration of traditional farming practices and modern farming methods as a gateway to sustainable development. In fact, Makunike and Mawere demonstrate 'that the potential and value of using indigenous *farming practices* in combination with modern scientific techniques to enhance the sustainable management and productive use of land is immense'. Besides, the duo advances the important argument that past attitude of scepticism and contempt for local farmers' knowledge and farming practices have been the cause of many government and aid sponsored failures, and have contributed to mistrust and suspicion of local people towards officialdom. Thus going beyond labelling and finger pointing between 'traditional farmers' and the so-called 'modern farmers', Makunike and Mawere advocate the acknowledgement of diversity and the integration of different farming practices, whether from the so-called 'modern farmers' or 'local farmers', if at all communities are to develop sustainable systems for greater self-reliance and sustainable development.

Lastly, chapter 13 by Martin Q Amlor rips open the rich contents of indigenous knowledge such as cultural norms and values. For Amlor, cultural norms and values traditionally played (and in many other African societies continue to play) a pivotal role in fostering sustainable development at local community, national and even global levels. Yet, in the face of Westernisation, Amlor observes that the recognition of these knowledge forms in the contemporary society of Ghana is daunting such that 'indigenous education and prospects for cultural survival' continue to dwindle day-by-day. This is, thus, in spite of the fact that indigenous knowledges are central to the political and socio-economic growth and development of any society, state, or nation. Amlor makes another critical observation that Ghana 'being a developing country struggling to enter the middle income bracket, there is a wide gap between the rich and poor, and between those who can and cannot access opportunities' resulting in high levels of unemployment and poverty. In a bid to rescue the majority jobless and poverty-stricken Ghanaians, Amlor proposes a change in attitude towards indigenous knowledge as a possible solution. He, thus, argues that scholars and researchers should make efforts 'to recreate awareness among the citizens that *indigenous knowledge* is a national heritage and a resource that can be harnessed for the *political and socio-economic* benefit of humanity'.

As is exemplified in the contributions that constitute this book, the merit of the present volume lies in their realisation that the tenets of African indigenous knowledge overlap with those of other knowledge forms such as Western science such that they should not be viewed as mutual enemies but complementary forms of knowledge with the same goal of generating and advancing knowledge to improve human society.

References

Bernheims, Marc and Evelyne. 1968. *From bush to city: A look at the NewAfrica,* New Harcourt, Brace and World Inc.; new York.

Constantino, R. 1978. *Neo-colonial identity and counter consciousness,* Merlin Press: London.

Fadipe, N.A. 1991. *The sociology of the Yoruba,* (Edited by Okediji, Francis Olu. and Okediji, Oladejo O.). Ibadan University Press.

Fairhead, J. and Leach, M. 1996. *Misreading the African landscapes: Society and ecology in a forest-savanna Mosaic,* Cambridge University Press: Cambridge.

Hawthorne, T. 1986. *Windows on science and faith*, Leicester: Inter-Varsity Press.

Herodotus. 1942. *The Persian Wars*, The Modern Library: New York.

Iwara. A.U. 1994. 'Falsified and Stolen Legacies', In Andah, Bassey W. and Bolarinwa. Kunle A. (eds.). *A Celebration of Africa's Roots and Legacy*. Ibandan: Fajee Publications Ltd. Pp. 22-27.

Jacobs, N. 2006. Intimate politics of ornithology, *Society for Comparative Study of Society and History* 48 (3): 564-603.

James, G. 1954. *Stolen legacy*, Available at: sacred-texts.com

Levine, G. 1996. 'What is science studies for and who cares?' In Ross, A. (Ed.), *Science wars*, Duke University Press, North Carolina.

Macedo, D. 1999. 'Decolonising indigenous knowledge', In Semali, L. and Kincheloe, J. *What is indigenous knowledge? Voices from the academy*, Falmer Press, New York.

Mbiti. J. S. 1969. *African Religions and Philosophy 2nd revised Ed*, London, Ibadan, and Nairobi: Heinemann.

Olopoenia, R.A. 1994. "Economics: A United 'African Descent' Market: State of Economic integrations in African", In Andah, Bassey W. and Bolarinwa Kunle, A. (eds). *A Celebration of Africa's Roots and Legacy*, Ibadan: Fajee Publications Ltd.

Opoku, K. A. 1978. *West African Traditional Religion*, Accra: FEP International Private Limited.

Parrinder, E.G. 1961. *West African Religion: A study of the Beliefs and Practices of Akan, Ewe, Yoruba, Ibo and Kindred peoples*, London: Epworth Press.

Semali, L. and Kincheloe, J. 1999. 'Introduction: What is indigenous knowledge and why should we study it?' In *What is indigenous knowledge? Voices from the academy*, Falmer Press, New York.

Sponsel, L. 1992. Information asymmetry and the democratisation of anthropology, *Human Organisation*, 51 (3): 299-301.

Chapter 2

Indigenous Knowledge for Disaster Risk Management in Africa: Some showcases from Zimbabwe

Munyaradzi Mawere

Introduction

Traditionally, Africa is a cultural context based on indigenous epistemology for its survival and development. In Zimbabwe, for example, as in many other communities in Africa, indigenous knowledge (IK) has been, since time immemorial, used in all spheres of life which include but not limited to environmental management, political governance, economic development and disaster risk management, particularly governance of disaster risks, disaster management, risk perceptions and social vulnerability to natural hazards. The knowledge that Africans possessed, and is still possessed by some, served to facilitate the communities in Zimbabwe to sustainably manage their environments, establish early warning indicators, predict and prepare for oncoming disaster(s), respond to impending disaster(s), and mitigate in a way that make the disaster(s) less severe, that is, the knowledge helped them for disaster risk management. By disaster risk management, I mean the organisation and administration of resources and responsibilities for dealing with all aspects of emergencies, including disaster prevention and mitigation, but especially disaster preparedness, response and recovery (see also Holloway 2003). Disaster risk management, thus, may be seen as a formalised body of knowledge for dealing with difficult moments that result from certain events.

Yet with the advent of colonialism, Western-based scientific knowledge was introduced but at the expense of African-based knowledge forms across the continent. Africa-based scientific knowledge bequeathed to the sons and daughters of Africa by their ancestors found itself undermined to the extent of being labelled as

19

irrational, superstitious, anti-development and unscientific. As if this pejorative labelling was not enough, many African societies were either encouraged to unlearn or forced to abandon their indigenous knowledge and adopt Western-based scientific knowledge that was swiftly introduced in schools to replace traditional education. This posed a serious threat to sustainable development on the continent given that indigenous knowledge has always been traditionally used to foster development and sustainability, among other uses.

With the ushering in of political independence in many parts of Africa, majority of the African Governments vowed to change this impasse and restore their people's heritage. Surprisingly, more than three decades after majority of the African countries attained their political independence, not so much have been done to restore the African people's soiled indigenous knowledge; worse still, to integrate indigenous knowledge into the mainstream educational curricular and developmental projects. Many African countries continue with Western-based scientific knowledge at the centre of their education curricular and national developmental projects. This is in spite of the burgeoning realisation by some scholars and organisations (see Steiner 2008; Singh 2011; Shizha 2013; Beinart and Brown 2013; FAO 1998) alike that indigenous knowledge is intrinsically linked to sustainable development, and also that sophisticated scientific knowledge of the natural world is not confined to Western science. In fact, at global level, there is an increasing acknowledgement of the relevance and efficacy of indigenous knowledge as an under-utilised, underestimated and despised yet an invaluable knowledge used to control, monitor, manage natural risk disaster and other such systems (see for example, FAO 1998; Beinart and Brown 2013). This entails that the potential role that indigenous peoples and their knowledge can play in addressing many of the problems that haunt humanity even at global level, across the world, is increasingly emerging as part of international discourse. No wonder that, both the 1987 "Brundtland Report" and Chapter 26 of Agenda 21 have formally recognised the contributions that indigenous peoples can make in global sustainable development.

Nevertheless, evidence on the ground is not too clear if governments across the world especially African governments appreciate this urgent call. Worse still, due to the fact that indigenous knowledge continues to be side-lined and despised in many spheres of life, there is general lack of documented information as well as understanding of the relevance and efficacy of indigenous knowledge by policy makers and implementers in environmental conservation, climate adaptation, good governance, sustainable development, poverty reduction, and risk disaster management-related institutions. The general lack of information and understanding of the relevance and efficacy of indigenous knowledge has drastic effects on Zimbabwean societies and Africa in general. Due to lack of information and comprehensive research on indigenous knowledge, much of the continent's valuable indigenous knowledge about ways of living sustainably is being lost. Achim Steiner (2008: 4), the Executive Director for United Nations Environment Programme in Kenya, confirms this when he notes that "indigenous knowledge is still intact among indigenous or local communities in many parts of Africa. However, this knowledge is not well documented and it stands in danger of being lost as its custodians are passing away". For the same claim also see Awuah-Nyamekye (2009). This observation is critical as it suggests that that a lot more still needs to be done on the African continent, for example in Zimbabwe, to encourage or even to convince respective governments to adopt indigenous knowledge to foster sustainable development, reduce poverty, and manage risks and natural disasters in their communities.

This chapter seeks to explore different ways through which indigenous knowledge was used (and continue to be used) by some communities in Zimbabwe to control, master, and predict early warning indicators of risk disaster and environmentally threatening circumstances. The chapter goes further to enumerate some of the 'concrete' showcases, as was gathered from fieldwork data in south-eastern Zimbabwe, that are still used in some communities in Zimbabwe to ensure continued survival of their environments and to predict early indicators of impending disasters such as floods, droughts, famine, diseases, and danger.

Objectives and methodological issues: A brief overview

The main aim of this study was to provide information and showcases of indigenous knowledge that were (and are still) used in some communities in Zimbabwe for risk natural disaster preparedness and mitigation. The study, which was largely inspired by my research and teaching experiences over the years and the need to document indigenous knowledge used in disaster preparedness and mitigation to avoid it being lost, was carried out in south-eastern Zimbabwe between August and October 2014. Various data collection techniques were used in gathering data for the present study. These included focus group discussions, open interviews, observations and library research. I relied on a variety of interlocutors who included elders, traditional medical practitioners, and traditional African leaders such as chiefs and headmen. These interlocutors were selected as they were believed to be the custodians of the African traditional values and indigenous knowledge systems.

Before discussing the findings of this study, I should point out that indigenous knowledge as a concept is widely discussed (see Altieri 1995; Semali 1999; Odora-Hoppers 2001, 2002; Mapara 2009; Mawere 2012, 2014; Shizha 2010, 2013; Ocholla 2007). As such, in this chapter, I will not delve much into the controversies and debates surrounding the concept of indigenous knowledge except to offer a brief conceptualisation of the term and, indeed what I understand to be such. The chapter further enumerates and elaborates some of the showcases of indigenous knowledge that were (and are still) used in some communities especially those in hazard-prone areas in Zimbabwe, particularly to ensure continued survival of their environments and to achieve disaster risk reduction.

Understanding indigenous knowledge

Indigenous knowledge has been understood differently by different research groups and scholars across disciplines (see Altieri 1995; Melchias 2001; Odora-Hoppers 2001, 2002; Mawere 2012, 2013; Ocholla 2007; Mapara 2009; Shizha 2013). For this reason, among others, indigenous knowledge is known by other names such as: indigenous ways of knowing, traditional knowledge, indigenous technical knowledge, rural knowledge, ethnoscience/people's science (Altieri 1995). It is important, however, to underline that though vary in their articulation, all these names try to explain one and the same thing which in this chapter shall be referred to as indigenous knowledge.

For scholars such as Melchias (2001), indigenous knowledge refers to practices that have evolved for generation through trial and error and proved flexible enough to cope with change. As can be seen, this definition emphasises the colonial racist idea that indigenous knowledge is a monopoly of trials and error while Western science is characterised by laboratory experimentations. I should underscore, however, that Melchias' conception of indigenous knowledge is flawed in that he fails to note that even indigenous knowledge itself is also characterised by observations and experiments. It is only that observations and experiments for indigenous knowledge were not documented but preserved under cultural institutional framework and practices.

Altieri (1995) provides a somewhat similar definition. He defines indigenous knowledge as knowledge form that has originated locally and naturally, and has failed to die despite the racial and colonial onslaught that it has suffered at the hands of Western imperialism and arrogance (see Altieri 1995: 114). Altieri's understanding of indigenous knowledge implies that indigenous knowledge exist only in those areas that were affected by colonialism. In this chapter, I go beyond Altieri to argue that indigenous knowledge exist in all human societies including those of the former European colonisers and so-called developed world.

I should be quick to point out that there are a myriad of definitions that have proffered over the years in an attempt to explain what indigenous knowledge really is. For this study, indigenous knowledge refers to a set of ideas and practices (some of which have indigenous religious underpinnings) of indigenous people of a specific locale that has been used by its people to interact with their environment and other people over a long period of time.

The use of indigenous knowledge in Zimbabwe

The lifetime experiences (events, facts, practices, beliefs, and social norms), loosely referred to as indigenous knowledge, stored in human beings' memories have always facilitated humans' continued existence on the face of this world (see also Beinart and Brown 2013). This entails that indigenous knowledge, which is what people in a particular geographical location have known and done for generations, is as old as humankind, and has persisted through time. Researches show that even in the present time as was in the past, indigenous knowledge has provided basic knowledge in natural resource management, veterinary medicine, agriculture, forestry conservation, disaster risk management, and weather forecasting (see Beinart and Brown 2013). Citing Beinart (2007), Beinart and Brown (2013), for example, explain how early settlers in South Africa benefitted from "Khoisan pastoralists about the value of trekking between sweetveld and sourveld" (p. 16) in preventing fatal diseases such as *lamsieke*. The duo go on to show how early veterinarians in South Africa benefitted from indigenous African farmers' knowledge of livestock diseases such that they even adopted the Zulu word *"nagana"* for the disease caused by tsetse flies.

Internationally, the use and relevance of indigenous knowledge has been acknowledged in conventions such as the Brundtland Commission, the Biodiversity Convention, Agenda 21, and the Rio Declaration, and the World Summit on Sustainable Development. This means that though the use of indigenous knowledge may not be supported by national law and policies especially in many African countries, the use of indigenous knowledge has international support. Although constantly evolving, indigenous knowledge has been used across communities since time immemorial. In Zimbabwe, as in many other parts of Africa and beyond, indigenous knowledge was used (and continue to be used across communities) in political governance, environmental conservation, economic development, socialisation, health care delivery, among other uses, which ensured continued survival of societies and sustainable exploitation of resources (Personal Communication 23 September 2014). In many communities across the country, especially in the rural areas, the use of indigenous knowledge remains high (see Mapara 2009; Shizha 2010; Mawere 2012, 2014). The continued use of indigenous knowledge implies its efficacy, its ability to adapt and to interact with new type of information and knowledge forms. Even in recent researches (Mawere 2014; Nyong *et al* 2007; King *et al* 2008; Gearheard *et al* 2009; Actalliance n.d), it has been established that there are many advantages associated with using indigenous knowledge especially in environmental conservation, good governance, and community development projects. Actalliance (n.d), for example, have outlined four advantages to using indigenous knowledge and practices in humanitarian response work in Africa:

■ Indigenous practices and strategies can be generalised to other communities in similar situations.

■ Integration of indigenous knowledge into practices and policies encourages and empowers community members to play a leading role in disaster preparedness.

■ Indigenous knowledge provides valuable information about the context of a disaster such that mitigation or intervention becomes much easier.

■ The informal method of sharing indigenous knowledge can be used to disseminate other education material on disaster preparedness.

In Zimbabwe, the deployment of indigenous knowledge was, however, diminished with the advent of colonialism and globalisation, forces which in many ways have been criticised for their urge to thwart all indigenous practices and efforts especially from the southern hemisphere. The dawn of national independence in Zimbabwe, saw some significant changes towards perceptions on indigenous knowledge and other such practices. At national level, at least three state universities, University of Zimbabwe (UZ), Midlands State University (MSU), and Great Zimbabwe University (GZU) have established culture and heritage studies degree programmes as a gesture that the country is committed to restore and advance the image and dignity of the African people and their indigenous practices. However, to date, little if not no effort has been made by these institutions' research units to come up with a data base for all indigenous knowledge and practices bequeathed to the Zimbabwean people by their ancestors. There is, therefore, lack of information and understanding especially by the young generation on the relevance and efficacy of some indigenous knowledge. This realisation entails that a lot more is still desired to be done at national level to ensure that the relevance and efficacy of indigenous knowledge is fully understood and realised by all.

Showcases of indigenous knowledge for disaster risk prediction and mitigation

As highlighted in the preceding discussion, a myriad of indigenous knowledge was (and continued to be) used to control, master, and predict early indicators of disaster risks. These were used in conjunction with environmental resources such as plants, animals, water, land and the solar system as well as the state of the atmosphere. Numerous as they are, it will be overzealous to promise readers to discuss all of them in just a single chapter as this. A voluminous text is actually required for this task. As such, this chapter discusses at least eight indigenous knowledges that were (and continued to be) used in relation to risk disaster management.

■ *Bird behaviour*
Some birds are naturally endowed with the gift of predicting weather changes, what others call biotic weather forecasting. Indigenous people of Zimbabwe, for a long time, studied behaviours of such birds and observed their patterns of behaviour. The bird, *Dendera's* (hornbill) hooting, for example, is used in south-east Zimbabwe to predict drizzle in the near future.

In south-east Zimbabwe, a bird locally known as *Teererwa* is used to predict floods. My interlocutors informed me that the bird normally lays its eggs in holes along rivers banks and dongas. However, when there is an impending flood, the bird lays its eggs on trees. In Swaziland, some local communities use the height of the nests of the *Emahlokohloko* bird (*Ploceus spp.*) on trees to predict floods (see Mwaura 2008: 9; Manyatsi 2011). Manyatsi (2011), for example, affirmed that indigenous knowledge about bird behaviour is used to predict floods. This behaviour is observed in nest building especially for birds that normally construct their nests along rivers. In his study, Manyatsi (2011) established that these birds have a tendency of building their nests at lower positions during years when there are no floods. But on years when there are floods, the birds tend to build their nests at higher points. In this sense, some birds are used to predict floods. This pattern has also been observed elsewhere in Africa, particularly in western Mozambique (personal communication). The patterns were (and are still) used to mitigate the effects of impending disasters, in this case, floods once predictions were made. In Banyala Community in Budalangi on the shores of Lake Victoria in Kenya, for example, it is reported that one of the mitigating strategy used to control the effects of impending floods was that each community was required to dig out trenches to control the water around the homesteads and farmlands. Those living on the highlands were (are) also expected to accommodate neighbours displaced (or are likely to be displaced) by floods in the lowlands, which were flood prone areas. (see Mwaura 2008).

The use of knowledge of bird behaviour is not unique to Africa alone. As reported by FAO (1998), Lapwing bird (*Tatihari*) found in Australia is used by the Aborigines for biotic weather forecast and for facilitating disaster risk management. When the bird lays its eggs on the upper part of the field, it is an indicator for a good rain season and vice-versa when it lays its eggs on the lower part of the field. More so, the same source reports that if the bird lays one egg it is an indicator that rains will fall for only one month instead of the four months expected of a normal rain season in Australia. If it lays two eggs, rains will fall for only two months instead of the four months expected for the Australian rain season. Thus using such indicators, the Aborigines know how to prepare for the impending drought well before it strikes.

■ *Wind direction*

In the modern sense of the term climatologist, one could safely say that the forebears of African were very good 'climatologists'. They could predict weather in the next few hours and even days by mere observation of wind patterns. The blowing of wind called *nhurura* (incessant, cool, freshly winds) from north-west direction, for example, meant heavy rains were imminent. This reminds me of the time I was growing up, in the 1980s. I was the youngest boy in the family, bearing the task of herding some dozens of cattle and goats. Sometimes, I would take my cattle to as far away as 6 kms, looking for good pastures. My mother would, one morning, wake up only to warn me not to go with the cattle too far as there will be heavy down pours in the afternoon. We had no radio in the home those days. Worse still television set. I would wonder how she knew all this. But once she warns this, her words certainly come to pass. Heavy down pours would be received before day end. She only revealed the secret behind her knowledge one evening when she said: 'Munya, you know you go herding cattle all these days. You need to know that when we receive incessant winds from the south-eastern direction we will receive *guti* (drizzle). If the winds come from a north-western direction we will receive heavy rains normally associated with thunder and lightning. So you shouldn't go herding far those days'. The observation of what my mother revealed that day helped me coping with weather changes and to prepare my schedule ahead of time. I would no longer wait to be warned by mother whether I should take my cattle far or near. During this research, several elderly people in south-eastern Zimbabwe, majority of them in their 80s confirmed the same observation. This entails that people use their indigenous knowledge of wind movements to forecast weather. This knowledge is not only unique to people of south-eastern Zimbabwe. Elsewhere (see Singh 2011), it has been reported that among the 2004 tsunami survivors were the Moken of the Andaman Sea because they knew the tidal wave was coming. These nomads are reported to have a legend about the Laboon, that is, 'wave that eats people'. According to these people's ancient lore, before the tsunami arrives, the sea recedes and the loud singing of cicadas is silenced as happened before the 2004 tidal wave. One member of the Moken noticed the silence and warned everyone in their group prompting their whole community to move to higher ground long before the first wave struck. This is how the Moken people were saved from the tsunami.

■ Colour of clouds

People in south-eastern Zimbabwe, do not only have knowledge of local rain corridors, but also the type of rain associated with different clouds merely from the colour of the clouds. For instance, when the rain season approaches they knew it would appear a *mvumi yemvura* which is a white, thick, and stable cloud that looks like a pool of water around the sun (if during the day) and moon (if during the night). Once this rain bearing cloud appears, elders would know that some heavy rains are imminent. As such, they would prepare their activities accordingly. This indigenous knowledge was acquired through series of observations such that the knowledge became factual to the people who use it. One interlocutor in her early 80s, for example, had this to say to me during field work for this research:

Long ago when rainfall used to be reliable, we used to tell the kind of rainfall merely from the colour of clouds in the sky. We would know that thick black clouds normally bring hailstones, thunder and lightning. Once observing such clouds, we would prepare accordingly by taking cover or staying indoors.

From the foregoing, it is clear that people used (and some continue to use) their indigenous knowledge to prepare for an impending disaster.

■ *Shape of crescent moon*

Astronomy is not only studied in universities but even informally in communities. As such, knowledge of stars and the moon, have always been used by some communities in Zimbabwe to predict risk disasters such as diseases. In south-eastern Zimbabwe where the bulk of this research was carried out, it was confirmed by some elders that the position of the crescent moon is a very important phenomenon. As one interlocutor revealed 'when we grew up our elders used to tell us that when you see the crescent moon upside down or in a sliding position, it is a warning sign for the impending widespread pandemics such as malaria, fever, and influenza, among others'.

■ *Behaviour of some animals*

The forebears of Africans were great observers of nature. Environmental resources such as animals, reptiles, and amphibians had some religious underpinnings associated with them such that the resources would help the African peoples to predict their near future. In Zaka and Bikita, where part of this research was carried out, some of my interlocutors told me a number of animals they use to predict the safety of their journey. I was told, for example, that when travelling, if a baboon crosses your way twice, this is a warning sign for impending danger or a prediction that your journey will be unsafe. This obtains as well for the animal, *hovo/chikovo* (slender mongoose). While for other creatures such as a chameleon, I was told if it crosses your way just once, it is a warning signal of impending danger or a prediction that your journey will be unsafe. Crossing your way means cancelling your journey. In the past, it was said, once this happens, those on the journey would either go back home or plead with their ancestors and God to intervene and stop the danger.

The behaviour of tortoises is also important in biotic weather forecasting especially in the cosmology of the Shona people of south-eastern Zimbabwe. From what I gathered during fieldwork for this in south-eastern Zimbabwe, some elders claimed that the behaviour of tortoise help them to predict weather patterns. Tortoise is naturally a slow moving animal. When they see tortoises speedily crawling up the hills or mountains, they said, it is an early warning of impending heavy rains which will result in floods or destruction of crops and properties. The appearance of a white frog, with long legs, on tree trunks as well as its croaking was known to be a sign of imminent heavy torrential rainfall.

The other creature that is known by people in south-eastern Zimbabwe to be a messenger of impending disaster is a *gwavava* (Large rock lizard) which people in some parts of south-eastern Zimbabwe such as Gutu call it *gwereveshe* (Square-nosed monitor lizard). This reptile lives in rocks especially the dwalas and kopjes. It rarely visits human compounds, and if it does visit one's compound it is a warning sign that a close relative to the visited compound will pass away. While people confirmed this during my fieldwork in south-eastern Zimbabwe, I was not certain if this really happens. My doubts were put to rest when I witnessed a visit of one such a lizard at Nyamandi High School where my wife was teaching. It happened that one morning, a large rock lizard visited one of the teachers' houses. Many people including myself were perplexed by this occurrence. By evening, the owner of the visited house had already received news that her nephew had passed away earlier that morning. My research findings, thus, were confirmed.

■ *Yields of certain wild fruit trees*

In south-eastern Zimbabwe, the yields of certain wild fruit trees such as *muchakata (Parinari curatellifolia), mushuku (Uapaca kirkiana)* and *muhumbukumbu (Lannea discolour)* were for a long time understood to be among the arrays of early warning or predictors for the next season. When the yields of these trees are abundant, it is an indicator of an impending drought. Once observing this, local communities devised a variety of measures such as growing drought-resistant crops, early maturing crop varieties, engage in wetland cultivation, gather fruits and vegetables and preserve some for future use. Vegetables, for example, were cut into small pieces before they are cooked and dried in the sun as *mufushwa* (dried vegetables). Some fruits, such as *chakata (Parinari curatellifolia* fruit) were also among those fruits that were dried for later use once early warnings for drought were observed. It was also revealed that administrative structures to deal with disasters such as drought were always present in the form of a council of elders with *mapurisa aMambo* (Chief's policemen) who would urgently communicate messages about hunger striking whenever the need arises among members of the community. This is germane to observation made in Kenya where it was reported (Mwaura 2008: 8) "in Kenya a council of elders had at its disposal the speed and strength of numerous warriors that could be used to investigate a particular phenomenon or to pass urgent messages upon need".

Why the hour hand is ticking towards modern science?

As demonstrated from the data presented above, there is no doubt that some communities in Zimbabwe, as elsewhere in Africa, have for generations, generated a vast body of indigenous knowledge on disaster prevention, management and mitigation. This knowledge, unlike the bulk of Western science (the so-called modern science), is the sum total facts that learned from experience (such as observation and careful study) over time. The knowledge is indigenous in so far as it is handed down from one generation to another in particular communities or geographical locations. Yet, this is not to mean that this kind of knowledge is not applicable to other communities as the knowledge is dynamic and not static.

The global scientific community, as demonstrated during the World Conference on Science held in Budapest, Hungary from 29 June to 1 July 1999, endorse and acknowledge the relevance and efficacy of indigenous knowledge (see Steiner 2008). Between 2004 and 2006, the United Nations Environment Programme (UNEP) sponsored a study of indigenous knowledge in four countries namely Kenya, South Africa, Swaziland and Tanzania. Unfortunately, in many other countries in Africa such as Zimbabwe, no such projects have taken place thus far.

The major challenge of popularising indigenous knowledge and even integrating it with modern knowledge systems such as modern science is the continued disregard and looking down upon of indigenous knowledge by pro-modern science partisans, most of whom were educated in the West or Western-based institutions. No wonder some scholars (Selin 1993; Abonyi, Achimugu, and Adibe 2014; Ajikobi and Bello 1991; Atwater 1993) have urged all parties concerned with the production of knowledge (in institutions such as universities), current studies on methods of science instruction, and implementation of policies to do with indigenous knowledge in Africa, to desist from the habit of paying lip service.

Recommendations

This study recognises the value, relevance and efficacy of indigenous knowledge not only in disaster risk preparedness and mitigation, but also in other areas such as environmental conservation, political governance, economic development, among others. Yet, much of indigenous knowledge in Zimbabwe has not been documented in written form. Neither is indigenous knowledge taught in schools especially primary and secondary schools. It is only known orally, and unfortunately most of the custodians of this knowledge are passing away threatening the continued existence of indigenous knowledge in the future. And due to the lasting effects of westernisation and globalisations, many people in Zimbabwe now shun their belief systems including their indigenous knowledges especially those with religious underpinnings. In view of this realisation, this study makes as one of its recommendations that a study to come up with a data base of all indigenous knowledge systems used in Zimbabwe be carried out at national level. This will ensure the continued existence of indigenous knowledge across the country.

Second, the study recommends that indigenous knowledge data banks and networks be established in Zimbabwe to ensure the continued existence, full application, and copyright security of indigenous knowledge in the country. While some information on indigenous knowledge in Zimbabwe could be found, there is data bank for this valuable knowledge. Yet, it is known that indigenous knowledge has the risk of being lost forever given that most of its custodians are passing on, and that the present generation in Zimbabwe has become more migratory than ever mainly due to economic cataclysm since the past two decades or so.

Third, indigenous knowledge should be incorporated in education curricular at all level from primary education through secondary and tertiary education. In fact, the understanding that indigenous knowledge is an important phenomenon in influencing behaviour and even the lives of people for the better in all spheres of life ranging from political governance, environmental conservation, economic development, among others, can only be realised if indigenous knowledge, just like other subjects such as Mathematics, History, Geography etc. are studied and examined in schools. Denying children the right to learn this subject is no different from denying them the right to see and express their worldviews and vision in their own terms. It is no different from blinding their eyes. It is no different from denying them the right to inherit what is rightfully theirs: it is unduly denying them their epistemic right. It is no different from cutting them from their origins – their own roots, and it is well known that a tree without roots can be easily fallen by the weakest blows of wind. I submit, therefore, that it is only when serious teaching of indigenous knowledge is done that everyone would indeed see that the government of Zimbabwe is determined to restore the *lost* dignity of its people and advance their heritage of all forms. This is what the Tanzanian pan-African scholar, Ladislaus Semali, yearned for when he wrote lamenting about his own experiences at school during the colonial era, of course in relation to indigenous languages, that:

Then, I went to school, a colonial school, and this harmony was broken. The language of my education was no longer the language of my culture. I first went to Iwa Primary school. Our language of education was not Kiswahili. My struggle began at a very early age constantly trying to find parallels in my culture with what was being taught in the classroom. In school, we followed the British colonial syllabus. The books we read in class had been written by Mrs. Bryce, mostly adapted and translated into Kiswahili from British curricula. We read stories and sung songs about having tea in an English garden, taking a ride on the train, sailing in the open seas, and walking the streets of town. These were unfortunately stories far removed from our life experiences. As expected, we memorised them even though they were meaningless *to us*. By the time I was in fifth grade, Swahili was no longer the medium of instruction. English had taken over and Kiswahili was only a subject taught once a week. Kichagga was not to be spoken at any time and if caught speaking we were severely punished (Macedo 1999: xii-xiii).

Fourth, indigenous knowledge should be incorporated into national development plans such that it complements efforts by other knowledge forms such as modern science to improve the lives of humanity in the country.

The government of Zimbabwe should find ways of integrating indigenous knowledge with modern science and ensure that appropriate laws to protect intellectual property in indigenous knowledge are put in place.

Conclusion

In Africa, local communities had well-developed indigenous knowledge systems they used for disaster preparedness and mitigation. These knowledge systems did not only make African societies more resilient but also helped them to manage their resources in a more sustainable manner. Yet, it is only of recent that disaster preparedness programmes have realised the value and potency of indigenous knowledge as a significant contributor to disaster preparedness and mitigation. Using showcases and findings from south-eastern Zimbabwe, this chapter has not only argued that indigenous knowledge in Africa has a high sustainability potential, but demonstrated the legitimacy of the claim that African communities always had well-developed indigenous knowledge systems for disaster risk management including disaster risk preparedness and mitigation. It has been underscored in the chapter, however, that these knowledge systems are understudied and in many cases remain undocumented such that they risk being lost and extinct, especially considering that the Zimbabwean young generation has over the years become more migratory than ever. Most young Zimbabweans no longer grow up in their respective communities such that spontaneous handing over of the indigenous knowledge from one generation to the other is now disrupted. In view of this observation, the chapter has urged the Zimbabwean government of Zimbabwe to embark on indigenous knowledge systems' research to create a national indigenous knowledge data base that will be catalogued in indigenous knowledge data banks or libraries. This will go a long way to ensure that indigenous knowledge systems of all kind are harnessed and preserved for the present and future generations.

References

Actalliance, n.d. 'Indigenous knowledge in capacity building and psychological guide', Available at: psychological.actalliance.org/default .../ (Retrieved: 4 November 2014).

Abonyi, S. O., Achimugu, A. L., and Adibe, I. M. 2014. Innovations in science and technology education: A case for ethno-science based science classrooms, *International Journal of Scientific and Engineering Research*, 5 (1): 1-5.

Ajikobi, S. O., and Bello, G. 1991. Nigerian societal beliefs and language effect on the teaching and learning process in science, *32nd Annual Conference Proceedings of STAN Cultural Dimensions: Indigenous Knowledge Systems*, Intermediate Technology Publishers.

Altieri, M.A. 1995. *Agro-ecology: The Science of Sustainable Agriculture,* 2nd Edition. London: IT Publications.

Atwater, M. M. 1993. Multicultural science education; Assumptions and alternative view, *The Science Teacher* 60 (3): 32-37.

Awuah-Nyamekye, S. 2009. Teaching Sustainable Development from the Perspective of Indigenous Spiritualities of Ghana. In: Cathrien de Pater and Irene Dankelman (eds.) *Religion and Sustainable Development Opportunities and Challenges for Higher Education.* 25-39. Berlin: Lit Verlag.

Beinart, W. and Brown, K. 2013. *African local knowledge and livestock health: Diseases and treatments in South Africa,* Wits University Press, Johannesburg: South Africa.

Food and Agriculture Organisation (FAO). 1998. Indigenous knowledge for watershed management in the Upper North West of Australia, Available at: http://www.fao.org/docrep/X5672e09htm. (Retrieved: 2 November 2014).

Gearheard, S., Pocernich, M., Stewart, R., Sanguya, J., and Huntington, H. P. 2009. Linking Intuitive knowledge and meteorological station observations to understand changing wind patterns at Clyde River, *Nunavut. Clim Change.* Available at: doi10.1007/s10584-009-9587-1. (Retrieved: 2 Nov 2014).

Holloway, A. 2003. Disaster risk reduction in Southern Africa: Hot rhetoric-cold reality, *African Security Review* 12 (1). Available at: http://www.iisd.org/koetter_land_&_disastermanagement.htm /ster_preparedness/disaster_pre paredness.pdf. (Retrieved: 3 November 2014).

King, D. N. T., Skipper, A., and Tawhai, W. B., 2008. Māori environmental knowledge of local weather and climate change in Aotearoa – New Zealand, *Climatic Change* 90 (4):385–409.

Macedo, D. 1999. 'Decolonising indigenous knowledge', In Semali, L. M. and Kincheloe, J. L. (Eds). *What is indigenous knowledge? Voices from the academy,* Falmer Press, New York.

Manyatsi, A. M. 2011. Application of indigenous knowledge systems in hydrological disaster management in Swaziland, *Current Research Journal of Social Sciences,* 3 (4): 353-357.

Mapara, J. 2009. Indigenous Knowledge Systems in Zimbabwe: Juxtaposing Postcolonial Theory, *Journal of Pan African Studies,* 3 (1): 139-155.

Mawere, M. 2012. *The struggle of African indigenous knowledge systems in an age of globalisation – A case for children's traditional games in South-eastern Zimbabwe,* Langaa RPCIG Publishers: Bamenda.

Mawere, M. 2014. *Culture, indigenous knowledge and development in Africa: Reviving interconnections for sustainable development,* Langaa RPCIG Publishers: Bamenda.

Melchias, G. 2001. *Biodiversity and conservation,* Enfield: Science Publishers.

Mwaura, P. (Ed). 2008. *Indigenous knowledge in disaster management in Africa,* United Nations Environment Programme, Kenya.

Nyong A, Adesina F and Elasha BO. 2007. The value of indigenous knowledge in climate change mitigation and adaptation strategies in the African Sahel, *Mitigation Adaptation and Strategic Change,* 2007; 12:787-797. DOI 10.1007/s11027-007-9099-0.

Ocholla, D. 2007. Marginalized Knowledge: An agenda for Indigenous Knowledge development and integration with other forms of knowledge, *International Review of Information Ethics,* 7(09), 1-10.

Odora-Hoppers, C. 2001. *Indigenous knowledge and the integration of knowledge systems: Towards a conceptual and methodological Framework,* HSRC: Pretoria, South Africa.

Odora Hoppers, C. A. 2002. Introduction. In Odora Hoppers, C. A. (Ed). 2002. *Indigenous knowledge and the integration of knowledge systems,* pp. vii-xiv, Claremont: New Africa Books.

Selin, H. 1993. Science across culture: African and native American achievements, *The Science Teacher,* 60 (3): 38-44.

Semali, L. M. Community as classroom: (Re)Valuing indigenous literacy, In Semali L. M., and Kincheloe, J. L. (Eds). 1999. *What is indigenous knowledge? Voices from the academy,* Falmer Press: New York.

Semali, L. M. and Kincheloe, J. L. 1999. Introduction: What is indigenous knowledge and why should we study it? In Semali L. M. and Kincheloe, J. L. (Eds). 1999. *What is indigenous knowledge? Voices from the academy,* Falmer Press: New York.

Shizha, E. 2010. The interface of neoliberal globalisation, science education and indigenous African knowledges in Africa, *Journal of Alternative Perspectives in the Social Sciences*, 2 (1): 27-58.

Shizha, E. 2013. Reclaiming our indigenous voices: The problem with postcolonial sub-Saharan African School curriculum, *Journal of Indigenous Social Development*, 2 (1): 1-18.

Singh, D. (9/08/2011). *The wave that eats people: The value of indigenous knowledge for disaster risk reduction,* United Nations Office for Disaster Risk Reduction (UNISDR).

Steiner, A. 2008. 'Foreword', In Mwaura, P. (Ed). *Indigenous knowledge in disaster management in Africa,* United Nations Environment Programme, Kenya.

Chapter 3

An Evaluation of African Traditional Scientific Knowledge and Technological Devices

Pius Oyeniran Abioje

Introduction

The question of whether traditional Africans had scientific and technological knowledge has engaged the attention of some scholars, since the colonial era, coupled with the ascendance of Islam and Christianity over African Traditional Religion (ATR) and culture. The three foreign forces: Islam, colonialism, and Christianity have been out, for the most part, to upstage traditional African civilisation, through both subtle and violent means. The subtle means included trade interactions with ancient Africans by some Arab and European merchants, and building of churches, establishment of schools and hospitals by some Christian missionaries from Western Europe and North America. The violent means had featured in form of Muslim jihad (such as by Usman Dan Fodio in northern Nigeria, 1804) and now in form of violence that is visited on some adherents of ATR by some Christians and Muslims, to prevent them (the former) from celebrating some of their festivals, with particular reference to those that require curfew or restriction of women to indoor, such as in the case of Orò and Agemo festivals in Yorubaland, Nigeria.

Toward annihilating traditional African civilisation, the Arab Muslims and Christian colonialists paint African culture (including ATR) in demonic colours. Nothing good was expected to come from Africa, whether adequate knowledge of God, authentic religion, philosophy, or science and technology that is in focus in this chapter. Unfortunately, many Africans have swallowed hook, line, and sinker, the derogation visited on traditional Africans as sub-human and primitive. Such Africans who appear to be in the majority today, as Christians and Muslims, claim that traditional

Africa lacks a standard culture, including scientific and technological knowledge. This chapter reviews critically the arguments. The study is based on review of literature, and participant observation, as issued in my experience as a Yoruba, from southwest Nigeria. The research is, therefore, phenomenological, exploratory, descriptive, and expository at the same time.

The Backwardness of Traditional Africa

Given the advancement of Europeans and North Americans in the area of science and technology, one can hardly deny that traditional Africa is backward. Ehusani (1992:1) refers to "modern Western technological civilization" as "the most glamorous civilization in the history of humankind", viewed from the "tremendous breakthroughs in medical care, in communication, in agriculture and in economics". There are some other areas not listed by Ehusani, e.g. transportation by road, water and air. But, to what extent is Oyebola (1982: *Preface*) right, arguing that:

> We must admit the fact of our backwardness. We must ignore the liberal white scholars who exaggerate our past contributions to civilisation. After all, if our Black ancestors were as civilised as some liberal scholars would want us to believe, we must be able to find unmistakable evidence of their concrete achievements in Africa. For instance, the English, the Chinese, the Egyptians or the Japanese can point to their ancestors' great achievements in terms of buildings, works of art and inventions.

Obviously, Oyebola betrays his ignorance of the facts. He limits the meaning of civilisation to 'great achievements in terms of buildings, works of art and inventions', to the exclusion of the fundamental art of living in peace and harmony, or what Hume (1988: title page and content) refers to as 'civilisation of love', without which no human progress is possible. Human unity, peace, and progress rely on societal, community, clan, and family organisational acumen, and the content of a people's character, for which many scholars, Africans and non-Africans, have commended African ancestors. That is not to say, of course, that traditional Africans were perfect but their credit and meritorious contribution to world civilisation should not be underestimated.

Most outstanding among the achievements of African ancestors are the welfarist nature of the extended family system (Bernheims 1968:13-14): the checks and balance forms of governance (Fadipe 1991:198-242): environmental conservation (Mawere 2014a); economic integration (Olopoenia 1994:81-83); and what Iwara (1994:42) refers to as the 'stolen legacies'. As Iwara notes, the history of Africa is full of examples of deliberate falsification and plundering of the continent's works of art in their various forms, such as bronze, wooden and stone images. The Bernheims (p. 51) also note that:

> Metal, stone, and terracotta objects have been found, the oldest being terracotta heads of the Nok culture, estimated to date from 900 B.C. to 200 A.D. Bronze, ivory, and terracotta pieces belonging to the Ife and Benin cultures of Southern Nigeria and dating back to the thirteenth century A.D., are among the most precious in African art. The first pieces were brought to England in 1897 and bought up by German and British museums.... Today the great African collections are at the Musée de l'Homme, Paris; the British Museum, London; the Museum of Primitive Art, New York City; and the University Museum, Philadelphia.

On the same page, the Bernheims writes on how 'dissatisfied with the decadence of impressionistic painting, the new French artists found in the vitality of African sculpture the inspiration that led them to create the Cubist movement'. The essential point to note of course is that Africa had contributed to world civilisation in originality terms. The advancement of "African art" should not be dissociated from African science and technology, since, as Hawthorne (1986: 15) tells us, there is a thin line between the two fields of human knowledge. He explains that "the word 'science' comes from the Latin for knowledge", even though "nowadays it means the study of nature, natural science", with a method which "relies on observation and experiment." Beyond that, Hawthorne notes on the same page that more often than not, "something akin to the inspiration of an artist may help the scientist to make sense of his observations." It is thus inappropriate to separate, thoroughly, African "metal, stone, terracotta, bronze, and ivory objects" mentioned above from scientific observation and manipulation of nature. What's more, life appears to be a continuous seam (as between art and science), rather than in absolute compartments as such.

From the explanation given by Hawthorne, who is himself a scientist, it seems difficult sometimes to say where science or art begins and ends, if at all such a demarcation can be made. That is explicit in the statement that "the word 'science' comes from the Latin for knowledge" (above). Thus, the original meaning of science is knowledge, and in modern understanding, it still refers to sure knowledge or certainty, as different from guess, myth, assumption, hallucination, or anything in that category. To that extent, traditional Africans cannot be said to lack scientific knowledge and technological devices. There is no doubt that they erected structures, engaged in mining, made farming and hunting implements from stone, and then from metal, progressively speaking, for instance. With specific reference to architecture, Rodney (2005:75) refers to 'the constructions in brick' in Zimbabwe which are said to date back to around the 14th century, and are still standing (cf. Mawere 2014a, 2014b). This, as well as the aforementioned achievements of African ancestors, no doubt rubbishes any suggestion that Africa had no civilization or scientific knowledge before the advent of the Arabs and the Europeans. Yet, one cannot rule out the fact of Africa's backwardness, due to European and Arabic predators and their indigenous collaborators.

A brief history of Africa's backwardness

Three basic epochs are identifiable in the history of Africa: the pre-colonial period; the colonial period, and the post-colonial period. The first epoch, as Ogundele (2006: 697) notes, refers to the era before the advent of Arabs who represented Islam, as well as Europeans and North Americans who represented Christianity. The two religions are significant for Africa's disunity and destabilization. They were both associated with the Slave Trade, colonialism, and post-colonialism. The second epoch is the Slave Trade/colonial era characterized with the invasion, conquest and subjugation of African cultures (Mawere 2014c), while the third epoch is the post-colonial/neo-colonial era, which, like its colonial predecessor, is driven by both foreigners and their currently empowered African rulers. Both imperial forces (foreign and indigenous) have continued to rape Africa, collaboratively, despite the so-called political "independence".

Africa's scientific knowledge suffered (and, unfortunately, it is still suffering, largely) from both indigenous elitism and foreign dominance. As earlier noted, the aim of the Arabs who spread Islam to Africa, as well as Europeans and North Americans who brought Christianity was to replace ATR and culture with their own alternatives. On that score, Africa became a battleground, which in itself, was destabilising. There was the Slave Trade, for which different African rulers were incited by Arabs and Europeans to wage war against one another, so that they could get slaves to buy. As the Bernheims (1968: 73) note, the Slave Trade lasted for four centuries, from the sixteenth to the nineteenth centuries, and "an estimated fifty million Africans were captured or perished." And that refers mostly to able persons, which accentuated and propelled Africa's retrogression and socio-economic underdevelopment.

At the end of that inhuman trade, masterminded by people who brought "Godly" religions to Africa, the continent became occupied for colonization by European nations who partitioned her among themselves. From the Slave Trade, through colonisation and introduction of Islam and Christianity, until today, Africa has not been the same, in spite of "political independence". That is the historical trajectory that arrested Africa's civilisation, including her scientific and technological advancement. Ablade (1976: 25-26) is apt when he states that:

> Study the effects of environment on human nature. You place the White man in the slum, deprive him of educational advantages, arrange it so that he has to struggle hard to fulfil his instinct of self-respect, give him little physical privacy and less

leisure, and he would after a time assume the same characteristics he attaches to the Black man. These characteristics don't spring from whiteness or blackness but from a man's conditioning.

What does Ablade mean by the "characteristics" the "White man" attaches to the "Black man"? They include primitivism and backwardness. He has described the environment created for the Africans by the Westerners and the Arabs which was (and is still largely) responsible for the backwardness of Africa. The "environment" implies the Slave Trade, colonialism, and demonization of African culture by European Christians and Arabic Muslims. Ehusani (1992: 35) quotes Ngugi Wa Thiong'o as stating that "the cumulative effect of the experience of slavery and colonialism tantamount to a cultural bomb", whose effect "is to annihilate a people's belief in their names, in their language, in their heritage of struggle, in their unity, in their capacities and ultimately in themselves." When 'colonialism' is implicated in that way, both Christianity and Islam are included, since both religions try to 'annihilate' traditional African beliefs, names, and culture, generally. The 'environment' stifled, and has continued to stifle (in form of neo-colonialism, corruption, and self-aggrandizement) African civilization.

Some or many Christians may be quick to say that "colonialism" was not all a negative experience, and that it imported a lot of benefits. One would respond with an American journalist, David Lamb, quoted by Ehusani (p. 19), to the effect that:

> The colonialists left behind some schools and roads, some post offices and bureaucrats. But their cruellest legacy on the African continent was a lingering inferiority complex, a confused sense of identity. After all, when people are told for a century that they're not as clever or capable as their masters, they eventually start to believe it.

Ordinarily, one would think that whoever loses self-confidence or faith in oneself is a finished person. Beyond that, as Ablade (p. 27) notes, "The colonial and missionary education system has been fashioned to glorify European way of life', and "not to instil allegiance to truth and justice and the cause of enslaved humanity, but rather to create a petty of loyal running dogs who will respond more like machines than like human beings." Likewise, Pobee (1990: 202) quotes "Joseph Ephraim Caseley Hayford (1866-1930), one of the leaders of Aborigines Rights Protection Society (founded in 1897 in the Gold Coast)" as describing "the average product of the mission school as 'a black whiteman'." Consequently, many African "elites" today have abandoned African heritages in preference for those of "the whiteman". For instance, from religious point of view, a Christian Pastor, Ilupeju (2004: 34), who prides himself a theologian, insinuates that, "However sincere" the adherents of ATR "may think they are, they are ignorantly worshipping the devil". Quoting "1Tim 2:15" Ilupeju (p. 33) states that "There is no mediator between man and God apart from Jesus Christ." He no doubt represents numerous African Christians in that conviction. On a scientific note, Makinde (1988: 106) regrets how very many Western trained medical doctors seek ways of rubbishing and discouraging African traditional medical doctors, by painting them as having no standard, even though it was through the "traditional medicine" that "many of them were safely delivered, nurtured, and successfully treated until they grew up to be medical doctors." Otherwise, among African traditional values is creativity in all its ramifications, artistically and scientifically. As Gashash (2006: 69) notes:

> No country can progress without creative people leading it, finding new ways of solving problems, taking the things that are around them and creating something new from them, designing new plans and systems, etc. In order to preserve our culture, we need artists, we need scientists, we need all types of creativity in between these two.

To what extent could traditional Africans continue to be creative, when they are maligned and attacked by fellow Africans and their foreign accomplices? Too many Africans came to abandon traditional science, including the aspects of magic and medicine that sustained life in pre-colonial times. Not many Africans would say, as Ayandele (2006: 109) states that:

It is, indeed, presumptuous and unscientific to dismiss with levity our cultural heritage as ossified reactionary traditionalism irrelevant to evolution of Nigeria as a nation. The truth of the matter is that pre-colonial Nigerian society was rationally open, borrowing rationally and manfully from other communities.

What can be more scientific than for a people to be "rationally open, borrowing rationally and manfully from other communities", as Ayandele notes in that quotation? The implication is that traditional Africa is not as dogmatic as Christians and Muslims who hold that there is no other way than their own way. The latter are known for staunch opposition to whatever contradicts their own doctrines and claims. The Church's suppression of Galileo Galilei's confirmation of the observation of Nicholas Copernicus (1473-1543) that the sun is the centre of the planetary system and the earth revolves around it, is a popular case. Beyond that, Tarnas (1991: 318) notes how "The Christian injunction to love and serve all humanity and high valuation of the individual human soul now stood in sharp counterpoint to Christianity's long history of bigotry and violent intolerance – its forcible conversion of other peoples, its ruthless suppression of other cultural perspectives, its persecution of heretics", etc. That explains also how traditional Africa became suppressed and backward, scientifically and otherwise. What is worse, the Bernheims (1968: 29) note that under European domination, "Africans had to curb their personal ambitions and enter only those professions assigned to them: law and the civil service, religion, teaching, and medicine." According to their findings, "hardly any African who studied engineering or architecture in a European university could get a job back home under the colonial regime, since these were professions monopolized by the white man." So, where is the moral justification to blame traditional Africans for backwardness, when the Europeans and the Arabs were (and still are, to a large extent) responsible for her destabilisation? In sum, the latter perpetrated devastating Slave Trade, through incitement and war, and planted the divisive religions of Christianity and Islam, as well as neo-colonialism, due to all of which peace and unity are elusive in many African countries, such as Somalia, Nigeria, Central Africa, etc.

African science and technology in the pre-colonial era

A lot is known about pre-colonial Africa, because colonialism, including Christianity and Islam, has not destroyed African culture in its totality, due to the resilience of the latter. Even today, a lot of the culture can still be seen in villages and towns, only because old habits die-hard. It has been severally asserted that African culture is resilient. Hillman (1993: 8) notes that:

> Religious activity, aimed at displacing Africa's traditional religious symbol systems, and replacing them with foreign imports, was the greatest threat to the survival of African cultures. This is so, because these cultures are intimately bound up with the people's traditional religious experiences, perceptions and articulations. Moreover, the establishment of Christian congregations among the 'natives' lent an aura of respectability and a cloak of legitimacy to the morally reprehensible enterprise of colonialism.

Indubitably, the Christian (and Muslim) stratagems had worked, to a large extent. Yet, as Hillman (p. 46) further notes, "African cultures, even under the costly clothing of modernity, still show signs of vitality and varying degrees of relevance for the self-understanding of countless millions of people." That fact clearly indicates that the pre-colonial Africa was not intellectually, artistically, technologically, and scientifically bankrupt. As the Bernheims (p. 73) note:

> Africa before the arrival of the Europeans was not an isolated land mass. Since the seventh century, her East Coast carried on a flourishing trade with Arabia and China. Arab caravans searching for salt, gold, and slaves crisscrossed the Sahara. They linked West to North Africa and brought Islam to black kings. Since the eighth century, the great empires of

Ghana, Songhai, and Mali ruled in the upper reaches of West Africa. Each one of these states had a civilization perhaps superior to certain medieval kingdoms of Europe.

That is the historical trajectory unknown to many contemporary Africans (such as Oyebola, earlier quoted) who think that Africa has always been backward. Traditional African rulers were caught unaware because, as the Yoruba say, *A kìí ghón to eni to n ṣó ni* (You cannot be as wise as a person studying you clandestinely, to trick and exploit you). The politico-economic and religious beneficiaries of European and Arab heritages in Africa continue to malign African traditional heritages. Hence, for instance, very many African Christian and Muslim clerics would never see or say anything good in ATR, as they milk their congregations weekly, if not daily.

Otherwise, there is nothing to indicate, in any literature I have read, or field researches that I have conducted, that traditional Africans depended on Europeans and Arabs to reach God, or to survive as human beings, prior to the colonial era. African culture, before the advent of Arabs, Europeans and North Americans, was in a class of its own, in marriage and naming ceremonies, initiation and funeral rites, religious, moral, philosophical, political, judicial, scientific, medical, magical, etc. systems. Ayandele (2006: 90-91) explains why some enlightened Africans keep clamouring for return to African (valuable) heritages. He writes that:

> Unfortunately, judged by the results, neither Islamisation nor Christianisation effort has transplanted the healthy moralising role of traditional religion to the votaries of Islam and Christianity. For, by and large, the Crescent and the Cross have produced irredeemable hypocrites, that is baptised 'pagans' and counterfeit Muslim (sic). In our very eyes the facts testify that only a few Muslims and Christians have truly assimilated the moral values of their religions. Hence, the fact that, with very few exceptions, they contribute more to crimes than any other religious group.

Ayandele's last sentence (in that quotation) may be better appreciated if the level of Christo-Islamic materialism is assessed.

48

Smith (1972: 3) writes that, "Christianity, as Archbishop Temple used to contend, is the most avowedly materialistic of all the great religions of the East." And, according to Smith, Denis de Rougemont concurs, when the latter stated that: "Compared with the religions of the East, Christianity might be called materialism." In Smith's view, which I find incontestable, "Judaism and Islam should be ranked beside Christianity in these judgments." Coincidentally, both Christianity and Islam derived from the same family as Judaism, from Abrahamic ancestry. Evidently, Christians and Muslims need money to build churches and mosques, respectively, publish their holy books, engage in propagation and undertake missionary journeys, and so on, whereas ATR has never been so capital-intensive or money-centred.

From the scientific point of view, it is doubtful, that any nation or society can survive without a scientific mastery of the environment, coupled with certain technological devices to tame natural forces (cf. Mawere's book on African cultures, indigenous knowledge and development, 2014c). Africa had existed for many millennia before the birth of Jesus Christ, and had acquired her own scientific knowledge, comparable to what obtained in some European countries in the pre-colonial era, as the Bernheims earlier testified. Sadly, as Amewowo (2012: 9) notes, Africa has largely "lost or rejected with impunity, falsely in the name of Christianity, our scientific culture, science and technology that sustains and protects creation." Otherwise, as he further writes, "In the olden days, our culture and religion (African Traditional Religion) protected water sources, rivers, lakes and their banks", and "the entire hydrosphere was (treated as – emphasis mine) sacred." Unfortunately, continues Amewowo, "in the name of civilization and in the name of Christ who died for the salvation of the whole creation (cf. Rom 8: 19-23), the measures protecting the hydrosphere have been rejected as taboos" and, if I may add, superstitions. That is but an example of what has happened to our ancestral heritages –rejection and loss. Rather than learning more, selectively, from external sources, most contemporary Africans jettisoned African ancestral heritages in favour of external wisdom, even though no people are omniscient. In what way, for instance, are Christianity and Islam better than ATR, in fear of God and love of neighbour? Did adherents of ATR, for instance, engage in deception and violence, such as crusade and jihad, to propagate their religion? Do ATR clerics live on religion-ism, as do Christo-Islamic clerics? These are searching questions to which interested readers may try to find answers.

The pre-colonial Africa was not stagnant but progressive, scientifically. Ogundele (2006: 699) quoting Sinclair et al (1993) writes that traditional Africans were progressive, as obvious in the "transition from a hunting/gathering mode of economy to food production and from this level to metallurgy." That type of advancement would have been impossible without a scientific study of one's environment. Beyond that, it has been noted that science develops from magical knowledge, and Africa abounds in magical knowledge that could develop into scientific knowledge and technological devices. Smart (1981: 75), for instance, writes that "magic has tended to transform itself and to become science." Thus, as Smart further notes, "alchemy, which had many magical elements, became transformed into scientific chemistry, and astrology was replaced by astronomy." Moreover, writes Smart (p. 76), "we have more than once referred to magic as a kind of primitive technology, but it should not be supposed that a culture in which magical ideas and techniques flourish is thoroughly incompetent in dealing with the environment." I concur. From the Yoruba (African) point of view, Onibonoje (1976: 155-156) indicates that African science is magical in nature. In his words:

> In Yoruba indigenous science, it is common belief that every aspect of nature and creature has its primordial and authentic name which constitutes its very essence. Every time a Yoruba man is in confrontation with nature or creature, he overpowers and conquers it by pronouncing its primordial and authentic name. Even the most poisonous serpents, the dangers of fears of dark and dangerous night are confronted and tamed in this manner, at least in the consciousness of the Yoruba man.

That explanation goes beyond the Yoruba or African ideas and practices, if Smart's point earlier cited is anything to reckon with, and I suppose it is. The impression that belief in magical efficacy is peculiar to Africans is absurd. Indeed, there seems to be hardly anything human that is peculiar to any people. Needleman (1980: 91), an American who does not mention Africa or any African people in his book, writes that:

> True metaphysics works; true philosophy works; true mystery works. True magic works –through the phenomenon of resonance. One must know the exact words to say and one must say them in exactly the right place and the right time, and then forces may be called down from heaven.

That seems a perfect description of how incantations work. Magic and scientific-cum-technological devices work in identical ways. The device (remote control) which Westerners use to open and close heavy gates at a distance, or to put-on and off television, for instance, works magically. Likewise telephone, through which a person can just press some button and speak with somebody at an amazing distance, seems to operate magically. I witnessed some instances in which some Yoruba hunters, among whom I lived, spoke to some fellow hunters at a long distance, by blowing into a horn; certainly a magical horn. Then in a Yoruba play, *Saworo Ide*, which portrays African culture, a drummer used a feather to clean his ear. He then attached the feather to his talking drum, and when he beat the drum asking his son to come immediately, his son who was sojourning in an unknown land heard the drum calling him to hasten back home. He left the food he was eating, instantly, and went home to meet his father.

I would group radio and telephone in the same category. Television also, except that it carries talking images. From the traditional African point of view, I am aware that a magical expert can view and hear targeted persons, wherever they may be, by looking into a concoction, for instance. Beyond my personal experience, some friends also related their experiences to me in that respect. In the course of such exchanges, I heard the story of a son who was successful abroad, but was hiding his family (wife and children) from the glare of his villagers, including his own father, even though he was financially generous to the latter. On one occasion when he went to the village, his father called him into an inner room and asked him to look into a concoction. The son could not believe himself seeing his wife and children, what they were doing and saying, as they sat or moved around. His father said to him: 'I just want you to know that you are not hidden, and you should not think you can hide. I want you to be coming home with your wife and children. No harm or danger will befall them'. There is hardly anything to which magic does not apply. African traditional medical doctors don't usually perform sophisticated operations, such as cesarean operation, for instance, but they can use magic, in form of soap or incantation, to effect safe delivery, according to my findings. When a baby's hand or leg rather than head is forward in the womb, delivery is impossible without operation in the Western system. That is the point at which the woman will be given some magical soap to be washing her belly, externally. But some other African traditional doctors are believed to use incantation to solve the problem. A traditional medical doctor once recited the incantation to me, but I didn't record it. Before doing so, he looked around to see that no pregnant woman was around, because, according to him, the foetus would "come down" (i.e. be born), should she hear the incantation. And a woman actually testified to me that the soap solution worked for her and that within a few days, the baby's head was forward, in place of a hand earlier shown by scanning, and she had safe delivery in a university teaching hospital. Thus, wise Africans use both Western and African scientific solutions, as applicable to various life's predicaments. In Africa, there are incantations for burn, snake and scorpion bites, and some others, such as for extracting bullets from a shut person, etc., all in the manner described by Onibonoje and Needleman, above.

In the area of movement, traditional Africans are not known for any sophisticated means, for land, water, and air journeys, in my findings. But, they are said to have magic for reducing distance, which the Yoruba call *kánàkò*, with which a person can make in a few minutes, a journey of several hours by a car or lorry, for instance. Traditional Africans are also known for magic of multi-location, by which a person is found in many places at the same time. It is the type of magic used by night guards, for instance. Hence, a magically powerful person would guard a whole city, if he has magic for multi-location. He would be present everywhere at the same time in the city. It was based on that reality that one man called Eegungberiasa was singularly guarding my village, Iwere-ile, at night in the 1960s through 1980s, and there was never any incidence of theft. Iwere-ile is the current capital of Iwajowa local government of Oyo state, Nigeria. Night guards are also known for magic for arresting criminals, arms down, as well as amulets against cutlass (called òkígbé in Yoruba) and against gunshot (òògùn ìbọn).

That, in a nutshell, is the extent and power of African magic, which could have developed like Western magic into what we know as science and technology today. Of course, both magic and science can be put into negative uses, depending on the user and circumstances. That is the fact Christians and Muslims should have been addressing, to discourage people from unholy use of magical and scientific/technological devices, rather than indiscriminate demonization of African magic. While Western scientists break new grounds almost on daily basis, corruption and selfishness dominate the lives of most African countries, in addition to the maligning of African heritages of arts and sciences. Rather than building on African heritages, too many Africans are discouraged by Christians and Muslims who preach against them. In many instances, African children are taught in school drama that only Christian and Muslim prayers work, and that African traditional medical doctors are devilish agents. Whither Africa? That is the question for further research, in respect of traditional African magic, science and technology.

Moreover, I found that many Africans today (the exact percentage may never be known, even though, as Mawere - 2011:106 – following World Health Organisation Traditional Medicine Strategy 2002-2005 notes, about 80% in South Africa) believe that many traditional African medicines work effectively against various diseases, with particular reference to tropical diseases, such as malaria. One would not agree with Makinde (1988:103) in what seems a suggestion that it is only "the majority of Africans in the rural areas" who "look for treatment of diseases and illness (including mental illness) from the traditional healers who share the same experience with them and so understand their problems." The truth of the matter would seem to be that many

Africans in urban and rural areas patronize African traditional medicine, as well as Western medicine, because no system is perfect and self-sufficient. One only needs to see how many Africans live on selling traditional medicine in many towns, including Lagos, Accra, and other such (capital) towns. The question I would want my reader to ponder is whether it is possible for a people who are not scientifically knowledgeable and talented to discover effective medicines.

In Africa in 1957, when Ghana became the first Black African nation to gain independence, apart from Ethiopia that has never been colonized, and the other nations followed one after another. Nigeria attained hers in 1960. Why does the continent remain backward even in the twenty-first century? I observe that the Christians and Muslims who dominate many African countries, currently, perpetrate politicization of religion, divide and rule, materialism and self-aggrandizement, as opposed to the traditional African communal lifestyle. The Bernheims (p. 14) note that:

> For centuries, the Africans have maintained their own type of social security, opening their homes to less fortunate relatives. No member of the tribe ever feels alone. No woman is left unprotected. In certain tribes, widows traditionally marry their brothers-in-law. Motherless children are taken in by their relatives.

I crave the reader's indulgence that I illustrate the Bernheims' observation with my own personal example. My father, Oyinlọla Alabi Abiọje, died (in the second half of the 1950s) when I was too young to know him. Then my mother remarried outside the family. I was raised by my uncles (Ọjẹnikẹ and Ọlayiwọla), and an aunt (Eegunyọyin), the only sister my father had. Hence, I lament the individualism and self-aggrandizement that characterize African society today. How can any nation develop under a divisive environment, perpetrated by many Christians and Muslims, as it is the case in Nigeria, for instance? That is an issue a reader may consider for further research. It touches on why Africa remains backward, scientifically and technologically, generally speaking.

Conclusion

This chapter has examined the reality of African traditional science and technology. It advanced the argument that the Slave Trade, colonialism, Christianity and Islam, as well as neo-colonialism contributed in no small measure to the backwardness and underdevelopment of traditional African scientific and technological enterprise. One comes to the realisation that the onslaught on traditional African science and technology has continued unabated, even after the "independence" said to be attained by African countries. Many Christians and Muslims continue to preach against African magic, which has been described as African science by many scholars. Although many Africans (the percentage may never be known) continue to resort to African magic, there is no doubt that much knowledge has been lost. Knowledge is lost when children do not learn from their parents, and when experts die without trainees.

Nevertheless, another finding of this study is clamour in some quarters for a return to African heritages, to retrieve and conserve whatever is good and beneficial in them. For instance, there are good and evil types of magic. Sometimes, it depends on usage, to achieve a noble objective, such as to heal, arrest armed robbers, or, on the other hand, to harm. Africans should learn the nitty-gritty (practical details and implications), rather than a blanket condemnation or demonization of African heritages. That applies also to Western science and technology, to which one should not resort indiscriminately, such as applicable to explosives that can be ab-used, or harmful contraceptives that should be avoided. Western science and technology has made mobile telephone handsets and the social media possible in recent times. This study explains how distant communication is done magically in African traditional way; how magic is used by travellers to arrive quickly at their destinations; how magic is used in place of surgery in the Western medical system, etc. But, this researcher could not determine the extent to which such magical feats still exist today. The challenge is for interested readers to venture into that research area.

References

Ablade, N. A. K. 1976. "Racism – The Ideological Weapon of Imperialism", in G. O. Onibonoje, Kole Omotoso, and O. A. Lawal (eds), *The Indigenous for National Development*. Ibadan: Onibonoje Press and Book Industries (Nig.) Ltd., pp. 25-32.

Amewowo, Wynnand. 2012. "The Bible and Ecology", in JABS: Journal of African Biblical Studies, Vol. 4, October 2012, pp. 1-24.

Ayandele, E.A. 2006. "Chapter Three: Using Nigerian Culture for Nation Building", in *Perspectives in Nigeria's Cultural Diplomacy*, published by The (Nigerian) National Institute for Cultural Orientation (NICO), pp. 70-111.

Bernheims, Marc and Evelyne. 1968. *From Bush to City: A Look at The NewAfrica*. New York: Harcourt, Brace & World Inc.

Ehusani, George Omaku. 1992. *An Afro-Christian Vision: "QZQVEHE!": Toward A More Humanised World*. Iperu-Remo: The AMBASSADOR Publications.

Fadipe, N.A. 1991. *The Sociology of the Yoruba*. (Edited by Okediji, Francis Olu. and Okediji, Oladejo O.). Ibadan University Press.

Gashash, Mohammed Ibrahim. 2006. "Culture and Education for Peace", in *Culture and Education for Peac: Proceedings of A Two Day Seminar*, jointly organized by The (Nigerian) National Institute for Cultural Orientation (NICO) and United Nations Educational, Scientific and Cultural Organization (UNESCO), held on 27th& 28th June, 1996, pp. 65-75

Hawthorne, Tim. 1986. *Windows on Science and Faith*. Leicester: Inter-Varsity Press.

Hillman, Eugene. 1993. *Inculturation Applied: Toward An African Christianity*. New York: Paulist Press.

Hume, Basil. 1988. *Towards A Civilisation of Love: Being Church in Today's World*. London: Hodder & Stoughton.

Ilupeju, Kayode. 2004. "Chapter Two: African Traditional Religion", in Emiola Nihinlola & Mojisola Olaniyan (eds), *Discovering the Other Side: Challenges of Other Religions*. Ibadan: Fluorish Books Ltd., pp. 27-34.

Iwara. A.U. 1994. "Falsified and Stolen Legacies", in Andah, Bassey W. and Bolarinwa. Kunle A. (eds.). *A Celebration of Africa's Roots and Legacy.* Ibandan: Fajee Publications Ltd. Pp. 22-27.

Makinde, M. Akin. 1988. *African Philosophy, Culture, and Traditional Medicine. Ohio University Center for International Studies: Monographs in International Studies, Africa Series Number 53.*

Mawere, Munyaradzi. 2011. Ethical quandaries in spiritual healing and herbal medicine: A critical analysis of the morality of traditional medicine advertising in southern African urban societies, *Pan African Medical Journal,* 2011;10:6 Available online @ http://www.Panafrican-med-journal.com.content/article/10/6/full

Mawere, Munyaradzi. 2014a. *Environmental Conservation through ubuntu and other emerging perspectives.* Bamenda: Langaa Publishers.

Mawere, Munyaradzi. 2014b. "Western hegemony and conquest of Africa: Imperial hypocrisy and the invasion of African cultures", in Mawere, M. and Mubaya, R. (eds.), *African Cultures, Memory and Space: Living the Past Presence in Zimbabwean Heritge.* Bamenda: Langaa Publishers.

Mawere, Munyaradzi. 2014c. *Culture, indigenous knowledge and development in Africa: Reviving interconnections for sustainable development.* Bamenda: Langaa Publishers.

Needleman, Jacob. 1980. *Lost Christianity.* New York: Doubleday & Co., Inc.

Ogundele, S. Oluwole. 2006. "Quest for Our Ancestors: Some Reflections on Ancient African Heritages and Contemporary Politics", in Dapo Adelugba, Dan Izevbaye, and J. Egbe Ifie (Eds.), *Wole Soyinka at 70 Festschrift.* Place of publication not indicate. Published by LACE Occasional Publications & Dat & Partners logistics Ltd., pp. 689-730.

Olopoenia, R.A. 1994. "Economics: A United 'African Descent' Market: State of Economic integrations in African", in Andah, Bassey W. and Bolarinwa. 'Kunle A. (eds). *A Celebration of Africa's Roots and Legacy.* Ibadan: Fajee Publications Ltd.

Onibonoje, G. O. 1976. "The Concept of the Indigenous for National Development and the Urgent Need for Cultural Revolution", in G. O. Onibonoje, Kole Omotoso, and O. A.

Lawal (eds), *The Indigenous for National Development*. Ibadan: Onibonoje Press and Book Industries (Nig.) Ltd., pp. 155-163.

Oyebola, Areoye. 1982. *Black Man's Dilemma*. Ibadan: Board Publications.

Pobee, John S. "En Voie Theological Education in Africa", in J. S. Pobee and J. N. Kudadjie (eds), *Theological Education in Africa: Quo Vadimus?*. Accra: Asempa Publishers, pp. 193-228.

Rodney, Walter. 2005. *How Europe Underdeveloped Africa,* Abuja: PanafPublishing Inc.

Smart, Ninian. 1981. *The Religious Experience of Mankind.* New York: Collins Fount Paperbacks.

Smith, Huston. 1972. "Accents of the World's Religions", in John Bowman (ed), *Comparative Religion: The Charles Strong Trust lectures, 1961-1970*.Leiden: E. J. Brill, pp. 1-18.

Tarnas, Richard. 1991. *The Passion of the Western Mind: Understanding the Ideas that have Shaped Our World View,* New York: Harmony Books.

Chapter 4

Indigenous Knowledge, Conflation and Post-colonial Translation: Lessons from Fieldwork in Contemporary Rural Zimbabwe

Artwell Nhemachena

Introduction

This chapter explores matters of indigenous knowledge, translation, sublation and conflation in relation to fieldwork carried out in Zimbabwe. The chapter is motivated by contemporary debates on knowledge translation and postcoloniality. It is also motivated by efforts to explore ways in which the resilience of colonial epistemologies can be destabilised by revisiting and iterating indigenous knowledge systems and their roles in diverse African fields of life. The chapter explores ways in which indigenous knowledge systems were systematically sublated in the guise of colonial translation. It looks at ways in which various aspects of African modes of existence were erroneously conflated in ways that effaced the important distinctions for instance between African ancestors and the devil, Africans and animals. These modes of sublation, conflation and vilification, it is argued, were paradoxical in that the colonial settlers and the officials of the empires were appropriating the same African indigenous knowledge that they vilified as barbaric and devilish. The exploitation and appropriation of African indigenous knowledge continues, in the postcolonies, with very little acknowledgement of African indigenous intellectual property rights. With the colonial conflation of Africans with animals from the beginning of colonial scholarship and travel, Africans have been denied ownership of African resources including their own labour power which they were forced to provide to colonial industrialists under conditions of slavery or forced labour. This conflation of African modes of engagement in terms of animism is not supported by data yet the conflation had tremendous effects in facilitating the colonial project. This chapter looks at some aspects of animism that have, since the colonial period been used to mistranslate Africans. It argues that there is need to pay more attention to modes of translation that liberate Africa from colonial mind sets as well as from what Latin American scholars have called the coloniality of power in reference to continued subjection to imperial power of colonial subjects in the postcolonial eras. It argues for the need to pay attention, in matters of postcolonial translation in Africa, not only to linguistic issues but to broader cultural, political, social and economic issues.

Overview on Indigenous knowledge, animism and translation

This chapter is informed by contemporary debates on matters of knowledge and ontology by scholars around the world. Debates by Latin American scholars such as Mignolo (2007) about the decolonisation of knowledge and about the need to critique Euromodernity from its underside, that is, from subaltern knowledges (see Maldonado-Torres 2008) inform the arguments in this chapter. Contemporary scholarship is calling for the need to recognise the ways in which different epistemologies and ontologies with different metaphysical commitments play out together, connecting and separating (Verran 2013). The scholars like Turnbull (2000) and Verran (2013) for instance are also calling for the need to recognise that all forms of knowledge have their forms of rationality and ways of establishing objectivity (Turnbull 2001). Other scholars have called for critiques of dominant Eurocentric epistemologies which have been argued to have resulted in the colonisation of African knowledge and materialities, and which continue to take leading roles in shaping what constitutes progressive global values that are imposed on the African people (Ndlovu-Gatsheni 2013). For yet, other scholars like Hardin (1994), Eurocentric science is universal in the sense that it extracted valuable knowledge from other societies like India, Africa, China, Asia and Greece, that is, from colonised peoples. In this sense, it is argued that science continues to plunder other forms of knowledge including botanical knowledge, plant knowledge etc. yet it distributes costs and benefits unfairly.

The contestations about land ownership in Zimbabwe (see Raftopoluos 2009, Moyo 2008) and contestations about interpretations of recent recurrent droughts can be contextualised within broader debates on indigenous knowledge in relation to other kinds of knowledge heritages. Yet it was only in 2013 that the Zimbabwean Constitution, which is the Supreme law of the land, included a provision under section 16 that the state and all institutions and agencies of government at every level must promote and preserve cultural values and practices which enhance the dignity, wellbeing and equality of Zimbabweans. Under section 16, the state and all institutions and agencies of government at every level and all Zimbabwean citizens, must endeavour to preserve and protect Zimbabwean heritage. Section 16 further provides that the state and all institutions and agencies of government at every level must take measures to ensure due respect for the dignity of traditional institution. But other scholars, like McNeish (2005) have argued that despite interest in better engagement with indigenous populations and their knowledge, international development professionals and governments remain focused on development programmes initiated and funded by outsiders. As a result it has been argued that indigenous people's own initiatives and strategies have remained largely invisible except in cases where they can easily be capitalised on within the existing external industries and markets like biotechnology, organic products and crafts (McNeish 2005: 231). McNeish's (2005) remark is apt with respect to ways in which indigenous responses to droughts are interpreted, perceived and reacted to or ignored by different institutions and scholars that rely on schools of thought that do not pay much attention to everyday life modes of engagement.

Explanations, of the recurrent droughts in Zimbabwe, which appeared in the media showed that matters of causation of the droughts were not settled once and for all among the citizens of Zimbabwe. The explanations of the droughts underscore the fact that in coping with adversities people draw on indigenous as well as other cosmological and metaphysical resources before they act. One comment in the media explained the droughts in terms of the El Nino (which refers to abnormal heating of ocean waters that induces droughts and this El Nino is understood in Spanish as the little boy or Christ child) building up in the Pacific: *Zimbabwe: Experts predict drought* (The Herald, Harare 20 July 2009) but this explanation was contested by other accounts premised on the linkages between the droughts and the perpetration of violence in the country. The other explanations were that the droughts could only be averted by recourse to "traditional" ceremonies including *mukwerera* (literary meaning a request for rain but erroneously commonly known as "rainmaking") and "traditional" cleansing ceremonies to cleanse the nation of blood spilt during the liberation war fought in the 1970s: *Negation of Traditional Values Blasted* (The Herald, Harare 20 January 2003; *Zim "needs" cleansing ritual* (News 24.com AFP Special Report 28 April 2009: 13:19). Yet another explanation by the Zimbabwe Government was that the droughts were being caused by neo-imperialist Britain and the United States of America, that were opposed to the land reforms in Zimbabwe, and were thus alleged to be chemically doctoring the weather so as to arm twist governments in the Southern African region to capitulate to the whims of the world's super powers (BBC News, 28 June 2005: 15:13; UK, US caused Zimbabwe Droughts). These consternations by the Zimbabwe government have parallels in nearby Mozambique where the Renamo party has threatened that floods, which they admitted they caused by means of witchcraft, would not stop in Mozambique until the election fraud they alleged against the Frelimo party was addressed (Bertelsen (2004: 169-70). This connection between droughts and witchcraft is also evident in Schapera (1971: 49) who noted that a Kwena "rainmaker" in Botswana told the missionary David Livingstone in 1857 that: "other 'tribes' place medicines about our country to prevent rain, so that we may disperse and go to them and augment their power. We must dissolve their charms by our medicines".

While the explanations of the droughts in terms of the El Nino offered conventional "scientific" accounts, literature on Zimbabwean ethnography indicates that there are other ways of accounting for the droughts that link the everyday life of human beings to the environment and to politics. As pointed out above, in Zimbabwe, droughts have been explained by some citizens in terms of political and other conflicts deemed to disrupt the relations between human beings and entities held to be guardians (such as the *mhondoro* clan ancestors and intercessors) of the environment (Vujfhuizen 1997, Daneel 1998). Yet on the other hand, it has been reported that the (attempts to) expropriation of land from the whites for purposes of redistribution to black Zimbabweans was supported by "spirit mediums", the *mhondoro* guardians of the land, and *Mwari* (God) (see for instance Sadomba 2008; Daneel 1970). In Matabeleland region in the south west of Zimbabwe citizens are noted as having charged national leaders with neglecting the rain shrines after they came to power (Alexander et al 2000). The residents are further noted as having alleged that the leaders failed to report to shrines to thank "spirits" and *Mwali* (God) for their support in the liberation struggle. The interpretation by Alexander et al (2000) erroneously assumes, on the basis of western epistemologies of stasis, that God and ancestors are locked in shrines which national leaders are alleged to have neglected visiting. The leaders have been charged with failing to offer apologies for violence and for failing to lead the way in cleansing the nation of the effects of war (Alexander et al 2000), but this view by Alexander et al (2000) is oblivious to the fact that some forms of violence against injustice are deemed to be sanctioned by ancestors and God. It can also be noted here that scholarship seeking to understand such African cosmologies has also erroneously presumed that African ancestors and God are parochial enough not to see connections between (mis)governance in Africa and global (mis)governance. Thus there are erroneous assumptions that African ancestors and God get angry only with Africans yet in the moral geographies of Africa the causes of droughts and of ancestral anger can also be located outside Africa, in the realm of the global with which Africa has linkages.

Allegations that famine originated from conducts of governments have a long historical record. Historically the Ndebele, in the south western part of Zimbabwe, blamed the European settlers in the 1890s, when Zimbabwe was colonised by Britain, for the outbreak of rinderpests, for the droughts that ensued, for the grain famine which followed and for the swarms of locusts which invaded their lands. At the inception of colonialism the colonial settlers worsened the famine by setting African granaries on fire so as to make Africans dependent on the colonialist, during the 1893 war against colonialism (Kane 1954: 101-102; Chigodora 1997, LIiffe 1990). Indeed, the first Zimbabwean *Chimurenga* war of liberation from colonial rule, in the 1890s, was to protest against land seizures, hut tax. The droughts were also interpreted as resulting from the discriminatory practices of the colonists in matters of land legislation and other forms of maladministration, the confiscation of African cattle and land and the threats to sovereignty (Chitiyo 2004, Ranger 1979, Daneel 1998: 31). For Chitiyo (2004), the calamities were deemed by black inhabitants to be visited on the land by *Mwari* (God) who was displeased with colonial settlers' oppressive rule. While some may interpret these remarks by indigenous people as implying that it is the universe that is viewed as a Being other scholars have noted that views that the universe is a Being is a product of European Renaissance thinkers who described the cosmos as a chain of Being (Sheridan 2008: 16, Artigas 2001).

The ways of understanding the world are at the core of matters of translation. Translation for scholars like Law (2006) refers to the process of making two things that are not the same equivalent. With respect to this chapter, the challenge with conceptualisations of translation that focus on processes of mobilisation, betrayal and trials of strength (Callon 1986, Latour 2005) is that they do not help much to shed light on how postcolonial knowledge translation can be helpful to subjects of former colonies. Modes of engagement by colonial subjects have often been erroneously translated as animism or as involving the worship of personified objects of nature that colonial subjects were erroneously deemed to equate with human beings (Frazer 1926). Frazer's (1926) work makes it easy to reckon ways in which these animistic portrayals of colonial subjects collapsed human colonial subjects together with animals, and other fauna. By collapsing human beings with animals the animistic portrayals legitimised and facilitated slavery, exploitation and inhuman treatment of the Africans that were conflated with the animals. Yet other scholars such as Opoku (1978), Fontein (2006) and Bullock (1927) have shown that Africans do not consider every object to be animated but rather "spirits" can attach themselves to some objects which objects do not however become interchangeable with the "spirits". While some scholars like Garuba

(2013) argued that animism is beneficial to Africans, other scholars like Nyamnjoh (2012) have argued against the resilience of colonial epistemologies, such as epistemologies that attributed animism to Africa as a way to collapse human beings into animals to facilitate colonial projects. Nyamnjoh (2012) is apprehensive of ways in which Africans continue to be defined and understood within the Western matrix (see also Gyasi's (2008: 2). Eyebrows have been raised in translation studies with scholars like Robinson (1997: 10) noting that colonialists were keen to find ways not only to communicate with colonial subjects but also to develop new ways of subjecting them, converting them into docile subjects or 'cooperative' subjects.

One way in which to subject Africans and make them fit the Western matrix was to demonise African ancestors upon whom Africans relied in the struggles against colonialism. As Comaroff and Comaroff (2005: 505) noted Africans ancestors were erroneously portrayed as demons and as evil because this was part of the missionary ideology which unfortunately had the effect of colonising the consciousness of Africans who ended up accepting that their ancestors were demons. Yet even as colonial officials portrayed African ancestors as demons, they exploited Africans indigenous knowledge that was paradoxically deemed to originate from the ancestors. Though Africans continue to receive disapprobation in matters of development, epistemology and governance (see for instance Sachs 2005), their knowledge practices and their ancestral artefacts, which remain in European museums, have been expropriated for the benefit of western nations for long. African knowledge of architecture, writing, mathematics, agriculture, of plant medicines, of wild foods and vegetables, of mining and smelting and other manufacturing industries have been appropriated without acknowledgment for centuries (Hardin 1994, Ackroyd 2004, Herodotus 1942, Asante 2000, Onyewuenyi 2006, Koetsier and Bergams 2005, Ellert 1984, Kiggundu 2007, Segobye 2007, Posselt 1935, Suzuki et al 1992, Moahi 2007). The exploitation and appropriation of African epistemologies included the fact that in the history of Europe, European scholars were sent to Egypt to search for the origins of their ideas, institutions and practices and during the process Egyptian deities found their way into Greek and Roman pantheons. For scholars such as Kirkegard (2001), in 1240 statues of saints in the churches such as that of Magdeburg appeared for the first time with full African features and though the saints had always been known to be African they had been depicted with white European features. European scholars of various specialisations, such as those that were sent by Napoleon Bonaparte visited and stayed in Egypt for two years studying various practices and ideas of the Egyptians (Herodotus 1942: 130-1) but this is not acknowledged in Western scholarship. African scholars, who preceded Greek philosophers, (Asante 2000) taught philosophers such as Thales, Pythagoras, Aristotle, Plato all of whom lived in Africa and were taught by African priests and African scholars on Egyptian mystery system which formed the substantial beginnings of Greek philosophy (Onyewuenyi 2006). The indigenous mathematics which was a practical science that facilitated computation of the calendar, tax collection, harvests and public works on the banks of such rivers as the Ganges, Euphrates, Tigris, Indus have also been appropriated (Koetsier and Bergams 2005).The effacement of indigenous knowledge in the African territories has been witnessed in other places such as the Aztecs, Maya and Inca and other areas in Brazil and among Aborigines (Suzuki et al 1992). In areas such as Aztecs, Maya, Inca and Brazil indigenous agriculture, architecture, astronomy, mathematics that rivalled and surpassed fifteenth century European knowledge in these field have disappeared (Suzuki et al ibid: 7). Indigenous people who were able to identify plants, soil, insects and other elements in their environments have had their knowledge effaced in the same way yet the indigenous knowledge is relied on by Euro-Pharmaceutical organisations to extract medicinal plants and knowledge from Africa. Suzuki (1992:8) for instance notes that 270 Indian tribes along with their precious legacies of language and traditional knowledge have been erased from the face of the earth partly due to loss of their lands and due to cultural assimilation. If the fact that colonial officials exploited indigenous knowledge (Kiggundu 2007, Hardin 1994) is taken into cognisance, it becomes apparent that vilification of African indigenous knowledge was meant to distract Africans' attention from their own useful epistemologies which would have rendered Africans with lifelines or alternatives to hegemonising Western epistemologies.

These colonial processes, in so far as they subjugated African institutions, can be understood as sublational processes rather than merely translational processes: the objective was to reduce Africans and African institutions permanently to minority status in various fields. The unwillingness of colonial officials to admit that Africans had advanced knowledge and practices including pre-colonial industries is evident in Posselt (1935). Writing about colonial Zimbabwe, Posselt (1935: 3) for instance, argues that if colonial settlers attributed such works like the architecture at Great Zimbabwe entirely to Bantu that would mean accepting the view of a purely local Bantu civilisation of no mean order, yet Posselt (ibid: 8) admits that indigenous crafts, including furrow irrigation, mining and smelting have been supplanted by imported articles of European origin so the Bantu knew how to weave cloth from wild cotton in the pre-colonial period. This is supported by Ellert (1984) who notes that the culture including arts and crafts in pre-colonial Zimbabwe show that the people of Zimbabwe had developed technology appropriate for the manufacture of tools, implements, weapons, vessels, musical instruments, Cloth/*machira*, ornaments which demonstrated ingenuity and originality. For Ellert (ibid: 2) the idea that Africans possessed cultural values and civilisation independent of European culture was either inconceivable or suppressed as a threat to their own plans. The negative attitude was demonstrated in 1970 when the Rhodesian Front regime instructed that no official publication should state that Great Zimbabwe was without doubt an African creation. In spite of all this colonial vilification, Africans had an iron industry which flourished and reached a peak 50 years before the establishment of the British South African Company (BSA Co) administration and the Africans produced hoes, axes, spears, arrowheads, dagger, battle axes, *chigidi* (guns) as well as gun powder and bullets) etc. (Ellert 1984: 55, 57). This was deemed uneconomic and suppressed by the BSACo administration that however trotted the surviving smiths around the country to demonstrate their skills.

These processes of what I call colonial sublation rather than translation involved vertical colonial hegemonic epistemic relations.

These processes of sublation were evident with respect to colonial environmental epistemologies closely related to the environmental issues under discussion where Africans and other colonised peoples were interpreted as without human essence and as indistinct from animals and other fauna and flora in the environment and so were often included in museums together with reptiles and other animals (Vera 2001, Jacobson 2000). Such processes of sublation, collapsing and conflating Africans with animals and other creatures in the environment had the effect of legitimising colonial violence against the Africans deemed to be animals and therefore as without human essence to be protected by laws on human rights. Secondly the conflation of Africans with animals and other creatures had the effect of propping up the view that Africans, "without essence and like animals" could not be deemed to own assets including land which was coveted by the colonial powers and settlers. Thirdly, the conflation of Africans with such animals/creatures and denial of humanity to them had the effect of psychologically propping up colonial exploitation of Africans. In Zimbabwe for instance, African villages were referred to as "kraals" and as not distinct from cattle kraals and it was in these villages that the reserve labour for colonialist industries was located and tapped, as and when needed. In translation, one thing that needs attention is theories that are often recycled from colonial textbooks resulting in mistranslations of Africans. Some such recycled theories sublate, conflate and deflate Africans even as declarations and undertakings to postcoloniality are being made.

African modes of engagement, related to the environment including the droughts have been portrayed by some scholars in ways that presuppose animism. For instance, Ben Okri (1997: 132) argues that: "the gods of scientific certainty are yet to listen to the speech of poisoned dolphins, the cries of the stratosphere, the howls of the deforested earth, and the screams of people without hope and without food". On the other hand, other scholars have argued that the category of animism has been wrongly applied to Africa (Opoku 1978). Though other scholars conceive animism to be a way of overcoming modernist binaries there is evidence, as indicated below, to show that animism was in fact a product of Euro-modernity and was used by Europeans to colonise and subjugate other peoples that colonial officials alleged to be animals or close to animals. Defined as the endowment of "natural beings" with human dispositions and social attributes, and sometimes attributing to animals with culture, habits, rituals, songs, dances of their own (Descola 1996), animism presupposes the view that animals and other things are considered to be persons just like human beings. Defined by Descola (2005: 184-5 cited in Rival 2008) as the granting by humans, to nonhumans, of interiority identical to theirs. Such an attribution is understood, by Descola above, to humanise plants and above all animals because, he argues, the soul they are gifted with allows them not only to behave according to human social norms and ethical principles but also to communicate with each other

Other scholars have considered the increased invocation of the category animism by environmental/ecological movements as deriving from indigenous communities, postmodernism's relativistic epistemologies, new age spiritualism and from contemporary anthropologists speaking of relational epistemologies and different conceptions of personhood across cultures (Garuba 2013: 43). Yet other scholars note that animism can be traced to colonial modernist thinking, to Eurocentric epistemologies that include scientific naturalism (Oliver 1981; Kincaid 2013) and to European hylozoism cosmologies that deny God's transcendence as they presume that He is immanent or locked in nature (Smith 2001, Pearson 2001, Bryden 2001, Artigas 2001). Thus scholars like Garuba (2013: 43) who consider animism as an epistemological standpoint that is radically different from the modernist position appear not to be aware of arguments by scholars like Evensky (2005) that animism is a product of European eighteenth century deism when for Europeans "nature", viewed teleologically, became the polite word for God.

These observations pose questions about ways in which African cosmologies are translated particularly in Zimbabwe where during the liberation war of the 1970s, some guerrilla fighters are noted as having referred to themselves as *vana vevhu/ umtwana we lilabati* or sons of the soil (Mudzengi 2008, Fontein 2006) and the fighters also referred themselves as the bones of the dead ancestors that were now rising and fighting to reclaim the land from white colonial settlers (Kriger 1992). Such references would appear to support the assumptions of the European teleology and animism but on close analysis the assumptions of teleology are watered down. In Zimbabwe spirit mediums, and *mhondoro* ancestors, were also referred to as *vana vaMwari/abantwana BoMlimo* or Children of *Mwari*/God in so far as they were considered to be emanations from the Godhead (Bullock 1950: 145, 149). The *mhondoro* ancestors were also referred to as *varidzi vepasi/varidzi venzvimbo* or owners of the land/owners of the territories (Abraham 1966: 40, Daneel 1998: 23, Lan 1986): these references dissipate assumption that would conflate the *mhondoro* ancestors with the land that they own.

Other scholars have critiqued ways in which animistic portrayals of Africans by European travellers and scholars during the early contacts served to explain the other away as primitive, incapable of distinguishing the animate and the inanimate. For Boonzaier *et al* (2000: 10) European travellers and scholars portrayed the people they met as beastly, monstrous with faces on their chests and with sexual promiscuity. For Magubane (2007: 7, 10), the word savage as used to describe colonial subjects implied *inter alia*, "animal", "brute", "bestial", "heartlessness", "unfeeling", "childishness and buffoonery, laxity morally and mentally, "bloodthirsty", "cannibalism". In the light of all this some European travellers stated that Africans had sexual intercourse with baboons: the Africans were portrayed as half ape, descendants of baboons and resembling monkeys. In spite of these criticisms, other scholars such as Garuba (2013: 42) have argued that once considered as some kind of cognitive error, evidence of cognitive underdevelopment and epistemological failure, animism has once again become an object of discursive attention, a platform for political action particularly in relation to issues of ecology and environment. But for other scholars like Gifford (2012) and Brennan (2012), animism underpinned slavery, of which effects continue to be felt by Africans, in the sense that slaves were treated as beasts of burden to be driven like cattle and the slaves were considered useful precisely because they had the capacity to deal with complex order (Blackburn 1997: 12-20). This history of animism as applied to Africans by Europeans underscores that the colonial projects were premised on animistic portrayals of Africans as the dispensable animal-other. But then in the light of coloniality of power whereby imperial powers are understood to continue to exercise influence and power over former colonies (Ndlovu-Gatsheni 2013), the effects of animistic portrays of Africans continue to be felt even in postcolonies, with relations of inequality. The horse and rider relations proposed, between blacks and whites, by the colonial government, in the 1950s, in Zimbabwe (Mungazi 1996), underscore the animist portrayals of Africans in the imperial setting of the relations. Tracing human-environment relations in the context of the droughts allows one to appraise the discourses on animism and the effects of the application of animism as a category on African people.

This chapter dwells on the Shona indigenous idea of *mukwerera* (erroneously translated by early missionaries travelling to Africa as rainmaking) in relation to conventional weather modification (which was challenged in the Zimbabwean context of the crises noted above) as ways of surviving droughts. The problems that attend the translation of *mukwerera* as "rainmaking", in Eurocentric epistemologies and the ways in which the droughts were interpreted in the context of violence are germane in understanding indigenous knowledge in Zimbabwe. The chapter explores the kinds of connections, including with the environment, that were cultivated by villagers in Buhera, Zimbabwe, in their everyday life in struggles to cope with the droughts. In view of contemporary theoretical debates on animism, the paper also examines human-environment relationships and their import on debates about animism; the objective is also to explore the connections between meteorological practices in relation to indigenous drought coping mechanisms.

The worlds, entities and knowledge practices related to droughts and rains

Villagers in Buhera, a district in the south eastern part of Zimbabwe, related with entities of different kinds in their everyday life practices, at metaphysical, cosmological levels. Everyday life among the villagers, like healers and mediums, was lived on the basis of relations between human beings and other entities in the environment, and these entities such as the *mhondoro* and their mediums have been noted by scholar as having been instrumental in Zimbabwe's land redistribution exercise (see for instance Sadomba 2008). Interviews that I had in 2010 and 2011 with village heads Samuel and Bere, *mbuya* Magaya (who is a healer) and Monica who is a villager under Samuel indicated that human beings were connected not only to other human beings but also to entities like the *njuzu*, that were deemed to live under water; the human beings were also considered in such villagers' conceptions to be connected to other invisible ancestors. From the *njuzu* ancestors living in the underworld, humans were held to get *ruzivo*, a form of expertise for healing ailments, and the *njuzu* were also considered to be present in some streams, rivers, pools and springs which did not dry out even in the years of severe droughts. However, when humans violated the *njuzu* by using dirty, sooty or metal containers to fetch water from such rivers, springs, pools or streams, the *njuzu* migrate away in the form of "localised" whirlwind and the places subsequently run dry, since the springs, rivers, pools or streams were considered to be "*pamisha*", that is, the villages or headquarters of the *njuzu*. Villagers, like the healers and mediums, reported hearing sounds of cows mooing, sounds of drumming, singing and whistling in such rivers, streams, pools or springs which were home to the *njuzu* beings (see also McGregor 2003, Burbridge 1923, 1924). It is the character of *ukama* relations, as I will explain later in this chapter, with both the *njuzu* and other ancestors that were considered to affect rains or to bring about droughts.

It is such entities like *njuzu* and the rest of the African ancestors that were vilified and castigated a priori by European travellers, missionaries and scholars, as noted by Comaroff and Comaroff (2005), who were anxious to sublate African cultures and cosmologies under European ones. While African ancestors were deemed to punish their descendants, they were also deemed to be benevolent. But the benevolent part is what few early travellers who came to Africa noted. While Comaroff and Comaroff (2005) note that the missionary Moffat erroneously vilified African ancestors as demons, other scholars have noted the parallels between African ancestors and saints. One of the early travellers to pre-colonial Africa Manuel de Faria e Sousa (1674) noted, more than a hundred years before Zimbabwe was colonised by Britain, that people subject to Mutapa in pre-colonial Zimbabwe acknowledged only one God and they called upon royal *muzimos* (ancestors) as we (Europeans) the saints. Saints in Roman Catholic theology are presented as interceding with the Christian God so Faria e Sousa signified that the royal *mhondoro* spirits were conceived by the Shona of the precolonial period as intercessors with *Mwari* (Abraham 1966: 37). European kings also visited graves/sanctuaries of saints, in Europe, who they considered to be intercessors with God in order to venerate and adore them: the sanctuaries were deemed to be points of contact with the unseen worlds and to be resting places of the saints (Southern 1993: 133, 185-9). But the Europeans were not prepared to accept that Africans had their own intercessors (in the same logics of saints) with *Mwari* even if Africans also made pilgrimages to sacred places including to the famous Matopo Hills (Ranger 1999, Daneel 1970, Gelfand 1959, Bullock 1927, 1950, Ntholi 2006). Zimbabwean *mhondoro* such as Chaminuka and Nehanda, intercessors between human beings and God, who were considered to be "lions of the Heavens" (*mhondoro dzeMatenga*) (Garbett 1977: 57) were conceived by colonial scholars with disapprobation and scorn in spite of similarities with European conceptualisations of Heaven (see also Westerlund 2006 for the San who hold that deities or spirits of the dead stay in the sky/heaven with God).

But the ideas about visiting the Matopo Hills to hear the voice of *Mwari* in times of difficulties and the idea that *njuzu* stay in the underworld and manifest in rivers and pools have posed challenges for scholars trying to translate African cultures during the (post)colonial period. While some would seek to construe the rivers themselves as animate, it has been noted that the Shona people do not understand the rivers themselves as animate or as persons just like human beings (see also Bullock 1927). While Aborigines of Australia have been noted as conflating ancestors with nature, the Shona people do not consider the features to be animate and to be persons just like human beings (see also Fontein 2006). While other scholars would seek to construe the trees for instance under which rain petitioning ceremonies are conducted as animate and as persons just like human beings, the Shona do not consider trees and even the soil as persons but rather as resources (*nhaka*) from *Mwari* for use by humans (see for instance Moore 1993, Moyana 1984).

As hinted in the introduction, encounters in the early colonial period in Africa saw challenges of translation of different modes of engaging with the world, including ways of intervening to quell droughts, and what transpired during these early encounters helped shape the contemporary understandings of the world. Endfield and Nash's (2002) paper for instance, explores interactions and reactions, in the early colonial period, of missionaries and the people they encountered in African contexts of frequent droughts. The missionaries considered the introduction of irrigation technology and agricultural settlement as both moral and practical solutions to droughts but they were oblivious of the fact that such interventions as irrigation in pre-colonial Africa predated the arrival of the Europeans as there was evidence of furrow and other forms of irrigation in precolonial Africa (Posselt 1935, Manzungu et al 1996, Ackroyd 2004). It is pointed out in Endfield and Nash (2002) that the missionaries regarded the work of the "rainmaker" as erroneous, a folly, and a curse, with the result that "rainmaking" was ridiculed and scorned as a simple absurdity too ridiculous for sober argument but as Comaroff and Comaroff (2005) argue the missionaries were oblivious to parallels between praying for rain and the modes by which Africans requested for rain (for instance to God but via ancestors). In their turn the African people encountered in the region, by the missionaries, associated the droughts with the arrival of Europeans some of whom were alleged to have killed the Kings' animals such as the leopards associated with rains. The misunderstandings between the missionaries and the African inhabitants arose from the challenges of translation of the different modes of engagement with the world. The missionaries were meeting people who understood *Mwari* (God) as using rocks, caves or other aspects of the environment as vehicles through which He manifested (Daneel 1970). Observations such as this do not however preclude the use of pre-colonial Bibles, such as the original Ethiopian Bible which has just been returned to Ethiopia by the Europeans who had expropriated it (Kiggundu 2007: 28). In appropriating African original Bibles, European travellers, officials and scholars sought not only to monopolise material resources in

74

colonies but also to monopolise cosmological resources including access to God and to ensure only their portrayal of God and representations of God's word gained credence. But as is evident from the pre-colonial Zimbabwean Ndebele King, Lobengula's remarks to one early missionary, Africans subjected to colonial machinations were apprehensive of the ways in which the Bible was being used to colonise and to sublate African modes of Being and existence under Europeans ones. Lobengula said to Rev J B Thomson (a Scottish missionary) in 1870: "You say that he (God) made both black and white men and loves both equally, but only showed the one the means of salvation. If God meant the black man to be saved in the same way as the white man, he would have sent the same book to both and it seems to me that it is a great piece of presumption that you, a mere mortal, should come here to alter the working of God, whom you call good and wise" (Hromnik 1980: 22). It can be argued that Lobengula did not necessarily deny the existence of *Mwari*/God, since *Mwari* was understood by indigenous inhabitants to have been in existence even during the pre-colonial period, but what Lobengula questioned was the means of reaching out to God that the missionaries brought and claimed to be the sole means.

Understanding God only in terms of the written word in the missionaries' Bible partly explains the challenges of translation during and after the early encounters in that from the missionaries' point of view God was in essence detached from the African environment particularly from the African people who were erroneously considered by missionaries to be heathen and evil, savages and barbaric (even though pre-colonial Africans had their own conceptions of God known as *Mwari/Nyadenga/Musikavanhu/Mwali/Mlimo* that was not only accessible via missionaries). For scholarship on (pre-)colonial Zimbabwe the African inhabitants also held that God communicated with human beings via the word, but it was often the spoken word via the oracular voice at the Matopo Hills in south western Zimbabwe that was of great significance and that was visited by inhabitants from far and wide in Africa. Scholars like Daneel (1970), McGonagle (2007), Ranger (1999), Werbner cited in Ranger (1977) have indicated the significance of the voice speaking from the cave at Matopo Hills in south western Zimbabwe. The contestations between early missionaries and the Africans whom they called "rainmakers" created enduring categories such as "rainmaker" and "rainmaking" which I will argue do not speak to the ways in which *mukwerera* are done in Buhera. It is necessary to do some conceptual clarification, that is, clarify that the categories "rainmaking" and "rainmaker" as used by some missionaries for instance cited in Endfield and Nash (2002) above do not accurately describe *mukwerera* ceremonies in Buhera.

The concepts "rainmaking" and "rainmaker" for example erroneously imply that there is production or manufacturing of rain and that the *svikiro* mediums are the makers or producers of the rains. The concepts further erroneously imply that the people who perform the ceremonies can put together or assemble all the ingredients, material and cosmological; to produce the rain much like what manufacturers might do when making things or objects. As I will argue below, the *mukwerera* ceremonies involved petitions for rain from the *mhondoro* entities understood to manifest in the form of wind. Although mention is scantily made in some literature of requests to the *mweya/mhepo* for rain (see for instance Gelfand 1962) emphasis has often been placed on material "objects" used to make such requests such as rain stones (see for instance Dah-Lokonon 1997). The emphasis I contend should not be merely on the "objects" but on the *mweya/mhepo* (air/wind) of the *mhondoro* (considered to have similar subjectivities as humans) as understood by the petitioners for rain.

Contrary to what the concepts "rainmaking" and "rainmaker" suggest, villagers in Buhera did not engage in "rainmaking" but rather in petitioning for rain. Even the *svikiro* medium in Buhera did not profess to be a "rainmaker" or to engage in "rainmaking" as portrayed by other scholars (see for instance Chitehwe 1954, Gelfand 1962, and Vuifhuizen 1997), elsewhere in Zimbabwe. In response to my question about what is commonly understood as "rainmaking" ceremonies, the *svikiro* said: *tinokumbira mvura kubva kumhepo*: "we request for rain from the wind", in this sense referring to ancestors understood in indigenous knowledge and in Catholic theology (see Daneel 1970) as intermediaries between God and humans. The word they used for the request for rain was *mukwerera*.

They gathered, under the *muchakata* tree for the *mukwerera*, to petition for rain from the *mhondoro*. A petition being subject to action or inaction (delayed or otherwise) by the petitioned appears closer to the requests for rain, and the rain was not invariably regarded as a thing as children sang to rain so that it would falls and they could have plenty. The *mukwerera* were not simple requests; however as will be explained below, there had to be a number of people and other entities present to make the petitions effective. In the rain petitioning ceremonies, it is the *mhondoro* who is petitioned to intercede between villagers and *Mwari* to request for rain: the villagers do not request the rain itself or to clouds the *mhondoro* responsible for rain and with oversight of particular territories. Human beings understood the environment from different angles and so the different views do not reflect errors, irrationalities or failure of logic but different sides of the same thing. This implies that understandings of the world are necessarily partial depending on time and the place one begins to make an inquiry about it. Interesting emerging ideas related to the weather from the sciences that the wind, the clouds and the rain are not merely physical phenomena but that they are also biological and full of life in that in the wind, the clouds and rain there are bacteria which are understood as "rainmaking bacteria"(National Geographic News 12 January 2009, Rainmaking Bacteria Ride Clouds to "Colonise" the Earth1; Lousiana State University, 29 February 2008, Evidence of Rainmaking Bacteria Discovered in Atmosphere and Snow2) underline varieties of life related to rains and droughts. Both the scientists and the *svikiro* mediums reveal that there are ordinarily invisible life forms which are crucial for precipitation though they differ in their characterisation of the life (in terms of bacteria and in terms of *mhondoro* ancestors) and the ways in which they engage with the life forms to enhance rainfall.

As will be explained below approaches to quell droughts have differed with the meteorological sciences initial interventions through pluviculture in Europe and America involving shooting silver iodide into the air by some antiaircraft equipment into the stratosphere or through bombardments of clouds or cannonading or by concussion believing that since heavy rains followed great battles so cannonading would enhance rainfall (Fleming 2007,

Spence 1961). On the other hand, other interventions involved prayers for rain in various parts of the world including European countries such as Greece and Rome where it has for instance, been noted that citizens did not necessarily pray to clouds and to the wind (though it was held that the inhabitants prayed to the god Jupiter) because these were not deemed to act independently but the prayers were rather to a god called Zues deemed to have power in matters of weather (Morgan 1901: 100). But the debate in so far as it bears on translation in past and contemporary eras is whether or not Africans practise animism treating objects of nature as persons in the same way as human beings so this subject will be pursued, in this paper, with reference to rain petitioning ceremonies.

To petition for rainfall, the villagers in Buhera gathered under the *muchakata* tree and there were many *michakata* (plural for *muchakata*) trees in the villages in spite of deforestation because villagers shied away from cutting the *michakata* trees for reasons I will explain shortly. The *muchakata* tree under which they assembled for the petitioning of the *mhondoro* were not just trees or sacred places but villages of the *mhondoro* ancestors, which seem to be what have been translated by other scholars Bourdillon (1976, 1999) as shrines, in the same way some rivers and pools were regarded by the villagers as villages of *njuzu* entities. Although all *michakata* trees were revered it was the particular *muchakata* tree under which *mukwerera* ceremonies were held which was given more importance because that was where ceremonies were conducted. For instance, the *svikiro* said: *"panzvimbo idzodzi pamisha yevamwe vanhu saka panotogara pachitsvairwa"* (such places are the villages of other people (referring to *mhondoro* ancestral beings) so we regularly sweep them). It appears what they did was not a mere ceremony or ritual but a petition that interweaves worlds. During the performances the entities of the supposed past in the form of the *mhondoro* ancestors and founders of the clan were regarded as present, petition-able and as manifesting their presence by speaking through their mediums or by appearing in the form of lions. Thus the performances operated outside rigid dichotomies in that humans/other entities, the past/present, the visible present/the invisible present were held to partake.

Although the ceremonies to petition for the rains were open to villagers, not all of them partook or stuck to the expectations of the *mhondoro* ancestor who was understood by some villagers to mediate between the villagers and God in the petitions for rain. Christians such as Brian and Maria who belonged to the Apostolic Faith Mission and the Apostolic sect of Masowe described the ceremonies as *zvinhu zvemweya yetsvina* (things that are related to ill winds) so they preferred to pray for rain. Although they argued that they relied only on the Bible to pray, they also placed significance on place in the sense that their prayers for rains were done on the Gombe Mountain which as will be explained below was considered by some villagers as inhabited by the deceased people of the *hera* totem. In this way, they sought to break from *chivanhu* but only succeeded partially in that they remained connected in some way. While the Pentecostals contended that they talk to God directly without using intermediaries such as ancestors, the *svikiro* medium and *mbuya* Magaya, a healer, had different views. From their points of view, the church members simply replaced ancestors with their church leaders and prophets who replaced ancestors as intermediaries between them and God. In many ways, these contestations by the villagers resembled contesting and often conflicting interpretations of the relations between Shona *mhondoro* and God, who has been known from pre-colonial times among the Shona as *Mwari, Musikavanhu, Nyadenga, Mutangakugara, Dzivaguru or Chikara* Bourdillon (1976). Some missionaries regarded the ways of the people they met in early colonial Zimbabwe as heathen and sought to reduce God to the word in the Bible which the missionaries brought (see Jeater 2007) but other missionaries noted that *Mwari's* attributes were those of God (Bullock 1927) only that among the Shona, the *mhondoro* mediated between *Mwari* and the people. For these reasons, *svikiro* mediums were considered by some scholars to have been prophets (Mutswairo 1983, Gelfand 1956) and to be likened to the Bishops and Archbishops in a Christian society (Gelfand 1956: 17). Thus, Crawford (1967: 87) argued: "For a person who believes in the *mhondoro*, the possession of a prophet of the Pentecostal churches by the spirit of God, Christ or the Apostles, appears in no way untoward". In fact, as is evident in the villagers' conceptualisation of *Mwari*, ancestors are conceived as mediating between descendants and *Mwari*, the Creator and for this reason even in other parts of Zimbabwe, inhabitants refer to Heaven in their petitions for rain. Chitehwe (1954) noted that in north eastern Zimbabwe villagers state that: *"Dzivaguru, Ambuya Nehanda tipeiwo hore yemvura, imi varikumatenga musatifuratire, musati kangamwe mhuri yenyu. Tipeiwo mvura, nyika yenyu yaparara. Tinokumbira yi, O! Makombwe"* (Grandmother Nehanda give us rain bearing clouds, you who are in heaven do not ignore us, do not forget us your family. Give us rain, your country is dry. We request from you, give us of rain). The view that ancestors whether Christian or not interceded between the living and God is supported by Daneel's (2007) observation that in Catholic theology those ancestors who obeyed natural law are with God and therefore can be mediators irrespective of whether they are Christian ancestors or non-Christian ancestors. The mediatory functions in Shona cosmology were hinted by liberation fighters' (who engaged in war with the colonial authorities in the 1970s) arguments that they did not see any qualitative difference between the work of Christ and that of the pre-colonial Zimbabwean great prophet called Chaminuka who they said is mediator for Africans (Daneel 2007: 346). So at meetings, liberation fighters in Zimbabwe "made prayers" to the great pre-colonial prophet Chaminuka (also addressed by the Shona people as *mhondoro yedenga* (lion of the heaven)-see Garbett 1977: 57 above) but all in the name of God who is accepted in Shona history, from the pre-colonial era, as the almighty father over the Shona people (Kriger 1992). The contestations may well have arisen from the different interpretations of Chaminuka: whereas it appears that European scholars interpreted Chaminuka as an embodied human being, other scholars (Garbett 1977: 57, Bullock 1927, 1950) noted that he never had mortal existence and that he emanated directly from God albeit manifesting in bodies of selected Africans.

What both the Pentecostals and the rest of the villagers who attended the *mukwerera* ceremonies did appears to me to be petitioning for rain, the difference is one of the terms they used that is praying (which is arguably a way of requesting also) and *kukumbira* or requesting for rain. The practices are separated or different but related. These practices to avert droughts relied on relations between the visible and invisible entities such as ancestors for those who performed *mukwerera* and *ngirozi* deemed to be from the heavenly world for those who prayed for rain from God. However, the challenge in such villages where members had different ways of engaging with the weather world was to "democratise" the practices, to make space in order for the different knowledge practices to be considered without a priori dismissals. In terms of democratising knowledge heritages, scholarship is often mired in discourses on cultural hybridisation/creolisation/syncretisation; cultural polarisation and cultural homogenisation. Often scholars do not critically consider the implications of such notions on the majority of the (neo)colonial subjects, who unfortunately lacking the scholarly power to understand how they are often described in these ways, continues to suffer classifications some of which have the effect of attenuating, sublating or forcing acquiescence in the coloniality of their subordinate status. Such subjects of coloniality often continue to be subjects of colonial epistemologies, which deny them voices even well after the eras of direct colonialism.

Thus discourses that celebrate African cultures in terms of hybridisation, or intermixing of cultures, (see for instance, Boswell 2008) while suggesting European cultures including epistemologies as pure and purely European appear to ignore the realities in everyday life. The discourses in effect celebrate the colonial *fait accompli,* that is, the subordination of other cultures by the dominant European cultures of which subordination in postcolonial renditions is re-codenamed hybridisation. The idea of cultural homogenisation too is a sleight of hand that hides the subordinate/super ordinate relations created during the colonial period and that continue to operate in the postcolonial context where some dominant Western cultures are proselytised and cultures of subjects of coloniality are sublated. Both the ideas of hybridisation and homogenisation have the effect, similar to colonial tendencies noted in the introduction, of refusing to accept that African cultures and civilisations were freestanding and self-sustaining before colonisation and did not therefore have to depend on Europe so these discourses have the effect of sublating African culture under Europe and in terms of the coloniality of power that continues to exist in postcolonial Africa where African cosmologies and metaphysical renditions are sublated and continue to suffer ostracism and cynicism well after the era of direct colonial domination. The unfortunate result of such arguments about hybridisation/creolisation syncretisation and so forth is that they portray Africa as "impure" hybrid yet paradoxically treating Europe as pure. In terms of cosmologies thus Africa is portrayed as having only "impure" ancestors while Europe is portrayed as having only saints; equally in terms of cosmologies Africa is portrayed as the seat of the "impure" devil while Europe is portrayed as the seat of God. In such cosmologies Europe is portrayed as monopolising the heavens while "impure" African ancestors are excluded from heaven but occupy the caldrons of hell. In all these cosmologies and metaphysics the "impure" Africa is portrayed as fit for transcendence by the homogenising and universalising purity of Europe. Africa's own kinds or variants of purity are impatiently discarded and ignored while Europe's own impurities, for there is no conceivable place with a monopoly of purity, are downplayed. Also as evident among the villagers the question is not merely whether or not there is hybridity but whether particular forms of hybridity are accepted especially where inhabitants are wary of and conceive hybridity as impurities, dirty, pollution or as burdensome in the sense of facilitating integration into subordinate positions in the world.

Altering modes of engagement in the world including relations within the human domain without petitioning other entities in domains beyond but connected to the human often resulted in reprisals and disruption of relations of reciprocity among the beings and entities in the environment. It was not just the relations between the visible entities and beings that mattered in the well-being of human beings in Africa but the relations with the invisible entities also such as ancestors (see also White 2001) and for this reason, the past is often played in the present as ways to honour the ancestors. In this sense, an emphasis on the linearity of time fractures relations of reciprocity within the environment and as Garuba (2013: 49) argues: "there is need to recognise the complex embeddedness of different temporalities, different discordant formations and different epistemological perspectives within the same historical moment". But in Zimbabwe, and in Buhera district in particular, rethinking Euromodernity implies not only a focus on its notions of time but also of work: invisible entities such as *mhondoro* ancestors were regarded as working during some days to ensure that humans and other entities had rains and they rested on other days. Normally each *mhondoro* has a rest day during which he is honoured and villagers are not permitted to work during the particular day when the *mhondoro* will also be resting. Failure to observe the *chisi* (rest-day) resulted in reprimands from the *mhondoro*. One example as narrated to me by a number of villagers and by the *svikiro* medium was when the chief failed to personally comply with the *mhondoro*'s expectations about the *mhondoro*'s *chisi* rest day, the *mhondoro* speaking through his *svikiro* medium reprimanded him and threatened to visit drought on the chief's area, even if a small area in the chiefdom. Such threats were issued by the *mhondoro*, speaking through his medium, to the chief in 2009: the chief had altered prior to 2009, the day of the *chisi* rest day from Thursdays to Fridays because his (the chief's) father had died on a Friday so he sought to honour him. The *mhondoro* founder of the clan was very angry about this change and, speaking through his medium, he summoned the chief and told him that it will not rain in his area until he restored the *chisi* rest day to Thursdays. The chief was told that on the day he changes the *chisi* it would rain in his area. The chief in turn summoned his headmen and village heads and told them that the *chisi* had reverted to Thursdays. He had initially altered the *chisi* rest day without seeking consent either from the *svikiro* medium or from the *mhondoro*. He did not request for such permission because he was scornful towards the *svikiro,* who had just succeeded her late father as a medium, on account of her being female, though scholars like Ranger (2003) have noted that in pre-colonial Zimbabwe, women held important public roles in the form of mediums. The demand by the *mhondoro* for his rest day, or for his leisure time to use Euro modernist conceptualisation, underlines to me the limited character of Euro modern understandings of work which has excluded other entities that are deemed in everyday life to perform activities or work that make it possible for human beings to survive or to have life. The work and activities of such other entities are simply taken for granted in the political economies which privilege human beings and treat other *mhondoro* as non-existent, if because they are invisible, yet the colonial scholars and authorities were prepared to recognise their own invisible entities such as states and other institutions which they set up to replace pre-colonial African institutions. Although mediums and their *mhondoro* are generally ignored in the literature on work, employment and labour they often expected and appreciated gifts and recognition of their work (see Mudege 2008: 145; Lan 1986: 32). The recognition of their work was not always expected to be in the form of money or other material assets but in terms of attending their ceremonies and partaking in them.

While the view that the *mhondoro* had his *chisi* day which had to be honoured by the villagers may appear in the renditions of other scholars to be "traditional" and to belong to the past, such perceptions that classify the modes of engagement as "traditional" and opposed to the "modern" appear to labour under the misapprehension that there is no "tradition" in "modernity" or "modernity" in "tradition". In any case, such perceptions fail for instance to notice that even the months in the modern calendar are in honour of deceased human beings albeit from outside Africa: the months of January (named by Romans after Janus a two faced god), June, July and August for instance, are named after Junius Caesar, Julius Caesar and Augustus (the Emperor of Rome) respectively. Furthermore, the days of the week are themselves named after certain western divinities or gods not that are not necessarily local African ones, for instance Delaney (2004: 88) notes that Saturday was dedicated by the Romans to Saturn hence it is Saturn day, Monday to Moon day, Tuesday to Tiw's day, after Tiw (in Latin, the god of war), Wednesday to Woden's day, Thursday to Thor's day (because it was deemed sacred to Thunor the English thunder god) and Friday to Fria's day (because it is deemed to be the day of the goddess Frig) and Sunday to Sun day (anciently dedicated to the sun). So with the suppression and sublation of local African intercessors between Africans descendants and God, of which God is variously named in Africa, there appears to have been replacement of such African intercessors with European ones. These replacements of African intercessors with European ones also underscore the fact that time which is misunderstood as linear, even in European renditions is not necessarily invariably so. There are parallels between what Europeans deemed to be backward and savage practices (including honouring the dead as well as divinities in the cosmos) and European modes of engagement. In fact the proselytization of European divinities indicates that such divinities are more honoured even outside their traditional localities and so the proselytization indicates that Europeans while derogatorily calling Africans traditional were in fact honouring their own traditions (within and outside Europe) even more than Africans were doing in restricted localities. The linearity of time, even in Europe, that is considered to be modern par excellence by some scholars is challenged by Hobsbawm (1984: 1) who argued that nothing appears more ancient and linked to the immemorial past than the pageantry which surrounds British monarchy in its public ceremonial manifestation. I would thus argue that while Europeans denied African ancestor heroes', the Europeans created and filled up Africa with European goddesses and gods. As Reynolds et al (1983: 6) note in the realm of justice the goddess *justicia* is deemed to reign. But it can be argued that *justicia* reigns even outside Europe, including in Africa where *mhondoro* are not recognised in spite of their enforcement, within indigenous knowledge systems, of environmental ethics, moralities and laws in everyday life. Suppositions are inferable that Eurocentric scholarship holds that there was no justice in pre-colonial Africa only because there was no goddess called *justicia* in Africa prior to colonisation. Yet as underscored in this chapter, the experiences with the *mhondoro* indicated that such ancestors ensured justice, law, morality and ethics in their territories.

The data I got in the interviews with the villagers indicated that in Buhera, attendance and participation in the *mukwerera* ceremonies was often poor not only because some villagers were disinclined on account of their membership in churches but other villagers simply did not attend or they chose to do other things. Some of the villagers did not even request for recusal and for this reason the *svikiro* medium was often dejected by the poor attendance or nonattendance in the ceremonies which ceremonies she contended benefited every villager when the rain eventually fell in the area. Attendance at the *mukwerera* was therefore so variable that when I intended and had agreed with the *svikiro* that I would attend one near her homestead in 2011, it was according to the *svikiro* medium aborted because villagers did not come in their numbers to partake. Instead the *svikiro* went on a different day to another village a distance away to assist in their *mukwerera*. To me the medium narrated how the *mukwerera* is done. The following is an account of how the *mukwerera* was performed.

After the *matakapona*, which is a gathering for thanks giving following harvests, people begin to prepare for the *mukwerera* which involves petitioning of the *mhondoro* for rains for the next season. Mature and married nephews of the paternal side cut firewood for the brewing of the beer. *Rapoko* grain is collected from the villages and the *mhondoro* is informed of the impending *mukwerera*. Elderly women soak the *rapoko* grain which is used for beer brewing. The people who cut the firewood have to abstain from sexual intercourse until the end of the *mukwerera* for the *mhondoro* considers sexual intercourse impure. Women who are breastfeeding are also not allowed to partake because breastfeeding is also considered to be impure because the *mhondoro* detests milk. After the beer has been brewed the *mhondoro* is informed that his beer is ready for consumption. During the *mukwerera* there is drumming, singing and clapping of hands. People have to kneel down and clap their hands when making the petitions. They also have to use Shona which is the vernacular language.

Headmen Samuel and Bere as well as the *svikiro* medium pointed out that it often rained even as people were about to leave the *rushanga*, at the *mukwerera* tree, for the homes.

During the *mukwerera* one clay pot full of beer reserved for the people of the *mhondoro*'s clan is placed into the *rushanga* (an enclosure of spaced poles which I saw around the *muchakata* tree where the *mukwerera* is held). A nephew of the clan pours a little of the beer in four directions around the *rushanga* and then he gives the remaining beer to the elders of the clan. The rest of the people then form a circle around the *rushanga* and each one is given a *mukombe* (a container made of gourd) full of beer. As each one drinks the beer, they sit down. The remaining beer is left in the *rushanga*. Clay pots and the *mukombe* are left in the *rushanga* and they are collected by elderly women the following morning. The elderly women have to ululate /*kupururudza* as they collect the items but they have to shrill even though there may not be anyone else visibly present since they regard the *mhondoro* beings to be present, though invisibly present.

The account above showed that the *mukwerera* was conducted through forms of relatedness understood as *ukama* between human beings and invisible entities such as ancestors. It is also necessary that villagers relate well together during the *mukwerera* and from the point of view of some villagers, even before and after the *mukwerera*, relations among different beings and entities if upset would result in droughts. For instance, Martin an elderly man who I met when he was taking a rest at the shopping centre in the village contended that the violence, in which some villagers and citizens of Zimbabwe had died during the decade from 2000, angered God who then visited the recurrent droughts on Zimbabwe.

Although in the vernacular mode of relating known as *ukama,* there is no radical distinction between human life and the lives of other entities such as the *mhondoro*, the *ukama* is not necessarily animism or animistic for a number of reasons including that animism emerged as a category from within Euromodernist ontologies that reduced God to nature on the presumption that God was immanent in nature, and not abiding in Heaven where He would exercise transcendence over nature, rather than the immanence in nature that the European scholars presumed. Animism has been defined in many but related ways as noted by Bird-David (1999: S67): it is defined as the belief that inside ordinary visible tangible bodies there is a normally invisible, normally intangible being: the spirit. Second, animism is a religious belief involving the attribution of life or divinity to such natural phenomena as trees, thunder, or celestial bodies. Third, animism is defined as the belief that all life is produced by a "spiritual" force, or that all natural phenomena have souls. Fourth, animism is defined as the belief in the existence of a separable soul-entity, potentially distinct and apart from any concrete embodiment in a living individual or material organism. Fifth, animism is defined as the system of beliefs about souls and spirits typically found among many preliterate societies. Lastly, animism is defined as the belief, common among many preliterate societies, that trees, mountains, rivers and other natural formations possess an animating power or spirit. As pointed out above the *svikiro* medium did not appear to me to consider the *mhondoro* that spoke through her as a mere "spirit", a soul or divinity but rather as a relation that is as grandfather. But the *sekuru* or grandfather was not conflated with her or with the aspects of nature through which he manifested himself as is suggested by the notion of immanence that is relied upon by some scholars to explain animism. The medium herself did not become "a *sekuru*/grandfather": this was because the *mhondoro* that "possessed" her would come and go. Equally the objects of nature which the *mhondoro* was considered to attach himself to did not become *mhondoro*: the *mhondoro* is essentially like air/wind, is mobile, comes and goes, attaches and detaches from objects and from the medium yet retains transcendence over them as well as over his territory.

The fact that the *mhondoro* was deemed to move in and out of his medium allowing the medium to recover her personality after the "possession" session has significant implications for understanding the idea of *kusvikirwa* (conventionally understood as to be "possessed" but literally translated as to be reached) in this case by the ancestors. The movements of the *mhondoro* in and out of the body of the medium imply that the personality of the medium is not incapacitated or mortified by the *mhondoro* but the medium's personality has room to recoil, to return to the initial position when she recovers herself after the sessions. Because the *mhondoro* moved in and out, there are no presumptions of animism in such Shona indigenous knowledge where ancestors such as the *mhondoro* are deemed to temporarily attach themselves to entities or objects which they use periodically as vehicles to exert their influence. In fact, there is no vernacular equivalent of animisms in the Shona language and so the term animism does not render itself to vernacular linguistic translation or to indigenous cultural translation. As noted above, in indigenous sessions of *kusvikirwa* there is no complete annihilation of the personality of the medium but rather such personality is given the chance to rebound, recoil or recover and this absence of conflation of the identities of the *mhondoro* and the medium rebuts notions that would mistranslate the ancestors as soil or as turning into landscapes or into animals. The implication is also that while some scholars argue that "there is need to embrace animality and to learn from the poor as a means to learn how to live with modest means" (de Castro 2013), in Shona cosmology there is a clear separation between notions of *kusvikirwa* and what scholars call animism.

Relations among villagers maintain openness for possibilities for such switches. But relations need not be unreliable or prevaricating. In fact the prevarications of the early Portuguese settlers who initially had friendly contacts with inhabitants of precolonial Zimbabwe attracted dismay. This was because the Portuguese subsequently manipulated the precolonial inhabitants of Zimbabwe and in the process they attracted the phrase, "*Mazungu manyoka haatani kuumbuka*" (the Portuguese are like inflamed bowels they are quick to change (Murphy et al 1978). The openness of the relations bears some resonance with Ingold's (2007) argument that in "animistic" cosmologies there is attribution of supreme importance to the winds and such "animism is not a system of beliefs about the world but a way of being in it characterised by openness rather than closure" and by the openness he alludes to sensitivity and responsiveness to an environment that is in flux. For Ingold, "there is no separation between the substances and the medium since the wind, rain and other weather phenomena enter into substances and the substances are in the wind, in the weather. That is substances and the medium are mingled in an open world with no insides and outsides but comings and goings" but this idea of absence of outside and insides is problematic in a context such as among the villagers as well as the broader Shona people in Zimbabwe where they have proverbs such as, "*mipanje iri kunze inodzivirira iri mukati*" (outer ridges guard what is inside). What such proverbs imply is that the Shona conceive a world with insides and outsides and they value such categories since for them the outside ridges protect the inside so doing away with the outer ridges implies exposure for them to risks, it implies removal of protection by such outer ridges.

If as scholars have flagged the necessity of not restricting translation to linguistics but broadening it to culture, social, political and economic realms then there is need to interpret the statements that guerrilla liberation fighters in Zimbabwe were *vana vevhu* or sons of the soil (Kriger 1992, Fontein 2006) not necessarily to mean that ancestors or parents were interchangeable with soil for if they were so walking on the soil or ploughing it would have, in local cosmologies, amounted to violence on and to killing the parents and the ancestors. It is rather that ancestors were deemed to be so near the human world during the liberation war that they were attached to the soil which they used as their vehicles to exercise influence in the human world.

But in addition to Ingold's (2007) notion of becomings, there were also what I call unbecomings in the world in that violence and the global modes of interferences that afflicted some villagers constituted the unbecomings. As noted above, such unbecoming do not only emanate from the local scene but are also a product of global processes that are considered to interfere with, to disrupt and erupt into the domain of everyday life moral geographies. For instance the liberalisation and legalisation of homosexuality have been contested in African moral geographies (see for instance Sunday Times March 2 2014 p 10 *South Africa's Zimbabwe Style Finesse for Uganda: Silent over Museveni, Government Now wants Talks about Rights*, Sunday Times March 2 2014 p 14 *Why Doesn't Obama Marry a Man?*) with for instance Uganda being denied aid by international organisations on the allegation that it had criminalised homosexuality. Thus while it is important to pay attention to local aspects of moral geographies, there are also extralocal aspects that are considered to impact on the moral geographies as well. In the villages where I carried out fieldwork, some villagers for instance pointed out that because their *ukama* had been ruptured by interparty violence in Zimbabwe, they could not coattend ceremonial parties and other gatherings together as they no longer saw eye to eye with their assailants. But Ingold's (1993, 2007) notion of an open world is problematic in that even in practices of rain petitioning, there is demarcation of space and place as noted in the narrative of how the rain petitioning is done in the villages. As noted by Schapera (1971: 50) there is often pegging of spaces to stop outsiders from entering the territories and spaces lest it fails to rain or the territories are bewitched by hostile or merely by unclean people that bring pollution in the areas. As noted above this violence on the moral geographies does not only include physical violence but also structural violence, including symbolic violence on Africa etiquette via colonial education and colonially induced habits.

The ways in which villagers connected with the environment had important partial connections with ways in which meteorological scientists connected with the weather phenomena and other places in the world. A look at the ways in which meteorological scientists operate reveals these connections.

Meteorological Sciences and Connections in the Indigenous Knowledge Systems: A Brief Note

A lot of scholarly work has been written on meteorological issues but sadly there has been neglect of the invisible aspects that meteorological sciences rely on. It is partly due to the neglect of such invisible aspects that the sciences vilify rain petitioning ceremonies. It is on the basis of observing the widespread reliance on invisible realms be they in so called traditional or modern societies that Gordon (2012: 1) has asserted that invisible forces mobilise us to action and such invisible forces are sometimes remote and absolute or proximate for instance the state and its laws. For Gordon (2012), invisible forces are sometimes conceived as spirits that possess bodies, incarnate the dead and guide the actions of the living. While westerners accept their own invisible worlds, and may seek to change, repress or simply ignore the invisible worlds of others, not all agents of invisible worlds are compatible but they have to be reckoned with. While villagers, in the rain petitioning ceremonies, rely on the *mhondoro* and on the *mweya/mhepo* (air/wind) meteorological sciences also rely on the air/wind to gauge temperatures, wind directions, wind speed and air pressure for instance. The meteorological sciences also rely on air waves to broadcast the weather reports and forecasts. They also rely on mathematical or statistical figures which they manipulate to forecast the weather and on the basis of such statistical/mathematical figures the sciences are often conceived as better able to predict weather than the villagers' local modes of predicting and foretelling the weather.

While such statistical/mathematical figures have acquired reverence with the ascendancy of colonial epistemologies that sublated indigenous epistemologies the foundations of the mathematical or statistical figures themselves have not been taken into cognisance by those who vilify indigenous knowledge. Tracing the foundations of mathematics and statistics for instance, Koetsier and Bergams (2005) note that for founding philosophers like Plato and Pythagoras the divine origins of all things in the universe are understood on the basis of mathematical principles. For such philosophers, mathematical techniques played a role in artificial divination while on the other hand shamans, in vernacular Shona *n'anga,* relied on natural divination messages that emerged directly from the "gods". For the philosophers therefore, mathematics has a ritual origin and counting was a means of calling the participants in a ritual onto the ritual scene in such a way that the announcements inviting the participants took the form of numbers. For other scholars numbers have been attributed with special, secret powers that make them fitting for magical conjurations and for astrological prognostications (Schimmel 1993: 10). It can therefore be argued that while divination by local *n'anga* in Zimbabwe for instance is often vilified as involving the throwing of "bones" (Jeater 2007) and throwing of sticks to foretell events, activities such as manipulating numbers/figures to foretell weather, by statisticians and mathematicians, share similar logics to divination by *n'anga.* Though the shaman, or in vernacular Shona the *n'anga,* are often vilified by "rational" philosophies as "irrational", Koetsier and Bergams (ibid) have argued that the shaman's trance and deliberate detachment of the occult self from the body has become the modern practice of mental withdrawal and concentration which is deemed to purify the rational soul.

Although the meteorological scientists in Zimbabwe whom I visited during fieldwork spent much of their time in the offices compiling and computing data, communication in the form of flows of the data among various stations underlie their relations. What they kept outside the offices were the apparatuses such as rain gauges, wind vane, wind roses, theodolites, radars and satellites for gathering data. At different atmospheric levels, radiosondes detected temperatures, pressures, humidity and wind direction. At the station or ground, satellite dishes tracked the movement of the radiosondes and fed data to a decoder at the base station. The meteorological scientists were in this sense separated from the weather world yet in *mukwerera* ceremonies, the mediums and the villagers operate in the open even under trees such as *muchakata*. While in *mukwerera* human mediums were relied upon to use their bodies as technology to sense the weather, the meteorological scientists indirectly accessed the weather world via the apparatuses such as the radiosondes, which were equipped with sensors, which they kept in the open or sent into atmospheric levels so that they brought or bore signals about the weather. The meteorological sciences separated the bodies (and bodily senses) of the meteorological scientists from the weather but apparatuses that they use such as radiosondes equipped with sensors hint at Crosson's (2013) argument that "spirits" did not disappear with modernity but rather they have become more and more transformed into modern technological mediums. It can be argued following Crosson (2013) that modernity appears to have deterritorialised kinds of mediumship from human beings and implanted them in pieces of technology disguised as entirely new and modern when in fact it merely circulated earlier pre-modern logics of mediumship. In the light of the proliferation of technologies modernity can be argued to have proliferated mediumship; but it was mediums that capital and colonialists could readily and easily control and exploit that were developed and nurtured. Modernity does not appear, as suggested by some scholars, like de Castro (2013) arguing for a posthuman turn, to have instantiated humanisation of life but rather in ways that were dehumanising to colonial subjects, it multiplied technological mediums while vilifying human mediums. Modernity was dehumanising for the colonial subjects who together with their indigenous knowledge were pilloried and vilified by colonisers who pretended to be civilising and modernising, while in fact arrogating all humanity to themselves. I will return to this argument below suffice it to note here that arguments by some scholars about the need to move towards the posthuman assume that everybody including subjects of colonialism as well as subjects of coloniality, has been equally humanised by modernity. Posthumanism erroneously assumes that everyone has been humanised in the modern sense by modernity.

In drought mitigation, meteorological scientists in Zimbabwe cloud seeded, in much the same logics as the cannonading or concussions in early experiments on pluviculture noted in the introduction, by shooting at the clouds so that rain fell, using flares to send small particles that served as hygroscopic nuclei in the form of sodium chloride, lithium carbonate or magnesium. The meteorological officers were accompanied by military personnel during the cloud seeding. It took 15-30 minutes after the shootings for it to rain. In this way the clouds were not mere passive "objects" of the shootings. The seeded clouds were also mobile and continued to "interact" with unseeded clouds in ways that made it hard to distinguish between naturally and artificially seeded clouds. The inexactness of weather predictions defies the categorisation of science as exact in sharp contrast to indigenous knowledge which is presumed to be inexact and merely based on belief and faith. But here, we note as villagers in Buhera did that weather predictions and forecasts refer often to provinces and districts rather than to specific villages and even to specific fields and this aspect generate inexactness of the forecasts which leaves the audiences of the forecasts wondering if it would for instance actually rain on their fields or in their villages of which it may not in spite of provincial or district level forecasts.

Conclusion

This chapter calls not only for the recognition of African voices but also the voices of African ancestors in postcolonial epistemologies. To enrich the debates on translating African indigenous knowledge, this chapter has called for the need to recognise the voices of African scholars and African research informants including, as Olukoshi and Nyamnjoh (2013) argue, the voices of African ancestors all of whom have been denied voices since the colonial period. All that is heard and read from colonial scholarship are the voices of such scholars lamenting that Africans were hopeless and Africa was a dark continent but we do not hear the voices of the African ancestors that have for long been denied the justice to speak and be heard since the beginning of colonialism. If Western scholars and ancestors are capacitated to speak and to have voice via textbooks to which references are always made around the world, one wonders why African ancestors should be denied voice even if they may speak differently and not through the written texts. Even within postcolonial eras little care is taken to develop ideas from within Africa and to desist from imposed notions some of which have no equivalence in African languages and cultures. It is important to note that concepts if arbitrarily transposed across linguistic domains hijack Africans' own trajectories including their quest for epistemic democracy and justice.

During the colonial era the mediums were labelled witchdoctors and proscribed from communicating with descendants as such communication was viewed as brewing insurrections against colonisers. In the area of drought alleviation interventions in indigenous knowledge systems, the disappearance of indigenous epistemologies incapacitates villagers and rural households to survive droughts. And without all the capacities to produce and to survive using indigenous knowledges, technologies and apparatuses the danger is that Africans continue to rely on aid. Without the capacities to cope, to produce and reproduce, including institutions, using indigenous knowledge systems and practices Africans risk assumptions by some scholars that they lacked institutions and therefore that they need to be perpetually grateful to colonisers that are erroneously deemed to have provided Africans with institutions and wherewithal to survive. As Jacobson (2000: 111) notes such (continuing) assessments made the ultimate appropriation or conquest of continents such as Africa as much a certainty as was the appropriation of North America, a land, in Owen Wister's words, "where Indians and wild animals lived unchained". Perhaps the dangerous assumptions in colonial modes of conflation of Africans with fauna are clearest in Vera (2001). Vera (2001) records Karen Buxen's statement about Africans thus: "When we really did break into the natives' existence they behaved like ants, when you poke a stick into their anthill they wiped out the damage with unwearied energy, swiftly and silently-as if obliterating an unseemly action (Karen Buxen, Out of Africa). Vera (2001) further pays attention to Joseph Conrad's statement about the colonial subjects that, "They work swiftly and silently, without communication for like ants, they are not heard to speak. Their language is incomprehensible". The point in so far as this chapter is concerned is that while Africans such as the villagers I studied did not conflate themselves with fauna, colonialists found it convenient for the colonial project to conflate colonial subjects with fauna so that the colonialists would not be bothered considering human rights and issues of justice for fellow humans that were being colonised.

As Yvonne Vera (2001) argued, in order to help Africa move forward it is necessary to trace and identify when and where the "rain started to beat us". With respect to this chapter the rain can be argued to have started to beat us when we did not get translated but when we were conflated and sublated in various ways many of which have not been addressed as yet in the postcolonial eras. It can be argued that in order to monopolise the realm of the future colonial translators misconceived and sublated African ancestors on the pretext that they belonged to the past. As is evident in the consultation of ancestors for rain, the African ancestors were consulted by their descendants in the knowledge that they were ahead of their descendants. The ancestors were thus in the realm of the future of their descendants rather than in the past to which colonisers erroneously consigned them. And all this pillorying of African ancestors was done even as the Europeans were busy not only ransacking the graves of the ancestors of Africans looting jewellery including gold and silver from the corpses (Ellert 1984; Posselt 1935) and even looting mummified bodies of the corpses of Africans. One wonders whether this sublation and consignment of Africans and African ancestors to the past was not a way of retrenching Africans and their ancestors from Africa's present and future. By a sleight of hand, the colonists sought to monopolise world affairs by retrenching colonial subjects and their ancestors from having voices in their present and futures. In the light of the above, it is necessary to enter into debates on the translation of Africa with minds that ask how and whether postcolonial translation assist Africa or it continues to conflate and weigh down postcolonial Africa with burdens of the past, that is, with colonial mistranslation. Africa conflated and conceptually weighed down by the burdens of colonising hegemonic languages assumes the role of a horse, in the horse and rider analogue, for such conceptual burdens of mistranslation. The free exploitation of indigenous knowledge by colonisers since the colonial period indicates that what is more at stake in Africa is not merely recognition of such knowledge but its protection and use to enhance postcolonial transformation and to the benefit of Africans. The vilification of indigenous knowledge systems by colonial officials did not by that fact alone constitute absence of recognition and exploitation of such knowledge. In fact vilification was meant to facilitate the exploitation not only of the indigenous knowledge but also of the indigenous populations possessing the indigenous knowledge. The critical issue for postcolonial Africa is therefore not merely securing the recognition of indigenous knowledge but ensuring its equitable mobilisation to benefit postcolonies. The challenge for postcolonies is with colonial histories where metropoles have been conflated with God and the good to such an extent that the periphery of the empire has been reduced to the opposite, of the metropole, and in such peripheries wars of various kinds with the devil (even if sometimes imagined and fabricated) are exported.

References

Abraham, D. P. 1966. The Role of Chaminuka and the *mhondoro* Cults in Shona Political History, in Stokes, E. and Brown, R. (eds). 1966. *The Zambezian Past: Studies in Central African History*, pp28-46 Manchester: Manchester University Press.

Ackroyd, P. 2004, *Kingdom of the Dead: Voyages Through Time.* London: Dorling Kindersley Ltd.

Albert, E. 2001. Deleuze's Impersonal Hylozoic Cosmology. in M Bryden, (ed) *Deleuze and Religion.* pp.184-195 London: Routledge: 184-195.

Alexander, J. et al. 2000, *Violence and Memory: One Hundred Years in the "Dark Forests" of Matabeleland.* James Currey, Heinemann.

Artigas, M. 2001, *The Mind of the Universe: Understanding Science and Religion.* Pennsylvania: Temple University Press.

Asante, M. K. 2000, *The Egyptian Philosophers: Ancient African Voices from Inhatep to Akhenaten,* Chicago: African American Images.

Bernard, P. 2003, Ecological Implications of Water Spirit Beliefs in southern Africa: The Need to Protect.

Bryden, M., 2001, Introduction, in Bryden, M., ed, *Deleuze and Religion.* London: Routledge: 1-6.

Bernard, P. 2007, Reuniting with the Kosmos. *Journal for the Study of Religion, Nature and Culture*.1.1: 109-129.

Bertelsen, B. E. 2004. It will Rain until we are in Power! Floods, Elections and memory in Mozambique, in H Englund and F B Nyamnjoh, (eds), *Rights and the Politics of Recognition in Africa*. London: Zed Books Ltd: 169-236.

Bird-David N., 1999, Animism Revisited: Personhood, Environment, and Relational Epistemology. *Current Anthropology* 40: S67-S91.

Boonzaier, E. et al., 2000, *The Cape Herders: A History of the Khoikhoi of Southern Africa*. Athens: Ohio University Press.

Boswell R., 2008, *Challenges in Identifying and Managing Intangible Cultural Heritage in Mauritius, Zanzibar and Seychelles*. Dakar: CODESRIA.

Bourdillon M F C., 1976, *The Shona People: An Ethnography of the Contemporary Shona with Special Reference to their Religion*. Gweru: Mambo Press.

Bourdillon, 1999, The cults of Dzivaguru and Karuva amongst the North Eastern Shona Peoples, in Schoffeleers J, ed, *Guardians of the Land*. Gweru: Mambo Press.

Brennan F., 2012, in Brennan F and Packer J Chattel Slavery.

Brennan, F., 2012, Slave Trade Reparations, Institutional Racisms and the Law, in Brennan, F. and Packer, J. C. ,eds, *Slavery, Reparations and Trade: Remedying the Past*. Abingdon: Routledge.

Bullock C., 1927, *The Mashona (The Indigenous Natives of Southern Rhodesia*. Cape Town: Juta and Co.

Burbridge A., 1923, How to Become a Witch Doctor. NADA. The Southern Rhodesia Native Affairs Department Annual. Vol 1: 94-100.

Burbridge A., 1924, In Spirit Bound Rhodesia. *NADA, Southern Rhodesia Native Affairs Department Annual*, 1-6: 17-28.

Dah-Lokonon G B., 1997, 'Rainmakers': Myth and Knowledge in Traditional Atmospheric Management Techniques, in Hountondji P., ed, *Endogenous Knowledge: Research Trails*, Dakar: CODESRIA.: 84-112.

Callon M., 1986, Some Elements of a Sociology of Translation: Domestication of the Scallops and the Fishermen of Ist

Brieuc Bay, in Law J, ed, *Power, Action and Belief: a New Sociology of Knowledge*. London: Routledge: 196-223.

Chakravarrty A., 2013, On the Prospects of naturalised Metaphysics, in Ross D et al., eds, *Scientific Metaphysics*. Oxford: Oxford University press: 27-50.

Chitehwe S S M., 1954, Rainmaking in Mashonaland: *NADA the Southern Rhodesian Native Affairs Department Annual* 31: 24-26.

Collins S L., 1989, *From Divine Cosmos to Sovereign State: An Intellectual History of Consciousness and the Idea of Order in Renaissance England.* Oxford: Oxford University Press.

Comaroff J and Comaroff J., 2005, The Colonisation of Consciousness, in Lambek M, ed, *A Reader in the Anthropology of Religion:* Oxford: Blackwell Publishing: 493-510.

Constitution of Zimbabwe (no 20) 2013, Harare: Zimbabwe.

Crawford J R., 1967, *Witchcraft and Sorcery in Rhodesia*, London: Oxford University Press.

Crosson J B., 2013, Anthropology of Invisibilities: Translating, Spirits of the Dead and thePolitics of Invisibility, Cultural Field notes, http://Prodn.culanth.org/fieldsipho/346-invisibilities-translation-spirits -of-the dead-and-the-politics-of-invisibility.

Daneel M., 1970, *The God of the Matopo Hills*. Leiden: Afrika-Studiecentrum.

Daneel M., 2007, All Things Hold Together: Holistic Theologies at the African Grassroots, UNISA.

De Castro E V., 2013, Economic Development and Cosmopolitical Re-involvement: From Necessity to Sufficiency. In Green L., ed, Contested Ecologies: Dialogues in the South on nature and Knowledge. Cape Town: HSRC Press.

De Castro, E. V., 2004, Perspectival Anthropology and the Method of Controlled Equivocation. *Tipiti Journal of the Society for Anthropology of Lowland South America* 2 (1): 3-22.

De la Cadena, M., 2010, Indigenous Cosmopolitics: Conceptual Reflections beyond "Politics", *Cultural Anthropology* vol. 25, Issue 2 p 334-370.

Descola, P., 1996, Constructing Natures: Symbolic Ecology and Social Practice, In Descola, P. and Palsson, G, eds, *Nature and Society: Anthropological Perspectives*. London: Routledge: 82-102.

Endfield G H and Nash D J., 2002, Missionaries and Morals: Climate Discourse in Nineteenth Century Central Southern Africa. *Annals of the Association of American Geographers* 92: 4, 727-742

Evensky, J., 2005, *Adam Smith's Moral Philosophy: A Historical and Contemporary Perspective on Markets, Law, Ethics and Culture.* Cambridge: Cambridge University Press.

Fleming J R., 2007, The Climate Change Engineers, *The Wilson Quarterly* Vol 31, No 2: 46-60.

Fontein, J., 2004, Traditional Connoisseurs of the Past: The Ambiguity of Spirit Mediums and the Performance of the Past in Southern Zimbabwe, University of Edinburgh Press, *occcasional Paper.*

Fontein, J., 2006, Language of Land, Water and Tradition around Lake Mutirikwi in Southern Zimbabwe, *The Journal of Modern African Studies* Vol 44, No 2. P223-249.

Fontein, J., 2006, *The Silence of Great Zimbabwe: Contested Landscapes and the Power of Heritage*, Abingdon: University College London Press.

Frazer, J, G., 1926, *The Worship of Nature.* Leiden: Macmillan and Co Ltd.

Garbett K. 1977. Disparate Regional Cults and a Unitary Ritual Field in Zimbabwe, in Werbner R. P, ed, Regional Cults. A.S.A Monographs 16, London and New York: Academic Press: 55-92.

Garuba, H., 2013, On Animism, Modernity/Colonialism, and the African Order of Knowledge: Provisional Reflections, in Green, L., ed, *Contested Ecologies: Dialogues in the South on Nature and Knowledge.* Cape Town: HSRC Press: 42-51.

Gelfand M., 1959, *Shona Religion with Special Reference to the Makorekore.* Cape Town: Juta and Co Ltd.

Gelfand M., 1956, *Medicine and Magic of the Mashona.* Cape Town: Juta and Company.

Gelfand M., 1959, *Shona Ritual with Special Reference to the Chaminuka Cult.* Cape Town: Juta and Company.

Gifford A., 2012, in Brennan F and Packer J, Colonialism, Slavery, Reparations and Trade: Remedying the Past. Canada: Routledge.

Gifford, A., 2012, Formulating the Case for Reparations, in Brennan, F., and Packer, J., *Colonialism, Slavery, Reparations and Trade: Remedying the Past.* Canada: Routledge.

Girard R., 1977, *Violence and the Sacred.* Maryland: John Hopkins University Press.

Gyasi K., 2008, Translation as a Postcolonial Practice: The African Writer as Translator, in Linn S et al, eds, *Translation and Interculturality: Africa and the West.* Frankfurt: Peter Lang Internationaler Verlag der Wissenschaffen: 1-13.

Hardin S., 1994, Is Science Multicultural? Challenges Resources, Opportunities, Uncertainties in *Configurations* 2.2: 301-330.

Herodotus., 1942, *The Persian Wars.* New York: The Modern Library

Hobsbawm E., 1984, Introduction: Inventing Traditions in Hobsbawm E and ranger T., eds, The Invention of Tradition. London: Cambridge University Press: 1-14.

Hornborg A., 2009, Zero-Sum World: Challenges in Conceptualising Environmental Load Displacement and Ecologically Unequal Exchange in the World-Systems, *Journal of Comparative Sociology* 50 (3-4): 236-261.

Hornung E., 1983, *Concept of god in Ancient Egypt: The One and the Many*, London: Routledge and Kegan Paul.

Hromnick C A., 1980, Africa before Livingstone. University of Cape Town Extra Mural Studies.

Ingold T., 2007, Earth, Sky, Wind and Weather. *Journal of the Royal Anthropological Institute 13 (S1): S19-S38.*

Ingold, T., 1993, The Art of Translation in a Continuous World, in Palsson, G.(ed) *Beyond Boundaries: Understanding, Translation and Anthropological Discourse.* Oxford: Berg, p 210-248.

Ingold, T., 2007, Materials against Materiality. *Archaeological Dialogues* 14:1: 1-16.

Ingold, T., 2008, Point, Line and Counterpoint: From Environment to Fluid Space, in Berthoz, A., Christen, Y., eds, Neurobiology of Umwelt: How Living Beings Perceive the World, Research and Perspectives in Neurosciences (c) Springer-Verlag. Berlin Heidelberg pp. 141-155.

Ingold, T., 2010, *Bringing Things to Life: Creative Entanglements in a World of Materials, ESRC National Centre for Research Methods:* Realities Working Paper # 15.

Ingold, T., 2010, Footprints through the Weather-World: Walking, Breathing, Knowing, *Journal of the Royal Anthropological Institute* (NS): S121-S139.

Ingold, T., 2011, Introduction. In Ingold, T., ed, *Redrawing Anthropology, Materials, Movements, Lines.* Surrey: Ashgate Publishing Ltd p1-20.

Jacobson M F., 2000, *Barbarian Virtues: the United States Encounter Foreign Peoples at Home and Abroad 1876-1917.* New York: Hill and Wang.

Jeater D., 2007, *Law, Language and Science: The Invention of the "Native Mind" in Southern Rhodesia,* Portsmouth: Heinemann.

Kane N S., 1954, The World's View: The Story of Southern Rhodesia. London: Cassell and Company Ltd.

Kiggundu, J., 2007, Intellectual Property Law and the Protection of Indigenous Knowledge, In Mazonde, I., and Thomas, P., eds, *Indigenous Knowledge Systems and Intellectual Property in the Twenty-first Century: Perspectives from the Southern Africa.* Dakar: CODESRIA: 26-47.

Kikergard A., 2001, Questioning the Origins of the Negative Image of Africa in Medieval Europe, in Palmerg M., ed, *Encounter Images in the Meeting Between Africa and Europe,* Uppsala Nordiska Afrikainstutet.

Knowledge, Nature and Resource Rights. *USDA Forest Service Proceedings RMRS-P-27*: 148-154.

Koetsier T, and Bergams L., 2005, Introduction, in Same, eds, *Mathematics and the Divine: A Historical Study.* Amsterdam: Elsevier B. V.

Kriger N J., 1992, *Zimbabwe's Guerrilla War: Peasant Voices.* Cambridge: Cambridge University Press.

Kroker A., 2004, *The Will to Technology and the Culture of Nihilism: Heidegger, Nietzsche and Marx,* Toronto: University of Toronto Press.

Kwon H., 2010, The Ghosts of War and the Ethics of memory, in Lambek M, ed, *Ordinary Ethics: Anthropology, Language and Action.* New York: Fordham University Press: 400-441.

Lan D., 1986, *Guns and Rain: Guerrillas and Spirit Mediums in Zimbabwe.* Berkeley and Los Angeles: University of California Press.

Latour B., 2004, *Politics of Nature: how to bring the sciences into democracy*, Cambridge: Harvard University Press.

Latour, B., 2006, On Recalling Actor Network Theory, in Law, J. and Hassard, J., eds, *Actor- Network Theory and After*. Oxford: Blackwell Publishing: 15-25.

Law, J., 2006, After ANT: Complexity, Naming and Topology, in Law, J. and Hassard, J., eds, *Actor-Network Theory and After*. Oxford: Blackwell Publishing: 1-14.

Lyons, T., 2004, *Guns and Guerrilla Girls*. Eritrea: Africa World Press Inc.

Magubane, B. M., 2007, *Race and the Construction of the Dispensable Other*. Pretoria: University of South Africa.

Malin B., 2006, Resilient Society, Vulnerable People: A Study of Disaster Response and Recovery from Floods in Central Vietnam. Uppsala Department of Urban Development, Faculty of Natural Resources and Agriculture Sciences: Swedish University of Agricultural Sciences Doctoral Thesis.

McNeish J A., 2005, Overview: Indigenous Peoples' Perspectives on Poverty and development, in Eversole R et al, eds, *Indigenous People and Poverty: An International Perspective*. London: Zed Books.

Mignolo W., 2007, The Splendour and Miseries of Science: Coloniality, Geopolitics and Epistemic Pluriversality, in de Sousa Santos B, ed, *Cognitive Justice in a Global World*. Plymouth, Lexington Books: 375-395.

Ming D G., 2013, Sinologism: An Alternative to Orientalism and Postcolonialism. Abingdon: Routledge.

Moahi, K. H., 2007, Copyright in the Digital Era ad Some Implications for Indigenous Knowledge, in Mazonde, I., ad Thomas, P., eds, *Indigenous Knowledge Systems and Intellectual Property Rights in the Twenty-first Century: Perspectives from Southern Africa*. Dakar: CODSRIA: 66-77.

Morgan, M. H., 1901, Greek and Roman Gods and Rain Charms, *Transactions and Proceedings of the American Philological Association* vol. 32: 83-109.

Motz, L. and Hane, J., 1995, *The Story of Astronomy*. New York and London: Planum Press.

Moyo, S., 2008, *African Land Questions, Agrarian Transitions and the State: Contradictions of Neoliberal Land Reforms.* Dakar: CODESRIA.

Mudzengi E., 2008, Expropriation is not Enough: Rights and Liberties is What Matters, In Moyo, S. et al, eds, *Contested Terrain: Land Reform and Civil Society in Contemporary Zimbabwe,* Pietermaritzburg: S and S Publishers.

Mungazi D A., 1996, *The Mind of Black Africa.* Westport: Praeger Publishers.

Muphree M W., 1969, *Christianity and the Shona.* New York: The Athlone Press.

Murphy I et al., 1978, *Rhodesian Legacy.* Cape Town/Johannesburg: C Struik Publishers.

Mutswairo S., 1983, *Chaminuka: Prophet of Zimbabwe.* Washington D C: Three Continents Press.

Ndlovu-Gatsheni, S. J., 2013, *Coloniality of Power in Postcolonial Africa: Myths of Decolonisation.* Dakar: CODESRIA.

Ntholi L, S., 2006, *Contesting Sacred Space: A Pilgrimage Study of the Mwali Cult of Southern Africa,* Eritrea: Africa World Press.

Numbers R L., 1985, Science and Religion. Osiris 2nd Series, vol. I: 59-80.

Okri, B., 1997, *A Way of Being Free.* London. Phoenix House.

Oliver, H. H., 1981, *A Relational Metaphysics.* London: Martin Nijhoff Publishers.

Paul, L. A., n.d, Category Priority and Category Collapse, http://lapaul.org/papers/categorical-priority-and collapse.pdf.

Onyewuenyi I, C., 2006, *The African Origins of Greek Philosophy: an Exercise in Afrocentrism,* University of Nigeria Press.

Opoku, K, A., 1978, *West African Traditional Religion,* Accra: FEP International Private Limited

Posselt F W T., 1935, *Fact and Fiction.* Salisbury: Government House.

Potter, J., 2003, Negotiating Local Knowledge: An Introduction, in Potter, J. et al., eds, *Negotiating Local Knowledge: Power and Identity in Development.* London: Pluto Press: 1-29.

Raftopoulos, B., 2009, Crisis in Zimbabwe 1998-2008, in Raftopoulos, B. and Mlambo, A.(eds)*Becoming Zimbabwe: A History from the Precolonial Period to 2008.* Harare: Weaver Press.

Ranger T O., 1979, Revolt in Southern Rhodesia 1896-7. London: Heinemann Educational Books Ltd.

Ranger, T. O., 1969, The Role of Ndebele and Shona Religious Authorities in the Rebellion of 1896 and 1897, in Stokes E and Brown R., eds, *The Zambezian Past: Studies in Central African History*. Manchester: Manchester University Press: 94-136

Ranger, T., 2003, Women and Environment in African Religion: The Case of Zimbabwe, in Beinart, W. and McGregor, J., eds, *Social History of African Environments*. Oxford: James Currey Ltd: 72-86.

Rattray, R. S., 1927, *Religion and Art in Ashanti*. Oxford: Clarendon Press.

Rattray, R. S., 1969, *Ashanti*. New York: Negro University Press.

Reynolds D A et al., 1983, *An Introduction to Law*. Harare: Government Printers.

Robertson T., 2005, Sacrifice and Secularisation: Derrida de Vries and the Future of Mourning in Sherwood Y and Hart K., eds, *Derrida and Religion: Other Testaments*. New York and London: Routledge: 263-275.

Robinson D., 1997, *Translation Theories Explained: Translation and Empire: Postcolonial Theories Explained*. Manchester: St Jerome Publishing.

Sachs J., 2005, *The End of Poverty: How We can Make it Happen in our Lifetime*. London: Penguin Books.

Schapera I., 1971, *Rainmaking Rites of Tswana Tribes*. Leiden Afrika-Studiecentrum.

Schimmel, A., 1993, *The Mystery of Numbers*. Oxford: Oxford University Press.

Segobye, A. K., 2007, The Gods are Resting there: Challenges to the Protection of Heritage Sites through Legislation and Local Knowledge, in Mazonde, I., and Thomas, P., eds, *Indigenous Knowledge Systems and Intellectual Property in the Twenty-first Century: Perspectives from Southern Africa*, Dakar: CODESRIA: 78-94.

Setiloane, G. M., 1975, *The Image of God Among the Sotho-Tswana*. Rotterdam: A.A balkema.

Simmons D., 2012, *Modernising Traditional Medicine in Zimbabwe: HIV/AIDS and Traditional Healers*, Nashville: Vanderbilt University Press.

Smith, D. W., 2001, The Doctrine of Univocity: Deleuze's Ontology of Immanence, in Bryden, M., ed, *Deleuze and Religion*. London: Routledge: 167-183.

Spence C C., 1961, The Dyrenforth Rainmaking Experiments: *A Government Venture in Pluviculture in Arizona and West,* Vol 3, No 3: 205-232.

Southern R W., 1993, *The Making of the Middle Ages.* London: Pinilico.

Stanner, W. E. H., 2005, Religion, Totemism and Symbolism, in Lambek, M., ed, *A Reader in the Anthropology of Religion.* Oxford: Blackwell. P 90-98.

Starr C, G., 1984, *The Ancient Greeks.* Oxford: Oxford University Press.

Stengers I., 2004, The Challenge of Complexity: Unfolding the Ethics of Science in Momoriam of Ilya Prigogine.

Stengers I., 2010, Comparison as a Matter of Concern, *Common Knowledge* 17: 1: 48-63.

Suzuki D et al., 1992, *Wisdom of the Elders: Sacred Nature Stories of Nature.* New York: Bantam Books.

Turnbull D., 2001, *Masons, Tricksters and Cartographers: Comparative Studies in the Sociology of Scientific and Indigenous Knowledge.* Amsterdam: Harwood Academic Publishers.

Udavardy M L. Et al., 2003, The TransAtlantic Trade in African Ancestors: Mijikenda Memorial Statues (Vigango) and the Ethics of Collecting and Circulating NonWestern Cultural Property, *American Anthropologist, New series* Vol 105, No 3: 566-580.

Vera Y., 2001, A Voyeur's Paradise: Images of Africa, in Palmerg M., ed, *Encounter Images in the Meeting Between Africa and Europe.* Uppsala Nordiska Afrikainstutet: 115-120.

Verdery K., 1999, *The Political Lives of Dead Bodies: Reburial and Postsocialist Change.* New York: Columbia University Press.

Verran H., 2013, Engagements between Disparate Knowledge Traditions: Towards Doing Difference generatively and in Good Faith, in Green L, ed, *Contested Ecologies: Dialogues in the South on Nature and Knowledge.* Cape Town: HSRC Press: 141-161.

Vuifhuizen C., 1997, Rainmaking, Political Conflict and Gender Images: a case of Mutema Chieftaincy in Zimbabwe. *Zambezia* XXIV (i): 31-49.

Westerlund D. 2008. African Indigenous Religions and Disease Causation: From Spiritual Beings to Living Humans. Boston: Brill.

White H., 2001, Tempora et Mores: Family Values and the Possession of a Post Apartheid Countryside. *Journal of Religion in Africa*. XXI (4): 457-479.

Chapter 5

Traditional Healers and Medicine in South Africa: A Quest for Legal and Scientific Recognition

Andile Mayekiso and Munyaradzi Mawere

Introduction

The advent of European imperialists in Africa and in South Africa specifically, gave supremacy not only to the imperialists' ideologies on how Africans should live but also to their health care system. In their mission to "civilise" Africans as they claimed, Western colonisers who indeed like sheep in wolves clothing "…despised African traditions, customs, belief systems, and indigenous knowledge systems as diabolic, barbaric, and backward" (Mawere, 2010:209). African traditional healers together with their traditional medicines were systematically side-lined from practicing in the mainstream health care system (see also Awuah-Nyamekye, 2010:47) as there was fear that these would compete (or even outcompete) directly with Western medicines and medical practitioners.

In many African countries, the atmosphere was charged and spirits high when political independence from the European colonialists was ushered in. The majority were filled with hope that their lives would be changed for the better and the value of their once castigated traditional values, religions, indigenous knowledges and traditional medicines restored. Many African governments, indeed, had made extraordinary affirmations full of hope – promises of milk and honey – before independence as they were mobilising support from the masses. In South Africa before independence in 1994, for example, promised an inclusive South Africa with equality before the law and a full democracy that would accommodate the values of all citizens. Unfortunately, some twenty years since black-majority rule begun and South Africa became a full democratic country, the same country remains one of the most unequal countries when it comes to the scientific and legal treatment of traditional medicines and their practitioners vis-a-vi Western-biased medicines (or mainstream medicine) and their practitioners. We should, however, be quick to point out that this is not a problem unique to South Africa alone, but a continental problem that affects the larger part of Africa. Despite legislations from the mother bodies such as African Union to protect and legalise African traditional healers and their medicines, African leadership continue lacking the political will to accord traditional medicines and the practitioners equal status to Western-biased medicines and their practitioners (the so-called medical doctors). This gives a big challenge to traditional medicine in particular and Indigenous Knowledge System (IKS) in general which should swiftly reopen crucial files that were closed in the process of false civilisation (or colonialism), modernisation and development in which the cultural, socio-economic life of indigenous peoples were maimed or soiled (Domfeh, 2007:41). The only consoling point is that evidence is abound which suggests that despite all attempts by the European colonialists to wipe out or eradicate African indigenous healing methods fell short. During the reign of Apartheid government in South Africa and even to date, indigenous Africans in South Africa, as elsewhere on the continent, continue to make use of traditional medicines and their practitioners' generation after generation.

In this chapter, we examine the legal and scientific standing of traditional medicine and its practitioners in South Africa. We examine the challenges encountered in seeking to pass into law the *Traditional Health Practitioners Act of 2007 (Act. 22 of 2007)* which was meant to legalise the status of traditional healers only to come into effect on 01 May 2014. We also examine the prospects of traditional medicine and its practitioners in South Africa in view of the *Traditional Health Practitioners Act* mentioned above.

Background to the use of Traditional Medicine in South Africa

Before the establishment of cosmopolitan medicine (commonly known as Western biomedicine, modern medicine), traditional medicine and its practitioners known in Africa as traditional healers was the dominant medical system for millions of people in Africa but the arrival of the Europeans was a noticeable turning point in the history of this ancient tradition and culture (Abdullahi, 2011). Traditional healers are established health care workers within their communities.

According to Karim *et al* (1994) medication or herbs used by African traditional healers in Africa could be categorised into three distinct groups. Firstly, is the preventive and prophylactic medication, which protect their patients from possible afflictions, traditional healers may perform acts, using medicine against disequilibrium, or wearing totemic objects. Among the Zulus, for example, medication for self-fortification is called *amaKhubalo*. *IzinGqunda* or *IziNtelezi* is sprinkled around and about the kraal to ward off lightning or to cause the *umthakathi* (witch) discomfort in his bad endeavours (Karim *et al*, 1994). Secondly, is the treatment for ailments, which could be prepared different forms such as in cold or hot infusions, decoctions, powders, poultices and lotions, and a variety of earthy ointments that comprise animal fat, clay and sometimes ashes. These formulations are made into different medicine mixtures (*umuthi* or *imbiza*). The recipes are usually a secret and are part of the knowledge that the healer will pass onto his apprentice (ibid). Thirdly, is the medications used to destroy the power in others. These medications target specific individuals. A concoction can, for example, be placed in the enemy's path and it is then believed that when the enemy passes by, he will contract a fatal disease. We should, however, be quick to point out that it is the abuse [by some traditional healers] of this element which normally makes some people confuse traditional healers' practices and those of sorceries which in fact is seriously abhorred in traditional African societies.

A number of reasons why people consult traditional healers have already been identified. It is argued that their availability and accessibility in conjunction with their familiarity with people's culture, their relationship with patients and families make them ideal (Kgoatla, 1997). Besides, in traditional African societies, payment for the treatment normally depends on its efficacy such that traditional healers normally do not request payment until after the treatment is given and positive results obtained (see also Mokaila, 2001). Other reasons include patients know their traditional healers quite well, belief that illness arise from supernatural causes and indicates the displeasure of ancestral gods or evil spirits or is the effect of black magic hence only traditional healers are better placed to treat it, traditional medicine and the various African cultures go together, lack of trust in the ability of Western medical doctors to effectively treat psychosocial problems, and lack of Western medical practitioners in the treatment of culture-bound syndromes (Kgoatla, 1997; Stanhope and Lancaster, 1988). In poor communities Western based health care facilities are known for lack of resources – often without medication, far from the people which makes it difficult to access when someone is really sick with no transportation, and bad attitude from the practitioners.

In South Africa, traditional healers are mainly 'indigenous' Africans with spiritual gifts to treat various conditions (ailments/diseases) including resolving many other health related problems. They normally treat their patients using both herbs and spiritual powers. Partisans of Traditional African medicine differ in perspective from those of Western medicine in that they believe illness is not derived from chance occurrences but from social imbalance, witchcraft or spiritual imbalance. It is this difference in perspective that when European settlers came to Africa with their Western medicines they found it difficult to collaborate with African Traditional medicine resulting in the latter being despised and even threatened to be banned. In fact, modern medicine (as is the case with the so-called modern science), has considered traditional medicine and methods of healing as backward and primitive (see also Conserve Africa Foundation Report 2002). In South Africa, as elsewhere in Africa, repressive laws against African Traditional medicine were enacted (see also Chavunduka 1980, 1982). And, due to these repressive apartheid laws and their after-effects on all institutions deemed traditional, traditional healers have a protracted sad and odious history. However, just like many other traditional institutions, values and traditions, traditional healing practices and the deployment of traditional medicine is known to be very resilient. Having existed many centuries prior to the arrival of the Dutch in South Africa around the 17th century (see Setswe

1999), traditional medicine and their practitioners have survived the harsh and repressive laws of the apartheid era and even the unjust laws with regard to the status they are accorded the modern South African.

Traditional healers in South Africa as healers elsewhere in Africa use African traditional medicines and herbs to heal physical, emotional and spiritual ailments. People consult them for protection against illness, to counter witchcraft activities, restore lost love, protect their homesteads from witchcraft and many other reasons. Mawere (2011:106), following The World Health Organisation Traditional Medicine Strategy 2002-2005 notes that about 80% of the people in South Africa believe that many traditional African medicines work effectively against various diseases, with particular reference to tropical diseases, such as malaria. It is further estimated that approximately 60% of South African babies are delivered by Traditional Birth Attendants (TBA) especially in rural areas (Karim *et al*, 1994:3; WHO, 2002:1; Njanji, 1999:1). In a survey conducted in Zimbabwe by the co-author of this chapter on the use of traditional medicine, it was found out 81 % of the Zimbabwean households favoured both public hospitals and traditional healing methods which included consulting prophets and traditional healers. The least options were pharmacies (1 %) and public clinics (2 %) (Survey 2014). WHO attribute the high utilisation of traditional medicine to its historical accessibility and affordability in comparison to the Western medicine, and also it being embedded within the wider belief systems in developing countries (2002:2). Though the exact percentage of the people relying on traditional medicine in Africa cannot be readily known, one would definitely disagree with Makinde (1988:103) in what seems a suggestion that it is only "the majority of Africans in the rural areas who look for treatment of diseases and illness (including mental illness) from the traditional healers who share the same experience with them and so understand their problems." From our personal experiences of having stayed in different large cities (and rural areas) across the Southern African region, the truth of the matter would seem to be that many African people, both in the rural and urban settings deploy African traditional medicine, as well as Western medicine, because of their understanding that neither of the two systems (African traditional medicine and Western medicine) is perfect and self-sufficient. We, however, second Makinde (1988) who regrets how most of the Western trained medical practitioners seek ways of discrediting African traditional medical doctors, by labelling them as unscientific and having no standard, even though it is well-known that it was through the same African traditional medicine that "many of them were safely delivered, nurtured, and successfully treated until they grew up to be medical doctors" (p. 106).

The continued deployment and belief in traditional medicine in many parts of Africa and elsewhere in the world resulted in World Health Organisation (WHO), in 1977, to formally recognise the importance of mainstream biomedicine to collaborate with traditional medicine and healers. This means that traditional medicines and their practitioners ought to occupy a vital role in social and political lives of the people in their communities, of course, following a sad history of traditional healers who during the colonial era, were outlawed because they were considered by the European imperialists as witches and pagans, and therefore their activities illegal. Following the WHO call for the recognition of traditional medicine and practitioners, the African Union (AU) also declared the period 2001-2010 as the Decade of African Traditional Medicine, and the New Partnership for Africa's Development (NEPAD) has noted traditional medicine as an important strategy in its Plan (African Union, 2001:2; NEPAD, 2001:31). However, even with these declarations in place the process of decriminalising and formally recognising African Traditional medicine and its practitioners have been slow throughout the continent. In South Africa, hot debates on the percentage of people consulting traditional medical practitioners remain even tense. In the ensuing paragraphs, we briefly highlight the debates.

Challenges to the use of Traditional Medicine in South Africa

The figures on the exact percentage of people using traditional medicine remain unknown not only in Africa as a whole but in many countries on the continent. In South Africa, for example, the 80 % (which started with WHO) has come under a lot of criticism with some claiming that they exaggerate traditional medicine and practitioners' usage. For instance, when the BBC News website early in 2013 carried an article about traditional healers in South Africa, arguing that *sangomas* "remain the first point of contact for physical and psychological ailments for about 80% of black South Africans", it came under a lot of criticism from Africa Check, a non-profit organisation which promotes accuracy in public debate (www.africacheck.org). Likewise, in 2012 the *South African Medical Journal* made a similar suggestion that some 80% of South Africans use traditional medicine to meet their primary healthcare needs. Unfortunately, even Stats South Africa Organisation is unable to shed light on this matter, which is an indication that they do not see the importance of such statistics as to how many people make use of indigenous medicines. Such work remains to be conducted. The situation in South Africa is perpetuated by the lack rigorous scholarly work. Also, one could argue that the sharp criticism of WHO on the 80 % figure is not only based on the lack of rigorous scholarly work but it is also motivated by the urge to promote modern medicine and create an impression that African traditional medicine is fast losing value before its own people. It is, in fact, difficult to imagine if ever similar criticisms were going to be raised had the 80 % figure was credited to modern medicine.

Nevertheless, in this chapter it will be a digression for us to seriously and vigorously engage in such a debate, suffice to say no one is disputing the fact that traditional healers play a critical role in the lives of black South Africans. In the light of this, our interest is to understand the dynamics involved in drafting and completing the *Traditional Health Practitioners Act of 2007 (Act 22 of 2007),* aimed at recognising traditional healers and their medicines especially because it was declared by the African National Congress (ANC) as early as 1994.

According to Pretorius (n.d:250) traditional healers do not all perform the same functions, nor do they all fall into the same category. Although traditional healers are known by different names in the different South Africa cultures (for example, *amagqira* in Xhosa, *ngaka* in Northern Sotho, *selaoli* in Southern Sotho and *mungome* in Venda and Tsonga) most South Africans generally refer to them as *sangomas* (from the Zulu word *izangoma*). Freeman and

Motsei (1992:1184) stated that there are broadly three types of traditional healers available to South African consumers. Firstly, the traditional doctor *(inyanga)*. This is generally a male who uses herbal and other medicinal preparations for treating disease. Secondly, the *dingaka* (Sotho) who is usually a woman; operating within a traditional religious supernatural context and acts as a medium with the ancestral shades. Thirdly, the faith healer who integrates Christian ritual and traditional practices (Freeman and Motsei, 1992:1184). The WHO Centre for Health Development defines African traditional medicines as

> The sum total of all knowledge and practices, whether explicable or not, used in diagnosis, prevention and elimination of physical, mental, or social imbalance, and relying exclusively on practical experience and observation handed down from generation to generation, whether verbally or in writing.

Likewise, Domfeh (2007:42) describe traditional medicines as ways of protecting and restoring health that were used by locals before the introduction of modern medicines. As the name suggests, these indigenous methodologies to health belong to the traditions of each country, and have been passed on from generation to generation. Indigenous Africans like other indigenous peoples elsewhere, rely on plant and animal based medicine to meet their health care requirements (ibid). Traditional medicine treatment includes medication therapies, which involve the use of herbal medicines, animal fats and/or minerals, while non-medication therapies include acupuncture, manual therapy and spiritual therapy (Amai 2002). As elsewhere in Africa, South African traditional healers play a significant role in the health care system (Peltzer 1998:191; Pretorious 1989:101), regardless of their legal status for decades which saw them remaining on the margins of the health care system. Among the key legislations that were passed by the Apartheid regime in South Africa to prohibit traditional healers from practising legally using their gifts include the Witchcraft Suppression Act of 1957 and the Witchcraft Suppression Amendment Act of 1970 (Richter 2003).

It is not only South Africa that has struggled to incorporate traditional medicines with Western biomedical into the health services. In Uganda, Mutabazi (2008:203) reports that despite all the efforts and recognition of the importance of traditional medicine, they have not been fully integrated into national health services and for some, it is even doubtful that the model of integration being pursued will yield the anticipated results. In Mozambique, when the country attained its national independence from Portugal in 1975, attempts to control traditional medicine went on. It went as far as sending traditional healers to re-education camps while modern medicine practitioners were allowed to freely built clinics and hospitals across the country. In fact, little was done even by post-independent government of Mozambique to investigate the legitimacy and validity (in their own terms not from the perspective of modern science) of practices by African traditional healers (see also Onwuanibe 1979).

Traditional Medicine in post-Apartheid South Africa

The recognition and integration of traditional medicine into the national health care system was part of the African National Congress's (ANC) 1994 Manifesto. It was promised that consumers would be allowed to choose whom they want to consult for their health care and legislation will be changed to facilitate controlled use of traditional practitioners (African National Congress, 1994). Indeed, when the ANC rose to power in 1994, it formalised this policy in its Reconstruction and Development Programme (RDP) (African National Congress, 1994:3-5). What remains surprising and makes the promise rhetorical is the realisation that some twenty years after independence, the policy is not yet put into full effect. A lingering question, therefore, remains: 'if there was such a commitment then from the ruling party, how come it took twenty years for the policy to come into effect?' We return to this point shortly so as to understand the struggles that have been encountered which might serve as lessons to other African countries.   It is said that there were approximately 200 000 traditional healers practising in South Africa in 1995, compared to 25 000 modern doctors (Setswe 1999; Kale 1995). In Sub-Saharan

Africa, the ratio of traditional healers to the general population is approximately 1:500, while doctors trained in "Western" medicine have a 1:40 000 ratio to the rest of the population. It is estimated that 70% to 80% of the population in Africa makes use of traditional medicine (Setswe 1999; WHO 2002; Kale 1995; Mawere 2011). This is clear testimony that regardless of several campaigns especially by groups and individuals interested in modern medicine, the deployment of traditional medicine South Africa remains very high.

The first positive action by the South African Government towards legitimising African traditional medicine took place in November 1995, when the then National Health Minister and the Provincial MECs for Health called upon Provincial Governments to conduct public hearings on the feasibility of traditional health care (Pretorius, n.d:253). There was a long delay but eventually the hearings took place between May and June in 1997, resulting in a report at the end of that year, compiled by the National Council of Provinces and presented to the National Assembly's Portfolio Committee on Health. According to the report, all the provinces were in favour of a statutory council for traditional healers consisting of local representatives rather than persons appointed by the MECs for Health (ibid). The *White Paper for the Transformation of the Health System in South Africa 1997* stated that: "The regulation and control of traditional healers should be investigated for their legal empowerment. Criteria outlining standards of practice and an ethical code of conduct for traditional practitioners should be developed to facilitate their registration" (Ministry of Health, 1997:34). In 2003, the 'Traditional Health Practitioners Bill' of 2003 was proposed. The Bill aimed to:

> Provide for the establishment of the Interim Traditional Health Practitioners Council of the Republic of South Africa; to provide for a regulatory framework to ensure the efficacy, safety and quality of traditional health care services; to provide for control over the registration, training and practice of Traditional Health Practitioners and to provide for matters incidental thereto (Preamble of the Bill, 2003).

In 2004, the *Traditional Health Practitioners Bill for South Africa* was unanimously approved in Parliament and was enacted on 11 February 2005 (Republic of South Africa, 2005). Although the WHO formally recognised the importance of collaborating with traditional healers in 1977 (Richter 2003), in South Africa, it was only in 2003 that a Traditional Health Practitioners Bill of 2003 was drafted. Certain sections of the Traditional Health Practitioners Act, Act 35 of 2004, came into operation on 13 January 2006. Besides, it is still clear that despite the approval of the *Traditional Health Practitioners Bill for South Africa,* the practices of traditional healers remain largely regulated by modern science through the Ministry of Health. In fact, as is stated in the Preamble of the Bill (2003), the Bill "... provide for a regulatory framework to ensure the efficacy, safety and quality of traditional health care services". But when one asks: By what standard or yardstick the Bill is going to measure the efficacy, safety and quality of services of the traditional heath care, one discovers that the measure is modern science (and in particular modern medicine). This shows that even in the presence of the Bill, the scientific recognition of African Traditional medicine remains a thorn in the flesh: it is still unresolved.

To date, the Traditional Healers Organisation (THO) is reportedly the biggest traditional healer umbrella organisation in South Africa and was established in 1970 (Richter 2003:11). It claims a staggering figure of 69 000 traditional healers in Southern Africa as its members, with 25 000 of those residing in South Africa. Traditional healers legible to join the THO have to attend a one-day workshop, which introduces them to THO activities, and a five-day workshop on traditional primary health care. Another requirement is that members have to produce a good character reference (ibid). Although African and Western health practitioners have worked side-by-side for decades in South Africa but there are still difficulties and challenges which harm any effective collaboration between the two systems. Hammond-Tooke (1989:185) identified the challenges in integrating Western and traditional medicine to the prejudicial notion that traditional African beliefs and practices are 'primitive' and 'savage'. Gumede (1990: 153) echoes this belief by pointing out that Western health practitioners' critical view of traditional medicine is based on notions which perceive traditional health practitioners as posing a danger to the health of their patients. Thus Euro-centric views of African Traditional medicine remain grafted and lingering in the minds of many, including some Africans especially the Western trained medical practitioners and scholars.

As alluded to above, in 2004, the *Traditional Health Practitioners Bill for South Africa* was unanimously approved in Parliament and was enacted on 11 February 2005 (Republic of South Africa, 2005). On the 30th of April 2014, President Jacob Zuma signed a Traditional Healers Act. The Act states that in terms of section 52 of the Traditional Health Practitioners Act, 2007 (Act No. 22 of 2007), determined that on 01 May 2014 would be the date on which Sections 4, 5, 6, 8, 9, 16, 17, 18-28, 29-41, 42-46, and 51 shall come into operation (2 May 2014).

Critique of the Act No. 22 of 2007

The bill allows for the establishment of an Interim Traditional Health Council that will eventually accredit all Traditional Healers *(sangomas)* and regulate the industry. The signing of this Act means that traditional healers are permitted to issue medical certificates for the purpose of paid sick leave if an employee consulted them provided the practitioner is registered with the Interim Health Practitioners Council of South Africa, in terms of the Main Agreement of the Act. While the Traditional Healers Act of 2014 seems to have eased the plight of Traditional Healers, a critical analysis of the Act shows that it is more of a lip service than it is a genuine act towards recognition of Traditional Healers and their services. This is because the coming into operation of the aforementioned sections of the Traditional Healers Act caused a lot of noise among employers in South Africa who feared that Traditional Healers would go on a rampage dishing out medical certificates unnecessarily to allow employees to recuperate at home. This is interesting to note but also shows that mainstream doctors will never accept traditional healers. It is interesting to note because the issue of medical certificates raised here appears to be an issue in view of traditional healers yet even the same mainstream doctors could also give out medical certificates illegally accepting bribes. We argue in this light, therefore, that the mistrust by employers is unwarranted and unfounded given that already they accept medical certificates from mainstream doctors who can also abuse their offices. The KwaZulu-Natal Traditional Healers Council President, Sazi Mhlongo, have also responded to these claims by employers urging that they [employers] need not fear because they have strict measures in place in the form of monitoring committees, both at district and sub-district levels (see Baloyi, 2014:1). Mhlongo clarified that most of their members are aware of the work requirements of their patients. He further argued that currently there is a rampant abuse of sick leave certificates being issued by conventional medical practitioners, and why this reaction against traditional healers (The Daily News, 12 August 2004). We argue that the approval of the Traditional Healers Act by Parliament and subsequently the President is by no means a victory for traditional health practitioners as is evidenced by the subsequent outcry by employers immediate after the approval of the Act in May 2014. In fact, the outcry by employers should not be taken lightly. It shows that it will take time, commitment and trust from all those involved to get traditional healers play the role in the health system in South Africa. In terms of Section 23(2) of the Basic Conditions of Employment Act (BCEA) of 1997, a medical certificate is only valid if issued and signed by a person who is certified to diagnose and treat patients. This person must be registered with a professional council established by an Act of Parliament, which means as things stand in South Africa at the moment employers do not have to recognise any medical certificate issued by traditional healers (Truter, 2014:1). This is because the Traditional Health Practitioners Act (THPA) still envisages several regulations to be made by the Minister of Health in consultation with the Council (ibid). It is important to note that we might have the THPA passed and approved by the President but the status of these practitioners remains the same if not worse. The Act basically shut them off, to stop making noise about their status. According to section 17 of the Medical, Dental and Supplementary Health Service Professionals Act of 1974 which is still in full force, a medical practitioner is a person entitled to practice as a medical practitioner according to this Act. This Act excludes traditional healers. It is thus; clear that section 23 of the

BCEA contains two requirements that should be met in order for a medical certificate to be valid. The first requirement is that it has to state that the employee was notable to perform his normal duties as a result of illness. The second requirement is that such a medical certificate should be issued by a medical practitioner (http://www.labourguide.co.za). It is unfortunate that indigenous South Africans themselves or rather those who worship Western supremacy over African indigenous knowledge such as Amanda Mokoena (2014:112) continue to label traditional healers as unprofessional. Mokoena uses Western standard to despise traditional healers, calling them not "professional" on the basis that their practices differ from those of the mainstream doctors in many respects. In view of Mokoena's position, we argue that her use of the word *(un-)professional* is highly contested given that one can still go to many automobile companies and find the so called 'technicians' working on peoples cars on daily basis because they have been trained to work on those cars but do not have any paper ('qualifications') from a 'formal' institution to perform that work. It is also a failure to appreciate cosmological pluralism, of which, African cosmology particularly as pertaining to African healing methods is one and that relating to the mainstream bio-medicine is also another one of its own kind.

The prospects of traditional medicine and its practitioners in South Africa

The so-called 'fly by night traditional healers' is putting a bad name for all African healers. There are those who claim, for instance, that they cure HIV/Aids and out of desperation people consult them especially people who are in denial about their HIV status. According to Pretorius (n.d:254) even though legislation and official recognition of African traditional health workers and their medicines have been lagging behind, the private sector companies have realised the need for involving the traditional sector, because of the preferences of their employees. For instance, Medscheme, South Africa's largest medical aid administrator has introduced limited traditional healer benefits, while Eskom has since 1994 allowed employees to claim a limited number of visits to traditional healers on the company's medical plan. Another example is the Medical and Burial Savings Scheme that has screened and recognised more than 40 healers that clients may consult should they so wish. The Chamber of Mines and the National Union of Mineworkers have also allowed a panel of traditional healers at mines and have granted their employees three days' leave to consult such healers. The length of time it took from the initial recognition in 1994 until 01 May 2014 when it was finally signed shows the lack of willingness from the ANC led government. It is not about the outcry from the white populace because the ANC has proven in other spheres that if they want to do something they have majority to go ahead. For instance, there was a huge public outcry when they wanted to disband the so-called 'Scorpions' but they went ahead and gotten rid of what has been the most effective crime intelligence unit similar to the FBI. It all boils down to political will from African governments.

There is a growing interest from 'medical doctors operating in the best equipped hospitals, top-level experts in surgery or paediatrics who would tell their patients to go back to the village and consult traditional healers' (Hountondji 2002: 23) which usually has cultural and religious undertone. In fact, big western companies make a lot of money from indigenous medicines which they get for free without paying any taxes or giving back to the communities. Mugabe (1998) emphasises this view:

> Biotechnology, pharmaceutical and human health care industries have increased their interest in natural products as sources of new biochemical compounds for drug, chemical and agro-products development ... Of the 119 drugs developed from higher plants and on the world market today, it is estimated that 74% were discovered from a pool of traditional herbal medicine.

By having regulations in place, African countries stand to benefit from these big companies hence plaguing back to the communities in return. A study that was conducted in South Africa to investigate attitude and knowledge of nurses towards traditional healing, faith healing and complementary therapies in Northern

Province found that in line with other studies by (Mohape and Peltzer 1998: 39) the majority of the psychiatric nurses favoured the integration of faith healing (98%), traditional healing (93%), and complementary medicine (77%) into the national health care system. These psychiatric nurses were all African South Africans; most were Protestants (60%), followed by Roman Catholics (19%) and other religious denominations such as Zion Christian Church and Jehovah's Witnesses (Peltzer and Khoza, 2002:37). The study also report that patients often consulted traditional healers before visiting clinics especially in conditions like tuberculosis, HIV/AIDS, cancer, renal failure, epilepsy and sexually transmitted diseases (ibid). These findings confirm the claims that are often made by WHO that Africans value traditional healers and their medicines and often consult them before going to doctors and clinics. This trust could be used by national government to build relationships with traditional healers and train them so that when they encounter cases of emergence they should feel confident to refer patients to hospitals before it is too late.

The South African Traditional Healers' Primary Health Care Handbook was produced in 1997 by the Traditional Medicines Research Programme of the University of Cape Town, an established research group of the Medical Research Council (Clarke, 1998:9). The handbook acts as a guide for the treatment of common diseases by traditional healers, both from a Western medical and traditional perspective. The South African handbook of traditional healers identifies the following categories of conditions which could be treated by traditional healers:

o Conditions of the respiratory system: for example colds and flu; hay fever; pneumonia; asthma; bronchitis; emphysema; tuberculosis.

o Conditions of the gastro-intestinal system: for example diarrhoea; dysentery; constipation; heartburn, indigestion; ulcers; haemorrhoids, worms.

o Conditions of the cardiovascular system: for example angina; high blood pressure; palpitations.

o Conditions of the central nervous system: for example headache; migraine; stroke.

124

o   Conditions of the skin and hair: for example acne; eczema; boils; insect bites and stings; ringworm; scabies.

o   Conditions of the blood: for example anaemia; blood cleansing (routinely given following treatment to help cleanse the body of the original cause of the disease).

o   Conditions of the urogenital system: for example sexually transmitted diseases; cystitis; menstrual pain; vaginitis.

o   Conditions of the eyes: for example "pink eye".

o   Conditions of the musculoskeletal system: for example arthritis; backache; muscular pain; gout; sprains and strains; rheumatism and many other illnesses (Pretorius, n.d:252).

The handbook is a response to the traditional healers request to have guidelines and it has been widely distributed to clinics, traditional healers' organisations and health workers across the country. Pretorius (n.d:254-5) argues that the challenges that have been encountered by traditional healers to formally participate in the mainstream health care system in South African cannot be attributed to the official opposition from the Western medical sector in the country. He asserts that the Medical Association of South Africa as early as June 1995 formulated guidelines for co-operation between modern and African Traditional Medical Practitioners, especially in the case of referrals. He further state that even the public sector cannot be blamed for the delay in fully incorporating traditional healers. Departments of Health have been actively involved in providing traditional healers and TBAs with PHC training, among others in respect of HIV/AIDS/STDs and TB. Yet Pretorius' opinion is difficult to dispute or accept because there is no other study that collaborate his views. Most of his work is based on personal communication with specific individuals within departments rather than on official reports. It seems traditional healers themselves have been divided in the country with some in favour of the collaboration while other wanted the Statutory Council to be established first so as that they could conduct discussions on an equal footing (ibid).

Conclusion

This chapter has critically examined the legal and scientific standing of traditional medicine and its practitioners in South Africa. On this note, we discussed the difficulties (both legal and criticism from scientific perspective beholders) being encountered by traditional healers in South Africa in their attempt to have the services they render to society formally [scientifically] and legally recognised by the government and the mainstream heath care in the country. We also examined the prospects of traditional medicine and its practitioners in South Africa in view of the *Traditional Health Practitioners Act* mentioned above. We have noted that despite dragging for such a long period to have the *Traditional Health Practitioners Act of 2007* passed, the South African government has ultimately shown commitment in trying to bring traditional healers and the mainstream practitioners working together for a common goal. It, however, remains a point that justice delayed is justice denied given that the incorporation of the traditional healers into the mainstream health care system is long overdue. And, while the importance and role of traditional healers in society is widely acknowledged, the mistrust of traditional healers by some interest groups coupled with continual criticism that traditional healers faces remain an indubitable challenge that hampers progress in the medical fraternity as a whole. The mistrust is in fact responsible for the hold-ups in the integration traditional healers into the mainstream biomedicine or at least in the harmonious working together of the two health arms. Pretorius exonerates the private sector in all these delays. Yet his opinion is difficult to dispute or accept because there is no other study that collaborate his views. Most of his work is based on personal communication with specific individuals within departments rather than on official reports. On this note, we conclude that more research is needed to find ways to harmoniously integrate traditional medicine with mainstream health care in Africa and particularly South Africa especially given the spiralling and escalating costs of biomedically-based health care, compounded with an ever-increasing burden of chronic and mental disorder at regional and global levels, which in turn calls for indigenous health-care alternatives.

References

Abdullahi, A. A. 2011. Trends and challenges of Traditional Medicine in Africa, *African Journal of Traditional, Complementary and Alternative Medicines*, 8 (5s). Available at doi:10.4314/ajtcam.v8i5s.5. (Retrieved: 12 October 2014).

African National Congress, 1994. *A national health plan for South Africa*, Johannesburg: South Africa.

African Union. 2001. Decisions and Declarations. Thirty-seventh Ordinary Session/ Fifth Ordinary Session of the Assembly of Heads of State and Government: 9-11 July 2001: Lusaka: Zambia.

Amai, C.A., 2002. *Medicinal plants and bio-diversity Report*, Ministry of Health, Kampala: Uganda.

Awuah-Nyamekye, S. 2010. The role of religion in indigenous health practice in Ghana: Implications for Ghanaian universities in Ghana's Development, *Journal of Theology for Southern Africa* (138), pp. 36-56.

Baloyi, M. 2014. *Sangomas* fight back in sick leave saga. A leading resource on health systems and primary health care in South Africa. Health Systems Trust. Also available online: http://www.hst.org.za/news/sangomas-fight-back-sick-note-saga?page=8

Chavunduka, G. 1980. Witchcraft and the law in Zimbabwe, *Zambezia Journal of the University of Zimbabwe*, VIII (129-147), Harare.

Chavunduka, G. 1982. Witches, witchcraft and the law in Zimbabwe, *Occasional Paper No. 1 (1982)*, ZINATHA, Harare.

Clarke, E. 1998. A prime example of collaboration between traditional healers and conventional medicine. In Traditional healers: HST Update: Issue No.37. http://www.hst.org.za

Conserve Africa Foundation, (04/04/ 2002). 'Medicinal plants and natural products', (Retrieved: 10 October 2014).

Domfeh, K.A. 2007.Indigenous Knowledge Systems and the Need for Policy and Institutional Reforms. Tribes and Tribals, Special Volume No. 1: pp.41-52.

Government Gazette No. 24704, Vol. 454 on 11 April 2003. Notice 979 of 2003.

Gumede, M. V. 1990. *Traditional Healers: a medical doctor's perspective*, Johannesburg: Blackshaws.

Freman, M. And Motsei, M. 1992. Planning health care in South Africa: is there a role for traditional healers? *Social Science& Medicine* 34: 1183-1090.

Hammond-Tooke, D. 1989. Rituals and medicines: indigenous healing in South Africa, Johannesburg: Ad Donker.

Hountondji, P. J. 2002.Knowledge appropriation in a post-colonial context. In: Odora-Hoppers, C. A. (ed.) *Indigenous knowledge and the integration of knowledge systems: towards a philosophy ofarticulation.* Claremont, South Africa: New Africa Books (Pty) Ltd, pp. 23-38.

Kale, R. 1995. South Africa's Health: Traditional healers in South Africa: a parallel health care system. *British Medical Journal*, 310 (6 May): 1182-1185.

Kgoatla, P. 1997.The use of traditional medicines by teenage mothers in Soshanguve.*Health SA Gesondheid*, 2 (3): 27-31.

Makinde, M. A. 1988. *African Philosophy, Culture, and Traditional Medicine. Ohio University Center for International Studies: Monographs in International Studies, Africa Series Number 53.*

Mawere, M. 2011. Ethical quandaries in spiritual healing and herbal medicine: A critical analysis of the morality of traditional medicine advertising in southern African urban societies, *Pan African Medical Journal*, 2011;10:6 Available online @ http://www.Panafrican-med-journal.com.content/article/10/6/full

Mawere, M. 2010. Indigenous knowledge systems (IKSs) potential for establishing a moral, virtuous society: lessons from selected IKSs in Zimbabwe and Mozambique. Journal of Sustainable Development in Africa, Vol. 12, No.7: pp. 209-221.

Minister of Health (South Africa).1997. White Paper for the Transformation of the Health System in South Africa. Cape Town: Ministry of Health.

Mokaila, A. 2001.*Traditional vs. Western medicine – African context*, Drury University: Missouri.

Mugabe, J. 1998. *Intellectual property protection and traditional knowledge: an exploration in international policy* discourse. Available: *http://www.wipo.int/tk/en/hr/paneldiscussion/papers/pdf/mugabe.pdf.* Accessed 2 September 2014.

NEPAD. 2001: The New Partnership for Africa's Development. South Africa: NEPAD.

Njanji, S 1999. AIDS-Africa-medicine: African traditional healers part of army to fight AIDS. [Internet] Agence France- Presse. Available from: c h ttp://w w w.aegis.com /news/afp /1999/AF990956.html> [Accessed on 08 Oct 2014].

Onwuanibe, R. 1979. The philosophy of African medical practice, *A Journal of Opinion* 9 (3): 25-28.

Peltzer, K. and Khoza, L.B. 2002.Attitudes and knowledge of nurse practitioners towards traditional healing, faith healing and complementary medicine in the Northern Province of South Africa, Curations.

Peltzer, K 1998: A community survey of traditional healers in South Africa (Northern Province), *South African Journal of Ethnology* 21: 191-197

Pretorius, E. 1989:

Skakelingtussentradisioneleenmodemegeneeskunde in Afrika: die dekadesedert Alma Ata, *Acta Academica*21: 101-129.

Republic of South Africa. 2005. Traditional Health Practitioners Act, 2004. *Government Gazette*, 476 (27275). Cape Town.

Richter, M. 2003.*Traditional Medicines and Traditional Healers in South Africa.* Discussion paper prepared for the Treatment Action Campaign and AIDS Law Project. Available on the web:http://www.tac.org.za/Documents/ResearchPapers/Tradi tional_Medicine_briefin .pdf (date accessed: 09 Oct 2014).

Setswe, G. 1999. The Role of Traditional Healers and Primary Health Care in South Africa. *Health SA Gesondheid*, 4 (2): 56-60.

Stanhope, M. and Lancaster, J. 1988.*Community Health Nursing: Process and Practice for Promoting Health.* St Louis: Mosby.

World Health Organisation. 2002. *Traditional Medicine Strategy 2002- 2005.* 2002. Geneva: World Health Organisation.

Mokoena, A, C, U. 2014. The legality of traditional healers' sick-notes in South Africa. Ethno Med, 8(2): pp. 111-117.

No. 29, 2014. Commencement of certain sections of the Traditional Health Practitioners Act, 2007 (Act No. 22 of 2007). Also available online: www.gpwonline.co.za.

The Daily News, 12 August 2004. Accessed on 16 Oct 2014.

Truter, J. 2014. Medical certificates by traditional healers. Available online: http://www.paarlpost.co.za/196424/news-details/medical-certificates-by-traditional- healers.

The South African Labour Guide 2014. From http://www.labourguide.co.za (Retrieved 17 October 2014).

Acts:

1. Act 56 of 1974.
2. The Basic Conditions of Employment Act.

Chapter 6

A History of Pre-colonial and Colonial Wildlife Conservation in Ghana

Kwame Osei Kwarteng

Introduction

This is a multi–sourced chapter which examines the history of conservation of both flora and fauna in pre–colonial and colonial Ghana. Concepts relating to preservation of the natural heritage of Ghana such as national park, game reserve and forest reserve may appear to have been introduced to Ghanaians by Europeans. But a critical examination of the cultural practices of the Akan and other peoples of Ghana clearly shows that these conservation practices predate British colonisation of the country. The chapter, therefore, explores some of the indigenous conservation practices among the Akan and other peoples of Ghana and juxtaposes them with the conservation practices which the colonial authorities introduced into the country after colonisation. Before I examine the traditional wildlife conservation practices among the people of Ghana in the pre–colonial times, it is imperative to first attempt an explanation of the concept conservation.

Conservation

According to Jones (1987:8) it is easier to explain conservation than to define it because definitions are prone to change. For this reason, he points out that a satisfactory definition of conservation must emphasise not only economic considerations, but also biological and ecological dimensions. He further notes that terms such as *preservation* (which in disciplines such as conservation sciences, environmental anthropology and the like, mean protecting from destruction without using, distinguishes preservation from conservation which usually means protection from destruction

131

while using the resource), *protection* or *control* (defence of an object or an overused commodity) and *conservation* are used arbitrarily and interchangeably to imply the act of conservation Jones (1987:8-9). Spellerberg (1996:3) also acknowledges that the concept of conservation means many things and is practiced in many ways. He describes conservation in its biological sense, as 'the continued existence of species, habitats and biological communities and the interactions between species and their environment.' For their part, Anderson and Grove (1987:1) contend that 'conservation is a much used term, its meaning ranging through a variety of contexts.' They explain:

> In the African context the view that has commonly identified conservation with the protection of species and habitats, with movements to preserve wildlife and wilderness, is giving way to a broader discussion linking conservation to the process of rural development and survival of agrarian societies in Africa Anderson and Grove (1987:1)

Having distinguished between the concepts conservation and preservation as well as having given insight into what they are all about, it is now imperative to focus the discussion and analysis on wildlife conservation in the pre–colonial era.

Wildlife Conservation in Pre–Colonial Times

The question to pose at this juncture is: Did the peoples who crystallised into Ghanaians have conservational practices before their encouter with the Western Europeans? The answer to this question is that in pre–colonial times, the people of Ghana practiced all kinds of conservation which included wildlife. This is exemplified by assertions made by Awere(2005:7-9) and Moses Sam(1998:5). The former maintains that: '...the cultures and traditions of Ghanaians, indeed, all Africans, are strictly attuned to wildlife conservation' Awere (2005: 9). On his part, the latter providing information on how the African elephant was conserved before the arrival of Europeans writes: 'early efforts at conserving African elephant in Ghana were initiated by traditional institutions.

Elephants were regarded by local chiefs as royal game and jealously protected through traditional bye–laws and myths' Sam(1998:5) The rulers as custodians of stool property(caretakers of all the assets of a chiefdom) were vested with the ultimate responsibility for wildlife resources in their states. Therefore, they made rules to regulate the exploitation of wildlife; but the enforcement of the regulation was the responsibility of every member of the community Wildlife Development Plan (1996-2000:182). Besides, Awuah –Nyamekye (2012:5) observes that the Akan have a firm belief that their physical life depends on the physical environment for which reason they have devised ways to ensure the sustainable use of the natural resources. These mechanisms of conservation which according to him included sacred groves and totemism clearly have religious undertones. The people, during pre–colonial days, were afraid of incurring the wrath of the gods and ancestors, therefore, nobody dared to flout the conservation laws in his/her community because of thsupposed divine injunction.

Following from the above, it is clear that the adoption of totems by the people of Ghana was another aspect of early conservation practices. Awuah–Nyamekye (2012:5) citing Rose, James and Watson (2003) explains the term 'totemism' as the "relationships of mutual life–giving between human beings and natural species (or rarely, other natural phenomena)" He further notes that among the Akan people of Ghana, totem in *Twi* (the language spoken by the Akan ethnic group) is called *akyeneboa,* comprises both animal and plant species and is literally translated as "an animal that one leans upon or relies on for spiritual protection". Further, he states that the origins of *akyeneboa* are expressed in myths and concretely manifest in rituals, ceremonies and festivals. Awuah Nyamekye's classification of *akyeneboa* as comprising both animal and plant species is contentious. The reason being that '*aboa*' in *Twi* means animal while plant is *dua*. In other words *aboa* (animal) is fauna while *dua* (plant) is flora. Therefore, I find it difficult to accept his explanation that *akyeneboa* comprises both animal and plant species. I will however agree with him if he says that totemism includes animal and plant species without making reference to or equating it to *akyeneboa*. According to a conservationist, Okyeame Ampadu Agyei (2003), who Oti Awere (2005:9) cites as saying that:

'... [totemism] has been one of the major traditional conservation tools which have helped to conserve many wildlife species to date....' Wildlife had played important socio–cultural function in Ghana and other parts of Africa. The social value of wildlife manifests in their adoption as totemic animals. In the three geographical zones of Ghana–coastal, forest and savannah–some families and communities have since time immemorial adopted wildlife as their totem and symbols of state respectively which are regarded as sacred. The totems which included animals and plants, were not only held sacred, but were also protected by the members of either a family, clan or state for their spiritual wellbeing, because they had the belief that any harm caused to the totem or their extinction would have a disastrous consequences on the entire society. Additionally, any member of a family or clan who killed, captured and consumed a totem either advertently or inadvertently would have calamity befalling him /her, and if it was discovered by the elders of the family, clan or community, then sacrifices and prayers would have to be offered to atone for the sacrilege and great spiritual offence that the individual had committed Oti Awere (2005:9). This is a clear indication of the extent to which totems were held in high esteem and protected in pre–colonial Ghana.

At this point, it is imperative to identify some of the common totems of the various people of Ghana and provide reasons for their adoption by people, families and states. It is significant to note that the people of Ghana whether the Akan or the Ga–Adangbe, or the Ewe or the Mole–Dagbani preference for a particular reptile, animal, bird and plant as a totem was contingent upon factors such as the attributes of the totem like bravery, courage and speed which ensured its continuous survival, and a mythology concerning a good deed the totem did to the ancestors of the people in the past Okyeame Ampadu Agyei (2003). Thus, the people of Agogo in Asante Akyem, Gwira, Bimbilla, Tuluwe, Akyem Kotoku and Abuakwa, Kwahu, Assin Apemanim, Enyan Abassa, Akatakyiman as well as Ofoase have the leopard as their principal totem because of the ferocious courage and fighting spirit of their ancestors as warriors Oti Awere (2005:9).

Oti Awere (2005:9) further examines some of the communities in the Savannah belt of Ghana where the Mole–Dagbani people

134

resided. He demonstrates how the people of Chiana–Paga traditional area and those of Kaleo chose the baboon as their totem for centuries, and revered it because; it saved their ancestors from slave raiders during the height of the Trans-Atlantic Slave. In Nandom, Guo, Builsa Nankong and Nabdam the Patas monkey has been the sacred totem of these communities from the earliest times and the people had never killed or eaten the animal. In the same vein, the people of Navrongo and Sirigu adopted the squirrel as their totem because, according to their tradition, it was a squirrel which ran over a chronic swollen leg of their founding ancestor that brought relief and healing to him. For this reason, these two communities chose the squirrel as their totem and had never killed or captured the animal thereby conserving the squirrel. The skins of Kayoro traditional area and the Mamprusi and Yinyuo traditional areas have the elephant as their totem. Though the Kayoro skin has twelve totems, the elephant was the most important of these. In both the Mamprusi and Yinyuo traditional areas, where the elephant was the symbol of authority, the Damba festival was celebrated annually in honour of the totem.

Having looked at some of the people in the northern Ghana and the rationale behind their adoption of certain totems, the emphasis is now shifted to the Volta Region where the elephant, lion, the royal antelope, mona monkey, python, vulture, crab and the Nile monitor lizard are seen as the principal totemic animals of some of the people. Whereas the people of Anfoega regarded the mona monkey as sacred and held it in high esteem, the people of Awudome on the other hand have had the python as their totem because it protected and guarded their paramount stool. The tradition of the people of Awudome indicates that in the course of their migration to their present home, their stool miraculously turned into a python to scare their enimies who springed a surprise attack on them. On the other hand, the people of Tapa and Nkonya adopted the crab as their principal totem because, according to their tradition, it was a crab that showed their ancestors during their migration to their current homes water and fertile lands. Other people like the Krakye, the Anlo, and the Buem the lion, the Nile monitor lizard and the vulture respectively have served as their totems. Whereas in all cases the people forbade the killing of the totemic animal, in the case of the Buem the opposite was the case. The Buem sacrificed the totem (vulture) and offered its blood to the gods on the orders of the chief priest Oti Awere (2005:9). Though Oti Awere does not proffer reasons for the chief priest's injunction which appears strange though, nonetheless, we may hazard a guess. Vultures in most cultures are not eaten, so they are never scarce. Again, they are also scavengers that feed mainly on incinerators and peck carcasses. Perhaps the vultures may have been pecking meat offered to the gods and thus defiling it, and to pacify the gods, the chief priest may have ordered the sacrifice of the vulture to atone for that.

The people of Old Ningo, Osudoku and Shai traditional areas in the Greater Accra Region, have adopted the elephant as their totem, and according to tradition of the Shai as recorded by Okyeame Ampadu–Agyei (2003:23), the people took the elephant as their totem because 'an elephant directed their ancestors to a river when they were thirsty in the course of a war.' For this reason, an annual festival known as *Pamyam* was instituted in honour of the totem. The Old Ningo and the Osudoku also adopted the elephant as their totem because of its benevolence to their ancestors in the past. Okyeame Ampadu–Agyei (2003:24) writes that Old Ningo tradition asserts that an elephant 'carried one of their ancestors to safety when he was abandoned after a war. The man fell asleep on the back [of] the elephant and the animal took him to a river.' Osudoku tradition also holds that an elephant cleared the way for the ancestors during their migration to settle at their present abode (ibid).

The Akan who inhabited the forest belt of Ghana and are currently found predominantly in the Ashanti, Brong Ahafo, Eastern, Western and Central Regions of Ghana comprised eight clans (families), and each one of them has a totem. The clans and their totems are: *Aduana*(dog), *Agona*(parrot), *Asakyiri*(vulture), *AseneE*(bat), *ɔyoko* (hawk), *Asona* (crow), *Bretuo* (leopard) and *Ekɔɔna* (buffalo)Nkansa Kyerematen (2010: 29). Apart from the totems of these eight families, the Akan chiefs who also belong to one of the eight families, adopted stool symbols in addition to the family totems. In the Central region for instance, the paramount chiefs of Denkyira, Eguafo, Abura, Ajumako and Abeaze have

136

elephants as their stool symbol Okyeame Ampadu–Agyei (2003:15-17). Denkyira was once a powerful state in the forest belt which, until 1701, was the super power in the forest belt; its subjects included Asante, Wassa, Sehwi, Twifo, Aowin and Adanse. Not surprisingly, Denkyira adopted the powerful elephant, 'the king of all animals', as its totem. Indeed, first stool (throne) of Denkyira, which was lost when the Denkyira army was crossing the Pra River after a war with the Twifo in the seventeenth century, was made of ivory Reindorf (1889:49).

For their part, the Eguafo of Central Region associated themselves with the elephant because, just like the Denkyira, they saw the elephant as the king of the forest. According to tradition, the first chief of Eguafo, Nana Kwamina Ansa I, rode an elephant. As regards the Abura traditional area, they adopted the elephant as their totem because as great warriors they equated their strength to that of the elephant. The Ajumako have the elephant and Bushbuck as the emblem of their paramount stool because both animals were common in the area.But, unlike Eguafo and Denkyira,the Ajumako regarded the bushbuck and not the elephant as the king of the forest. Both the Ajumako and the Abeaze people have instituted the Akwambo and Eguakese festivals, respectively, in honour of their totems Okyeame Ampadu–Agyei (2003:15-17).

Other Akan traditional areas which had the elephant as a totem are Offinso in Ashanti Region and Wassa Amenfi in Western Region. The ancestors of the Offinso people, according to tradition, originated from the belly of an elephant. For this reason, the elephant is the main symbol of the Offinso stool; the linguist staff or insignia is atopped by an elephant.(ibid:8). With respect to Wassa Amenfi, the adoption of the elephant as a totem was based on the Akan proverb that 'when an elephant steps on a trap it fails to spring back', which is taken to signify the ultimate authority of the paramount chief as the pre–eminent person in the Amenfi traditional area. Just like Offinso, the linguist staff of the traditional area has the elephant displayed on it.[1]

---

[1]   Ibid, p34, in all Ghanaian culture a chief is approached or spoken to through linguist. The linguist holds a long staff of about one yard long which is his symbol of authority. On top of these staffs are displayed the totem of the traditional area or the lineage of either the linguist or the chief.

In the pre–colonial era, the *ɔyoko* adopted the hawk as their totem because of the courage and strength of the bird. According to Oti Awere (2005:9), in those days, a clan required courage and strength to be able to survive. Therefore, when the *ɔyoko* noticed the hawk has these two attributes, they adopted it as their totem. The hawk according to an Akan proverb (*sɛ asansa fa adea ɔde kyerɛ -- (whenever a hawk catches a prey it displays it)*, demonstrates its courage and strength by always showing its prey. But besides the hawk, the Asantehene, who belonged to the *ɔyoko* family, has the porcupine (*Hystricomorph hystricidae*) (*kɔtokɔ*) as the symbol of Asanteman, of which, he is the overlord.

With respect to the plant totems, some few illustrations would suffice here. In Akwaboa, a village located in Atwima District of Asante, the founder of the village, Brefo Apau and his family are referred to as *Satiasefoɔ*, because according to their tradition, it was an *esa* tree that provided them shelter when they first settled in the area following their migration from Denkyira to Asante. Thus from the late sixteenth century when they settled in the area until the late 1940s when the said *esa* tree uprooted, the *Satiase* family and the people of the village regarded the *esa* tree sacred and even made a sacrifice of ram to the ancestors when the tree uprooted.

Further, Awuah Nyamekye (2012:6) provides some insight into plant totems among the Akan people of Ghana. In the first instance, he notes that in Nsuta traditional area, tradition indicates that *Atoa* (*Spondias mombin*) is the plant totem of the people because the plant saved the ancestors of the area from starvation during their migration to their present abode. The tradition continues that the food resources of the immigrants got finished before they could reach their final destination, but fortunately for them they came across the *Atoa* plant which had sufficient fruits to feed the hungry Nsuta people. As a result of this, the people of Nsuta had maintained a special relationship with this species. Apart from the Nsuta, the people of Akwapim traditional area regarded the *Odii* plant (*Okuobaka aubrevillei*) as their totem. The explanation proffered for the people of Akwapim adoption of the *Odii* plant as their totem was possibly because the plant is culturally known to be powerful and this power it possesses, certainly, may have influenced the Akwapim adoption of it as their totem, at least for protection. The

Odii plant possesses special qualities which have guaranteed its conservation by the Akan.

The Akan also hold in high esteem *Homakyem* (*Spiropetalum heterophyllum*), another power plant found in the forest belt where the Akan forest are domiciled. One unique thing about this plant is that the colour of the sap in it is like blood. Whenever part of it is cut, its sap oozes out the way blood comes out from the body of a person whenever he/she is injured. This easy association of red sap with blood is found in ancient European and pre–Semitic cultures and may be one of the reasons for recognising personhood in plants. The plant is medicinally valuable, but because of the powerful force the Akan believe it possesses, only people who are spiritually endowed traditional medicine practitioners could use it in their herbal preparations. Finally, the *Odum (Chlorophora excelsa)* is the totem of the people of Ekumfi traditional area in the Central region of Ghana. The account relating the Ekumfi people's association with the *Odum* is hazy. However, the *odum* tree it is believed can transform at night into human being and visit the chief and reveal mysteries to him. As a totemic plant of the people of Ekumfi, the *Odum* has been protected throughout the history of the people of Ekumfi.

The implications for the adoption of totems by the various peoples of Ghana as demonstrated above are shown in the sentences below : Oti Awere (2005:5) puts it thus, ' it was a way of life and source of family pride that gives an indelible lesson on traditional wildlife conservation.' He further notes that 'our ancestors were very much attuned to conservation of wildlife species' It should be noted however that the traditional rulers were not only concerned with the conservation of wildlife, but were concerned with the conservation of the entire environment. Kwarteng and Owusu(2010:85-98) also note that 'the use of totems as means of indigenous conservation resulted in a situation of high concentration of particular totomic animals in areas where particular species were regarded as *akyiwadee* (translated totemic)' Again, the adoption of wildlife by traditional rulers as totems emphasised not only the latter's historical and socio–cultural significance, but also stressed the symbolic quality of the species as well as providing evidence of indigenous pre–colonial conservation practice. The local chiefs revered these totemic animals and ensured that they were protected by traditional laws which had religious and spiritual foundation Ghana Wildlife Division Policy (2000:79). Consequently, it became taboo for anyone within any traditional area, state or kingdom to kill and eat a totemic animal of any other state or traditional authority.

In addition to the adoption of totems, the indigenous Gold Coasters knew the value of the their flora and fauna as well as their water resources which they made conscious effort to preserve as part of their natural and cultural heritage. The Gold Coasters in pre–colonial times knew that farmers should not farm closer to the banks of rivers, so as not to expose the rivers to direct rays of the sun, which could dry up the rivers completely through intense evaporation. Kwarteng and Owusu(2010:93), for instance, record an Akan tradition which indicates that the Akan evolved a concept of protecting the upper courses, and in some cases, the entire length of rivers which served as sources of drinking water. The people aware of the fact that the volumes of rivers in the Gold Coast swell during the rainy seasons and dry during the dry seasons, tackled the danger of their water sources drying up completely during the dry harmattan season, which would deprive them of water for domestic uses, by forbidding clearance of the vegetation along river banks. Thus, they also protected the rivers from the direct rays of the sun and the dry harmattan winds. In addition, Valerie Sackey(1997:18-21) notes that cultural practices in Ghana 'have for centuries recognised the need to sustain [the environment and wildlife] resource by regulating hunting.' She explains that a traditional chief regulated hunting in his area by either imposing a closed season on particular species or withholding permission for hunting in a particular area.(ibid) These traditional conservation practices seemed to be prevalent in the Northern Territories of Ghana, especially the area around the Mole National Park. In this area, there were practices which offered protection to specific ecosystems, for example sacred groves and rivers. This practice forbade people in the traditional area from entering the sacred groves to hunt or fish Ntiamoa–Baidu (1993:66–67). This strategy of traditional conservation regulated the exploitation of plant and animal resources of a particular community. At certain times of the year, a temporary ban was placed on hunting and fishing in a community for about one to three months, so that pregnant animals would not be destroyed and for fish to spawn. During the period, the ban was in force any member of the community who contravened the regulation was severely sanctioned by the chief and his elders, who imposed either a fine of a specified amount or made the offender slaughter a sheep (ram). And because these practices were shrouded in religious and cultural beliefs, Mole National Park: the Management Plan (1994:11) people feared that if they were flouted calamity would befall those responsible.

Though these pre–colonial conservation strategies may have their own shortcomings, as the values of these practices were limited to only the localities where the animals and plants were regarded as sacred. Nonetheless, all species were conserved in one way or the other as those that were not revered in one community would be revered in another community. Therefore, these strategies ensured sustainability as they checked extinction of some species as we have been witnessing these days in Africa. In sum, it can be said that the practice was an indication that the people of Ghana in pre–colonial times had conservation consciousness.

With regard to forest conservation, Kwarteng and Owusu (2010:93) argue that the concept did not originate from Europe to Africa and that prior to the advent of the Europeans into Ghana, the Akan who dwelt in the forest region of Ghana had developed their on concepts of forest management. They explain that at the time the Akan took occupancy of their present abode, they met a pristine forest and with the passage of time they came to a realization that intense human activity could result in total degradation of the environment. To forestall this imminent danger, the Akan:

> Devised strategies of conservation mostly shrouded in mystery. The system they evolved combined ecocentrism and theocentrism To this end, there emerged among the Akan, taboos folklore and proverbs heavily embedded in forest conservation principles. This entailed in some instances, setting certain portions of the forest aside calling it *kyiridade*: meaning no indigene of the community could ever dare to enter that

tract of land to harvest either flora or fauna or clear a portion for farming or settlement (ibid).

Thus, Kwarteng and Owusu contend that what the Akan meant by conservation was holistic conservation and not partial conservation. In order to give the conservation of the forest legal basis, the Akan set aside part of the forest as *kyiridade* and the land declared as an abode of the gods or ancestors (*nananom mpow*), and it was a taboo for any person or group of persons to enter that sacred grove. Anyone who flouted the taboo incurred the wrath of the gods and the offenders severely punished when apprehended. When the British colonised the Gold Coast, the colonial government did discard the indigenous conservation practices it met because it saw everything African as bad and evil, so the colonial authority introduced its own conservation policy or law to protect the African flora and fauna.

Wildlife Preservation Laws and the creation of Game Reserves during the colonial era

Clearly, the foregoing has demonstrated that afterall the concept conservation was not introduced to the people of Ghana by the British colonial authorities, and that the people of Ghana were familiar with the concept of conservation which was embedded in their cultural practices long before their contact with Europeans in the fifteenth century. British colonisation of Ghana which was in four phases effectively commenced in August 1874 when the British annexed the southern vassal states of Asante into a protectorate, and converted their forts and settlements on the coast into a British Crown Colony Adu. Boahen (1975:34) with a Legislative Council empowered to legislate for the whole of the Protected Territory Wilks (2004:138-142).

Following the effective British colonisation of the Gold Coast, the colonial adminstration began to introduce Wild Animals Preservation Ordinance of 1901 and created Game reserves based on European models. What necessitated the introduction of the Wild Animals Preservation Ordinance of 1901 and the establishment of the game reserves was the wanton killing of elephants by white hunters for sport or trophy. During the second half of the nineteenth century, White hunters in Africa, particularly in East, Central and Southern Africa, embarked on reckless killing of the African elephant which alarmed the Colonial Authorities who entertained the fear that this could endanger the species if appropriate measures were not taken to curtail the killings. Accordingly, in January 1900, through the instrumentality of Hermann von Wissmann, the former governor of German East Africa, Beachey (1967:286); Mackenzie (1988:206) representatives of Britain, France, Germany, Portugal, the Congo Free State, Italy and Spain met in London for the maiden international conference on wildlife to discuss the preservation of African game Wilson & Ayerst (1979:138); Mackenzie (1988:206-207). A convention which emerged from the conference, and was signed in May 1900 in London Beachey (1967:107), became the basis for the preservation of African wildlife Mackenzie (1988:208). However, most of the parties to the convention never ratified it. Thus, the execution of the convention was left to individual colonial administrators who had to promulgate their own laws to enforce it Wilson & Ayerst (1979:138).

The response of the Gold Coast administration to the 1900 convention was that in 1901 it promulgated the Wild Animals Preservation Ordinance of 1901, which became the legal framework for the conservation of wild animals, birds, and fish, and the establishment of game reserves in the colony, Ashanti and Northern Territories. The elephant and twenty four other animals, including the rhinoceros and hippopotamus, were classified under Schedule IV, and Article 2(4) of the Ordinance, which prohibited 'to some extent the destruction of any females, when they can be recognised as such....' (National Archives, CO 76/86). Further, Section 2(11) of the Ordinance stipulated 'the prohibition of hunting or killing young elephants and confiscation of all elephant tusks weighing less than ten pounds'(ibid).

The Wild Animals Preservation Ordinance of 1901 applied to Ashanti per Section 26 of the 'Ashanti Administration Ordinance,1902 (PRAAD, Kumasi, ARG1/1/33).' A year after its passage, Governor Matthew Nathan, exercising the authority conferred on him by the Wild Animals Preservation Ordinance,

1901, made an amendment to the Ashanti Administration Ordinance of 1902, by revoking Section 26 which dealt with preservation of wild animals in Ashanti, and replacing it with the Regulations of 30th June 1903 (PRAAD, Kumasi, ARG1/1/1/55).

In 1909 three game reserves, (Kwahu (Afram–Obosum), Obosom–Sene and Onyim–Sene) were constituted in the Afram Plains in interesting circumstances (PRAAD, Tamale, NRG8/6/107). In the event, as a solution to land disputes which had erupted between the people of Kwahu, Kumawu and Agogo (PRAAD, Kumasi ARG1 /1/107) the disputed land was constituted into game reserves. This suggests that the constitution of the game reserves was an opportunistic move rather than a direct response to the Ordinance of 1901. On 30th November, 1911, Governor James Thorburn signed a law giving legal backing to the reserves in Ashanti which were defined as:

> All that piece or parcel of land situated in Ashanti assigned by Agreement dated the 22nd day of October, 1909, to the Government of the Gold Coast Colony by Chiefs, Elders and people of Kwahu and Kumawu for the purpose of a reserve, and bounded as hereinafter described. On the North by the Sene River. On the East by a line cut due North from the point where the boundary between Ashanti and the colony meets the Obosum River to a point where the said line meets the Sene River. On the South by the Onyim River westwards to the point where the Onyim River crosses the path from Abene to Agogo thence. On the West from the above mentioned point by a line cut due North to a point where it meets the Sene River (PRAAD, Kumasi, ARG1/1/33).

The first reserve was located in the colony, while the other two were situated in Ashanti(PRAAD, Tamale, NRG 8/6/107). By the 'Order in Council of 2nd December 1911' the reserves in the colony also received legal backing and were selected as partially protected game reserve and forest reserve(PRAAD, Kumasi ARG1 /1/107). The Ordinance explained and stipulated that, within these protected game reserves 'it shall be unlawful to hunt, capture or kill any bird or other wild animal[within the reserves] except those which shall

144

be specially exempted from protection.'(ibid). This means that hunters could enter the reserves, but could not kill animals protected under the law.

Athough the intention of colonial administrators in conserving and managing wildlife in the Colony and Ashanti was laudable, W.B Collins, the Deputy Chief Conservator of Forest of the Gold Coast, in a report to the World Forestry Congress, criticised the attempt to preserve wild animals in the Gold Coast as 'the promulgation of a set of useless regulations'(Wildlife Development Plan, 1996–2020 II:182). This assessment was informed by his belief that the regulations which governed the reserves were not enforced, thus making it possible for inhabitants to encroach on the reserves with impunity. In part, this was due to an absence of conscious effort on the part of administrators to educate the people about the regulations and the subsequent creation of the reserves. According to official report people appeared to breach the regulations and, out of ignorance, hunted in the reserves. This was compounded by the fact that trade routes from the north to the south (coast) passed through the reserves, which also had several scattered villages located in them (PRAAD, Tamale, NRG 8/6/107).

The difficulty in enforcing the regulations was attributable to the fact that 'these initiatives were not backed by the necessary human and financial resources required for effective implementation'(Wildlife Development Plan, 1996–2020 II: 182). The available evidence indicates that no effort was made to set up a department which would take charge of wildlife protection; neither were any staff with expertise in wildlife preservation and management such as Game Warden, Rangers and Control Officers recruited, nor funds provided for protecting the wildlife reserves (ibid). No wonder an official of the colonial administration, in a memorandum to the Executive Council in 1948, acknowledged that:

> The attempt to preserve game in the Gold Coast has not met with success, largely because: (i) no steps have been taken to control game movements and game population; (ii) there has been no staff to enforce it and to educate public opinion in the

necessity for control measures(PRAAD, Tamale, NRG 8/6/107).

Additionally, the enforcement of the Wild Animal Preservation Ordinance was entrusted to 'departments that were already fully committed to other duties and staff under the District Commissioner'(Wildlife Development Plan, 1996–2020 II: 182). This undoubtedly resulted in a situation in which the officers were unable to devote adequate attention to effective wildlife preservation, in addition to generating a conflict of interest(PRAAD, Tamale, NRG 8/6/10).

In May 1914, representatives of Great Britain, Belgium, France, Italy, Germany, Portugal and Spain attended an International Conference held in London and once again, the subject of the preservation of the African fauna, particularly elephant and rhinoceros, came to the fore during the meeting. The delegates, with the exception of that from Germany, expressed satisfaction with the proposals made at the conference and were ready to sign the draft protocol, but decided to aim for a consensus. Unfortunately, negotiations with the Germans were still underway when WWI broke out, thus aborting the implementation of the conference protocol (PRAAD, Kumasi, ARG1/1/107). At the same time, the Society for the Preservation of the Fauna of the Empire expressed concern about the alarming rate at which African wildlife was being exploited and 'called attention to the urgency of taking measures for the protection of elephant and rhinoceros, and in particular elephant, in Africa'(ibid).

In 1920 the British Government decided to re–visit the question with the governments represented at the 1914 conference, with the exception of Germany which was no longer interested in the subject of the preservation of the African elephant. Before initiating any action on the matter, however, the British Foreign Office, knowing that the Gold Coast was an elephant range country, sent the draft protocol of the 1914 conference to Governor Guggisburg and other Governors of British dependencies in East and West Africa to ascertain whether the colonies had any serious objection to the provisions of the document (ibid).

The document titled 'scheme for the international regulation for the protection of the elephant and rhinoceros in Africa' stipulated in article 1 and its sub sections 1 to 3 that:

> It is forbidden for every person in Africa…to possess ivory or rhinoceros horn…to trade in these articles; and to export them from the continent except in the following cases: when they have been obtained in pursuance of a permit to hunt issued by the local Government…when they have been obtained from the local Government [and] when they have been obtained in an entirely different legal manner (PRAAD, Kumasi, ARG1/1/107).

The other provisions of the protocol were that: it was forbidden to possess tusks weighing an average of 22 1bs or less than ten kilogrammes; that every tusk not acquired legally, that is in conformity with the provisions of the above article, and every tusk weighing below 10 kilogrammes would be confiscated and disposed of by the local Government at its discretion; that legal owners should obtain a certificate called 'permit for free disposal' from the local Government before all ivory could be disposed of; that the local Government should issue hunting permit, and at its own discretion should specify the number of elephants a holder would be allowed to kill; that the Governments had the right to authorise the inhabitants or residents to hunt elephants without restriction, either on the number of animals or the weight of their tusks, if the destruction was in the interest of the population or to promote development; that a hunting permit would grant a holder the right to dispose of and export the tusks, but he would have to present the document to a competent authority to affix its mark or deliver a permit of free disposal, which would accompany the articles; and that every person accused of illegally selling, exporting or having exported ivory would be rigorously prosecuted in line with the law of the country(ibid).

Guggisburg, upon receipt of the draft protocol and directives, did not act unilaterally; he sought the opinion of experts and his subordinates. In the Northern Territories, Guggisburg referred to Watherston's report of 1909 on elephant crop raiding in Navrongo

District; he sought the legal advice of the Acting Attorney General; and, finally, read a report which J .T. Furley, the Secretary for Native Affairs, wrote to the Colonial Secretary on the subject of big game preservation. The opinions and ideas he sought from these sources informed the final decision of the Government.

At the Governor's request the Secretary for Native Affairs, Furley, wrote to the Colonial Secretary a comprehensive document on measures taken by past colonial administrators on the preservation of wild animals in the Gold Coast colony and its dependencies (PRAAD, Kumasi ARG1 /1/107). It emerged from this that a former Commissioner of the Eastern Province, Curling, repeatedly reported to the authorities that elephants in Kwahu were facing imminent danger of extermination, due mainly to indiscriminate killing. For these reasons, according to Furley, the original game regulations were strengthened to protect the elephant in the Gold Coast (ibid).

As a hunter, Furley was not favourably predisposed to any attempt to proscribe the hunting of game, particularly elephant. Therefore, he did not only jettison the regulations proposed by the International Conference as too stringent and far reaching to be enforced, he also noted that 'it does not seem that any further legislation is really necessary for the Colony or its dependencies: while the protection of the native from depredation by elephant, and the preservation of his ancient rights are at least as important as the protection of these animals from extermination' (ibid). Guggisburg found the contention of the Secretary for Native Affairs objectionable, for which reason he rejected it when taking the final decision. Instead, he accepted the legal counsel of Wilkinson, the Acting Attorney General, to whom the draft protocol was referred for advice.

On the basis of Wilkinson's legal advice, Guggisburg presented the position of the Gold Coast Government to the Secretary of State in a dispatch dated 29th May, 1920. The Governor agreed with all the terms or provisions of the draft protocol for the preservation of the African elephant and rhinoceros, but rejected the provision on ivory trade. He strongly recommended 'the introduction of a clause permitting...Government to authorise the destruction of animals in districts where their depredations constitute a source of great hardship to the natives' (PRAAD, Kumasi ARG1 /1/107). Apparently, Guggisburg was here making reference to the Northern Territories, where Chief Commissioner Watherston's report of 1909 had indicated widespread damage to crops and farms every year by elephants in the Navrongo District, particularly, in the Kangyaga areas. Watherston's report showed clearly that the destructive activities of elephants deprived many of the inhabitants of the affected areas of food for a season, thus compelling people 'to buy from others and reducing them and their people to penury and often practical slaves to the more fortunate ones whose crops are not destroyed' (ibid).

Meanwhile, the U.K Foreign Office negotiations with foreign governments aimed at arriving at an International Convention for the preservation of the African elephant and rhinoceros fell through (ibid). This turn of events neither deterred nor halted Britain's resolve to ensure the preservation of these animals. Consequently, the Foreign Office took another initiative, this time to collaborate with British Dependencies in West and East Africa, to consider whether or not those Dependencies could take action to ensure 'the protection which would have been secured by the Convention.'(ibid). To this end, on 26 January, 1922, the Secretary of State, Winston Churchill, wrote to Guggisburg: 'to enquire whether your Government would see any objection to action being taken on these lines.' Churchill continued: 'If no objection is seen, the draft of any legislation necessary for the purpose should be submitted for my consideration' (ibid).

Guggisburg solicited the views of the Chief Commissioner of Ashanti who, it appears, did not make any input in 1920. The Chief Commissioner in turn referred the Governor's request to the administrators in the Western Province of Ashanti at Sunyani, where both the Acting Commissioner and his deputy expressed opinions on the subject. In addition, the views of the Provincial Commissioners of Western Province of Ashanti were also sought, because Gyaman, Ahafo, Nkoranza, Kintampo and Abease, which were known for their large elephant populations, were all located in that province.

Both the Acting Provincial Commissioner and the Deputy Provincial Commissioner expressed similar views on the proposed legislation, although the Deputy Provincial Commissioner's appeared to be more elaborate than the Acting Chief Commissioner's. The Acting Chief Commissioner stated that the proposed legislation was inadvisable on the grounds that:

> The elephants in the country are very small and, being untameable, are useless for practical purposes such as transportation. The rights of the natives to shoot their own animals surely precede the view of the sentimentalists in England. The elephants cause more damage in farms than they themselves are worth alive. The dead elephant is the only compensation to the native for the damage done to his farms– his profit being derived from the meat more than the tusks. It seems that the protection is only desired by the European until their ivory is ensured–the native paying the premium. The network of roads which is contemplated in this country and the Mechanical Transport will assuredly drive these mammals beyond the jurisdiction of those who might enforce this legislation PRAAD, Kumasi, ARG1/1/107.

He saw conservation of the elephant as irrelevant and not in consonance with the realities of the lives of the natives. Besides, he cautioned that introduction of this legislation would be counter-productive since it had the potential of causing rupture in the cordial relations and peaceful cooperation that had existed between the natives and the Government. Finally, he cautioned that the legislation could not be enforced, because it would be a source of revenue for unscrupulous people, who might take advantage of the letter of the law (ibid), to amass wealth and thus defeat the purposes of the regulations.

For his part, the Deputy Provincial Commissioner, who also doubled as the Government Anthropologist, opined that 'the elephant is doomed in Ashanti to extinction in not very remote future' (ibid). In his estimation, the date for the disappearance of the elephant in Ashanti may be delayed, but would not be postponed indefinitely. He pointed out that the disappearance of the elephant would not be brought about entirely by the depredation of hunters, and agreed with his boss that government policy of progress with, and improvement of communications, such as the construction of motor roads and the use of motor cars, constituted a real threat to the survival of elephants confined in well–defined localities. The Deputy Commissioner also identified other causes of the decline of elephants, including establishment of new villages and establishment of farms or plantations (ibid). Consequently, he objected to any legislation intended to prohibit the killing and hunting of elephants in Ashanti. In his view:

> The Ashanti hunter, hunting in land which is his or his Chief's and not ours, has from time immemorial looked upon it as his right to hunt and kill elephants…to forbid him to hunt and kill elephant at all, in my humble opinion, would be ultravires on our part, and would be looked upon as an unwarranted interferance [sic][interference] with their just right (ibid).

The Appointment of a Game Warden and Establishment of a Wildlife Department

A major shortcoming of colonial efforts towards the preservation of wildlife, and the creation of Game reserves in the colony and Ashanti, was their failure to appoint a Game Warden and employ rangers and control officers, to ensure the implementation of the Wild Animal Preservation Ordinance of 1901 and subsidiary legislations. In 1922, a Deputy Provincial Commissioner in Western Ashanti realised this, and advised that 'the formation of game reserves, without game wardens must be in most cases of little use' (PRAAD, Kumasi ARG1 /1/107). However, the Colonial Government did not immediately give this constructive and wise counsel any serious consideration, probably because the government felt it was the first time that such an advice and proposition were being made or the government did not see the Deputy Provincial Commissioner as expert to advice on wildlife matters, so it had to be shelved until the issue of the appointment of a game warden was raised again ten years later by Colonel A.H.W. Haywood, following a visit to the Gold Coast under the auspices of the Society for the Preservation of the Fauna of the Empire in 1931–1932. He noted in his report that:

> With my previous knowledge of West Africa and as a result of my recent mission the depletion of wildlife during the past generation strikes me as alarming. The process of extermination due to the spread of civilization and the activities of the native hunter is proceeding relentlessly....A number of important species are rapidly approaching extermination (PRAAD, Tamale, NR8/6/107).

Accordingly, he made a number of recommendations to help in halting the rapid decline of the wildlife resources of the country and ensure their preservation. First, he called for the abolition of the existing reserves and their replacement with larger areas which he termed National Game Parks. He suggested that the Prah–Anum Forest Reserve and either the area north of Krachi or the north–east Kintampo be constituted into the new national game parks. Secondly, he suggested that as soon as possible, a Game Warden and a small staff of African rangers should be appointed (ibid). The Government's response to Colonel Haywood's recommendations was not the immediate abolition of the existing reserves or the appointment of game wardens. Instead, the Government responded by carrying out feasibility studies towards the acquisition of land north of Kintampo, one of the areas suggested by Colonel Haywood as suitable for the creation of a National Park. The Government was torn between making outright payment to cover the cost of the land, and securing it on a long lease basis. After a thorough investigation, the Acting Chief Commissioner of Ashanti strongly advocated a payment of yearly rental to the land owners who were Nkoranzahene and Abeasehene, instead of paying a lump sum of money, and suggested £50 per annum as the minimum compensation (PRAAD, Kumasi, ARG 1/1/159).

As the proposed area was the hunting ground of the Abease and Nkoranza people, the Chief Commissioner made it clear to the Governor that constituting it into a National Park, would provoke considerable opposition, because the people would not only be deprived of their farming rights, but also their hunting rights. He nevertheless explained that if the land was constituted into Forest Reserve instead, the opposition would be greatly minimised, because the hunting rights of the people would not be interfered with (ibid). Unfortunately, the whole idea of establishing a National Park in north–east Kintampo was abandoned after the feasibility studies, although no explanation was offered for the decision.

Despite this, the Society for the Preservation of the Fauna of the Empire did not relent in its crusade to ensure that endangered wildlife of the Gold Coast was protected. To this end, it again raised the issue in 1935 with the Governor, while he was on leave in London. However, the Executive Council resolved in December of the same year, that any action on the establishment of game sanctuaries would not be taken at that time, although the matter was to be borne in mind for consideration later(PRAAD, Tamale, NR8/6/107).

While the Executive Council was procrastinating in taking a firm decision on the concerns expressed by the Society for the Preservation of the Fauna of the Empire, further evidence emerged in 1936 and 1937 from Cansdale, an official of the Forestry Department, who confirmed that the reduction in the game population reported by Colonel Haywood five years earlier had continued. Cansdale attributed this to communal hunting, 'still' hunting, and night hunting with dazzle lamps; communal drives; and the use of imported steel game trap in almost all the villages. These uncontrolled practices resulted in a severe depreciation of the game population (ibid). The report revealed a horrendous account of how hunters set fire to the bush during the dry season; resulting in the killing of large numbers of smaller animals, females and young animals in Afram plains, which was formerly the hunting ground of the Kwaman, Kumawu and Agogo. The report concluded that as a result:

> Animals are now so scarce in some parts of the plains as to make hunting hardly profitable…. If slaughter on the present scale is allowed to continue, it is probable that some of the species will reach a condition in a few years from which recovery is impossible…. (ibid).

Clearly, this report indicates that the Division Bye–Laws No.19 made by Head Chiefs, Chiefs and Elders of all the Divisions in Ashanti under section 23 of the Native Jurisdiction Ordinance which banned night hunting with lights and company hunting was a complete flop in the Afram plains. It could not help in arresting the drastic decline of wildlife in that part of Ashanti. If the bad hunting practices it was intended to eradicate still persisted after four or five years, then the bye–laws could not be said to have been implemented in the Divisions with jurisdiction over the Afram plains. In any case, the report served as a wakeup call to the authorities, but owing to the absence of an expert to advise the Executive Council on the problem, it could not put any pragmatic programme in place to improve the situation, except the ban it imposed on the importation and possession of steel game traps (ibid).

Cansdale's report coincided with the ratification of an International Convention for Protection of African Fauna and Flora in 1936 by the British Government. In 1933, effective international co–operation on wildlife protection was achieved, when the international conference for the protection of the Fauna and Flora of Africa was convened in London. The Convention, according to Mackenzie (1988:217), provided for the establishment of national parks and the conservation of African wildlife, and common policies on restriction of hunting alongside tighter controls on the export of trophies, mainly ivory(Ibid; Wilson and Ayerst:1976138). The ratification of the convention, coupled with Cansdale's report, made it incumbent on the Executive Council of the Gold Coast not only to preserve game, but also to limit its movement (PRAAD, Tamale, NR8/6/107). The Acting Secretary for Rural Development in a memorandum to the Executive Council in 1948, during discussions about the creation of the post of Game Warden, identified two reasons for the control of wildlife in the Gold Coast: crop destruction by elephants and lion attack on domestic stock; and the role of game in promoting the breeding of the tsetse fly, which infected domestic animals and human beings with diseases like trypanosomiasis and rinderpest (ibid).

The problems were prevalent in the Northern Territories. For example, in 1944, the Government Entomologist, Dr Morris, reported that:

An investigation of the damage done by elephants was made in 7 Dagarti villages on the Black Volta last autumn. In each village one or more bush farms had been completely destroyed after planting, with total loss of both seed and labour to the owner. When the crops were ripe one quarter of all the compounds in the 7 villages lost from 75% to 10% of all the crops in their bush farms and were faced with serious food shortage in the coming year. The men spent their nights in inadequate shelters in the farms beating drums and blowing horns to keep the elephants away, this in the height of the rains, imposes extra strain and risk of ill health on a hardworking and ill-nourished people. In yam growing areas elephants cause enormous losses by uprooting seed yams out of the mounds in the dry season (ibid).

With respect to disease infection, game resources, particularly big game, provided important nourishment for the tsetse fly (*Glossinamorsitans*), the carrier of trypanosomiasis. In the Black Volta and Kamba basins, for instance, where there was plenty of game, it was discovered that the wild animals served as reservoir for the breeding of tsetse fly.

The Government made two incongruous policy decisions in 1949. In the first place it set up the Tsetse Fly Control Unit which was mandated to eradicate the Tsetse fly, the vector of Sleeping Sickness. This unit, popularly called the Tsetse Control Unit, was to cause 'the extirpation of thousands of herbivorous game animals' in the north (Wildlife Development Plan 1996–2020:182). The second policy was the creation of the Game Department (PRAAD, Tamale, NRG2/15/9), which was tasked to drive the game, if practicable, into special reserves in sparsely populated areas in the north (PRAAD, Tamale, NR8/6/107). The execution of this policy resulted in the appointment of a Game Warden, who had the requisite expertise in wildlife preservation and management (ibid).

The Game Warden was to review the situation and adopt the exact programme that he consider appropriate; but he was also expected to focus attention on:

■ The selection and constitution of sanctuaries, reserves or game parks in areas suitable and from the point of view of scarcity of human population, etc.,

■ The revision of legislation, bearing in mind particularly the part which Native Authorities can play in this matter.

■ Publicity, to educate public opinion as to the dual necessity for game preservation on the one hand and game control on the other (ibid).

Further, to avoid the recurrence of past experience, the Game Warden was required to train staff who would act as Game Rangers to enforce the purposes of the Reserves; he was also supposed to train Control Officers who would shoot game that strayed onto farms and caused havoc to crops or posed a threat to the lives of people(ibid).

The Game Warden arrived in the Gold Coast on 11th October, 1949 and by 20th October, 1949 he had arrived at Lawra in the Northern Territories where he stayed for a brief period before moving his headquarters to Bamberri in Gonjaland near Bole in January, 1950 (PRAAD, Tamale, NR8/6/107).

Between 11th October, 1949 when he arrived in Lawra and 31st March, 1950, he focused his attention on the selection of a Game Reserve, and recruitment and training of future Game scouts, who were later employed as Game Control Officers (PRAAD, Tamale, NR8/6/107). Also, the Game Warden, in consultation with the Acting Director of Tsetse Control (ibid), proposed the selection of an area comprising over 1,600 square kilometres(Wildlife Development Plan II 1996-2020:182) or approximately 600 square miles in the Western Gonja Area as the Black Volta Game Reserve. The Chief Commissioner and Central Land Planning Committee at Tamale discussed the selection report and approved it(PRAAD, Tamale, NR8/6/107), with the Chief Commissioner suggesting to the Ministry of Agriculture and Natural Resources that the proposed reserve be constituted under section 2(13) of Cap.203 of the Laws(ibid).

The reserve was described as an 'area in Gonja District bounded by the Sawla–Tamale road on the north; the western boundary of Oil Seed Area No.2 to the point where it meets the River Lambo and thence the River Lambo and the River Black Volta on the east; a line in a westerly direction to the north of Babatu to meet the Kumasi–Lawra motor road on the south; and the Kumasi–Lawra motor road on the west'(PRAAD, Tamale, NR8/6/107). However, according to the Wildlife Department of Ghana, 'no resources were made available to manage [the Black Volta Game Reserve] or any of the earlier reserves and the intensive hunting of the game continued both within and outside the reserves' (Wildlife Development Plan II 1996-2020:182). This seems to be corroborated by the Game Warden's report of 1950–51 which states:

> The Game Warden, the only established officer in the department was in charge throughout the year. The training of the Game Scouts for control purposes was hampered at the beginning of the year by lack of rifles and ammunition. Three 404 rifles and 1,500 rounds of ammunition were received in the middle of July but only one man of the six required for Game Control was passed as being fully–trained by the end of the year. No permanent labour force was employed: casual labour was used on the inspection of areas selected as Game Reserves (PRAAD, Tamale, NR8/6/107).

Clearly, the appointment of the Game Warden in 1949 did little to abate the killing of game in the Gold Coast; neither did it help in protecting the game reserve from encroachment by poachers, because of lack of personnel to protect the reserves.

On 1st April, 1950, the Game Department was established with its activities confined to the Northern Territories of the Gold Coast (PRAAD, Tamale, NR8/6/107). In 1953, however, game conservation was put directly under the supervision of the Tsetse Control Unit. Following attainment of independence in 1957, the Tsetse Control Unit was abolished and the Game Section of the Tsetse Control Unit was transferred to the Forestry Department (Wildlife Development Plan II 1996-2020:182). From the above narratives, discussions and analysis it is crystal clear that both the pre–colonial and colonial conservation practices had parallel underlying principles, to wit, to protect the wildlife (both flora and fauna) from destruction and ultimately from extinction, for which reasons laws were in both cases, enacted to protect animals as has been demonstrated in this work. There were however differences which had to do with the strategies employed by the two systems to realise their goals –sustainable conservation of the wildlife heritage of the pre–colonial and colonial state.

Though the main objectives of both pre–colonial and colonial conservation mechanisms were to ensure sustainable conservation of the wildlife heritage of Ghana, but a critical examination of the two practices shows that whereas the former which is indigenous ensured sustainability of the wildlife in the country, the latter which is foreign and supposed to be far better that the indigenous one failed woefully to protect the countries fauna and Fiona. In the pre–colonial times different species of wildlife (plants and animal) were found in the country, but since colonization and the introduction of western conservation methods most of the wildlife have become extinct or endangered, an indication that after all the European belief that everything European was superior to that of the African was false.

Conclusion

This chapter has examined both the indigenous conservation practices in pre–colonial times and the European conservation practices in Ghana from 1901 to 1957, and established that the indigenous people of the Gold Coast were familiar with the concept of conservation which was part of their socio–cultural practices long before their interactions with the Europeans. Though the indigenous conservation practices had their own inherent shortcomings as what was regarded as a totemic animal in one area was a delicacy in another community undermined the indigenous conservation practices. Nonetheless, the European conservation practices equally had their flaws as they could not guarantee the protection of most of the wildlife they were supposed to. Thus, we can say from the foregoing that it is a myth for anybody to suppose that it was the Europeans who taught Africans how to conserve their wildlife heritage.

In my estimation, the pre–colonial conservation practice was far better than the colonial conservation method. During the pre–colonial era, measures that were put in place, ensured that there were high concentration of the population of wildlife species in areas where a particular wildlife species was regarded as totem. Similarly, with respect to forest conservation, the *kyiridade* concept ensured total conservation, so none of the species–both flora and fauna–were never threatened of extinction as we have seen today under the colonial conservation practice. Though the colonial conservation practices cannot be described as absolute failure since we can still see many forests, game reserves and national parks in the country today. Nevertheless we have witnessed in the recent past the encroachment of these reserves with impunity, large scale poaching of wildlife and illegal harvesting of trees by chainsaw operators despite the fact that the forest and game reserves as well as the national parks are protected by laws. The laws are disobeyed with impunity and wanton exploitation of both flora and fauna went on every now and then, resulting in the extinction and listing of some species(birds, reptiles, animals, trees and the like) as endangered.

References

Books and Articles
Amenumey, D.E.K. 2008, *Ghana: A Concise History from Pre- Colonial Times to the 20th Century*, Woeli, Accra.

Ampadu–Agyei , O. 2003, Forward to Conservation International – Ghana (2003), *Handbook of Totems in Ghana: Traditional Mechanism for Biodiversity Conservation*, ii. Innolink, Accra.

Anderson, D and Grove, R., 1987, 'the scramble for Eden: past, present and future in African conservation', in *Conservation in Africa people, policies and practice*, Cambridge, Cambridge University Press.

Awuah –Nyamekye, S., 2012, 'Totemism, Akyeneboa, Ethics' *PAN: Philosophy, Activism, Nature* no. 9.

Beachey, R.W., 1967, 'The East African Ivory Trade in the Nineteenth Century' in *Journal of African History*, viii, 2.

Boahen, A.A. 1975. *Ghana: Evolution and Change in the Nineteenth Century*, Longmans, London.

Cardinall, W, 1971.*In Ashanti and Beyond*, Johnson Print Corporation, London.

Gareth E. J. 1987, *The Conservation of Ecosystems and Species*, , Croom Helm, London.

Kwarteng, K. O. 2004. 'Extension of British Rule to Ahafo, 1896-1914', Journal *of Philosophy and Culture*, Vol.1. No.1.

Kyeremateng, The, N. K., 2010, The Akan of Ghana: Their Custom, History and Institutions, Sebewie Ventures, Kumasi.

Mackenzie, J.M. 1988. *The Empire of Nature*, Manchester University Press, Manchester.

Ntiamoa–Baidu, 1993, 'Indigenous Protected Area Systems In Ghana' in_*African Biodiversity: Foundation for the Future*, Professional Printing, Beltsville.

Owusu M. A.S and Kwarteng, K.O, 2010,The Desparacidos: A study of local knowledge and forest culture in the development agenda of Ghana' in Polishing the Pearls of Ancient Wisdom: *Exploring the Relevance of Endogenous African Knowledge Systems for Sustainable Development in Postcolonial Africa: A Reader*, edited by Kuupole & Botchway, 85-98, University Printing Press, Cape Coast.

Reindorf, C.C.1889,*The History of the Gold Coast and Asante2nd* ,ed. Basel Mission Depot, Basel.

Rose, D. James and C. Watson, 2003, *Indigenous kinship with the Natural World in New South Wales*, New South.

Wales National Park and Wildlife Services. Accessed online 27/2/12.
http://www.environment.nsw.gov.au/resources/cultureheritage/IndigenousKinship.pdf

Sackey, V. 1997. 'The effects of Appendix I on Ghana's Elephants' in Proceedings of the African Elephant Conference, Johannesburg.

Spellerberg, I .F, 1996, ed. *Conservation Biology*, Essex, Longman.

Wilks, I. 1996. *One Nation, Many Histories Ghana Past and Present*, Accra, Ghana Universities Press.

Wilson, D. and Ayerst, P., 1976, *WHITE GOLD: the story of African Ivory*, London, Heinemann.

Archival Documents

The National Archives, Kew Gardens, CO 76/86, Wildlife Preservation Ordinance(1901).

PRAAD, Kumasi, ARG1/1/33, Regulations under 'the wild animals preservation ordinance, 1901' with reference to returns to be furnished by holders of licences in Ashanti, signed   by the Governor, John Rodgers, 9/01/1907.

PRAAD, Kumasi, ARG1/1/1/55, Ashanti. Regulations as to the Preservation of Wild Animals, Made by Matthew Nathan, 30th June, 1903.

PRAAD, Kumasi, ARG1/1/1/55, Preservation of Wild Animals in Ashanti,, 1903.

PRAAD, Kumasi, ARG1/1/107, Minutes by the Secretary for Native Affairs, J.T. Furley.

PRAAD, Kumasi, ARG1/1/33, Chief Commissioner, F.C. Fuller to the Colonial 3/11./ 1906.

PRAAD, Kumasi, ARG1/1/1/55, Ashanti .Regulations as to the Preservation of Wild Animals.

PRAAD, Kumasi, ARG1/1/1/55, Ashanti .Regulations as to the Preservation of Wild Animals.

PRAAD, Kumasi, ARG1/1/33, Regulations under 'the wild animals preservation ordinance, 1901' with reference to returns to be furnished by holders of licences in Ashanti.

PRAAD, Kumasi, ARG1/1/33, Regulations under 'the wild animals preservation ordinance, 1901' with reference to returns to be furnished by holders of licences in Ashanti.

PRAAD, Kumasi, ARG1/1/1/55, From the Chief Commissioner Ashanti, Coomassie to Governor, Victoriaborg, Accra , , Return of wild animals killed in Ashanti by non-natives for the first half year ending 30th June 1913; dated 28th July 1913.

PRAAD, Tamale, NRG8/6/107, from AG Secretary for Rural Development, Accra to Chief Commissioner, Northern Territories: Copy of a Memorandum, submitted to the Executive Council in 1948 during the discussion for the creation of the post of Game Warden, 6th April, 1950.

PRAAD, Kumasi ARG1 /1/107, from the Deputy Provincial Commissioner, Sunyani to the Chief Commissioner, Coomassie, 15th May, 1922.

PRAAD, Kumasi ARG1 /1/107, Minute by the Secretary for Native Affairs.

PRAAD, Kumasi, ARG1/1/33, From V. C F. Robertson, AG. Colonial Secretary to the Chief Commissioner, Ashanti, Coomassie, 2nd January, 1912. PRAAD, Tamale, NRG 8/6/107, Copy of Memoranda.

PRAAD, Kumasi ARG1 /1/107, Minute by the Secretary for Native Affairs. PRAAD, Kumasi, ARG1/1/33, the Game Reserve Regulations of 1911, signed by Governor Thorburn, November, 1911. See also PRAAD, Kumasi ARG1 /1/107, Minute by the Secretary for Native Affairs.

PRAAD, Kumasi, ARG1/1/107,from L.S. Amery, for Colonial Secretary, Downing Street, to Guggisburg, Accra, 6th March, 1920.

PRAAD, Kumasi, ARG1/1/107, Copy Scheme for International regulation for the protection of the elephant and rhinoceros in Africa.

PRAAD, Kumasi, ARG1/1/107, Minute by the Acting Attorney General, R.W.H. Wilkinson, 31st March, 1920.

PRAAD, Kumasi ARG1 /1/107, from Guggisburg, Accra, to Viscount Milner, Downing Street, 29th May, 1920.

PRAAD, Kumasi ARG1 /1/107, Extract, signed by A.E. Watherston, 1909.

PRAAD, Kumasi, ARG1/1/107, From Winston .S. Churchill, Downing Street to Guggisburg, Victoriaborg, 26th January, 1922.

PRAAD, Kumasi, ARG1/1/107, from Acting Commissioner, Western Province, Sunyani to Chief Commissioner, Coomassie, 31st May, 1922.

PRAAD, Kumasi, ARG1/1/107, From Deputy Provincial Commissioner, Sunyani to Chief Commissioner.

PRAAD, Kumasi, ARG1/1/107, From Ag Chief Commissioner, Coomassie to Ag. Colonial Secretary, Accra, 19th June, 1922.

PRAAD, Kumasi, ARG1/1/107, Regulation No.6 of 1923 under the Wild Animal Preservation Ordinance, 1923, See also

PRAAD, Kumasi, ARG1/1/107, From the Chief Commissioner, Coomassie to Colonial Secretary, Accra, 23rd September, 1924.

PRAAD, Kumasi, ARG 1/1/159, Extract from the minutes of a political conference held in the Chief Commissioner's office, Kumasi, 9th February, 1932.

PRAAD, Kumasi, ARG 1/1/159, From the Chief Commissioner of Ashanti, Kumasi, to the Attorney General, Accra, 11th May, 1932.

PRAAD, Kumasi, ARG 1/1/159 , From the Chief Commissioner, Kumasi t Assistant Chief   Ashanti, Kumasi, 25th May, 1932.

PRAAD, Kumasi, ARG 1/1/159, list showing Divisions which passed bye–laws on hunting in the night.

PRAAD, Kumasi, ARG 1/1/159, Ashanti Bye–Laws No.19.

PRAAD, Kumasi, ARG 1/1/159, control of Company hunting Bye–Laws.

PRAAD, Kumasi, ARG1/1/107, Extract: Watherston, the Chief Commissioner, Northern Territories, to the Colonial Secretary, 19th February, 1909.

PRAAD, Kumasi, ARG1/1/107,From the Deputy Provincial Commissioner and Government   Anthropologist of Ashanti, Sunyani to The Chief Commissioner Ashanti, Coomassie, 15th May, 1922.

PRAAD, Kumasi, ARG1/1/107, Extract.

PRAAD, Kumasi, ARG1/1/107, From F.O. Ballantine, Ag Chief Commissioner, Coomassie to the Chief Commissioner, Tamale, 18th January, 1924.

PRAAD, Kumasi, ARG1/1/107, From W.R. Danby, Coomassie to the Chief Commissioner,   Coomassie, 18th December, 1923.

PRAAD, Kumasi, ARG 1/1/159, From the Ag. Chief Commissioner, Kumasi to the Governor, Accra, 1st September, 1932.

PRAAD, Kumasi ARG1 /1/107, Deputy Provincial Commissioner, Sunyani.

PRAAD, Tamale, NR8/6/107, Memorandum.

PRAAD, Tamale, NRG2/15/9, From Ministry of Agriculture and Natural Resources, Accra to the Director of Tsetse Control, Wa 26th September, 1952.

PRAAD, Tamale, NR8/6/107, Memorandum.

PRAAD, Tamale, NR8/6/107, Game warden's Report from 11th October, 1949 to 31st March.

PRAAD, Tamale, NRG2/15/9, From Ministry of Agriculture and Natural Resources, Accra to the Director of Tsetse Control, Wa 26th September, 1952.

PRAAD, Tamale, NR8/6/107, Memorandum.

PRAAD, Tamale, NR8/6/107, Game warden's Report from 11th October, 1949 to 31st March, 1950.

PRAAD, Tamale, NR8/6/107, from the Game Warden, Lawra to the Chief Commissioner, Tamale, 9th January 1950.

PRAAD, Tamale, NR8/6/107, Game warden's Report.

PRAAD, Tamale, NR8/6/107, Report on the Game Department for the year 1950–1951.

PRAAD, Tamale, NR8/6/107, the Game Warden's Report.

PRAAD, Tamale, NR8/6/107, Report on the Game Department.

PRAAD, Tamale, NR8/6/107, Report on the Game Department for the year 1950-1951.

Oral Interviews

Interview with Nana Akwasi Manu, Kontihene of Mim Traditional Area, 80 years, Mim, 16th November, 2005.

Thesis

Moses Sam, An Assessment of Crop Damage by Elephant in Red Volta area of Ghana, thesis submitted to the Durrell Institute of Conservation and Ecology, University of Kent at Canterbury for the award of Master of Science in Conservation Biology, November, 1998.

Management and Development Plans /Reports

Digya National Park: the management plan, Wildlife Department, Accra, December, 1995.

Ghana Wildlife Division Policy for collaborative community based wildlife management, Accra, September, 2000.

Mole National Park: the Management Plan.

Wildlife Development Plan 1996–2020, volume 2, Institutional Reform, Wildlife Division, Accra, not dated.

Newspaper

Oti Awere, J. September 10, 2005 'Totemism and wildlife conservation: Ghanaians know your totem' in Daily Graphic.

Chapter 7

'Sheep in Sheep's Clothing or Wolves in Sheep's Clothing?' Interventions by Non-state Actors in a Changing Climatic Environment in Rural Zimbabwe

Munyaradzi Mawere and Christopher M. Mabeza

Introduction

It is widely acknowledged by many scholars (Dovie *et al* 2001; Ellis 1998; Cavendish 1999, 2001; Chambers and Conway 1992) that an approach premised on local narratives plays a pivotal role in the process of understanding resilience among the rural poor: it puts the last (rural poor) first (Chambers 1983). This approach builds on local innovations and capacities. The rural communities should be at the centre of the innovation process as they have superior knowledge of their production practices and social context. Scientific approaches in rural development replicate the top-down method of conventional development embodied in interventions by some non-state actors (NSAs) (see also Dovie *et al* 2001; Leach and Mearns 1996; Brockington and Homewood 1996). By science [scientific approaches], we mean knowledge forms mainly from the West that are foreign to local communities in contexts such as those of Africa. Such NSAs are wolves in sheep's clothing because their interventions are ephemeral and do not provide lasting benefits and relief to the rural communities. Unlike what Chambers (1983) suggests, they do not prioritise the poor. More often than not, these NSAs create a dependency syndrome and guillotine local attempts at innovations to a changing environment. Western – based science, in the hands of the state and some of the NSAs has become a strait jacket in which rural communities have to fit in matters of adaptation to environmental change. In this regard, science tends to work with people in ways that treat them as objects; actors to be taught rather than actors to engage with in a process of mutual learning that cements the idea of researcher and the researched as "co-selves". Yet there are other NSAs, the sheep in sheep's clothing whose interventions have made an indelible mark and assisted smallholders adapt to climate.

This chapter attempts to explore pathways to coping mechanisms to a changing climatic environment at the smallholder – non state – actor nexus in rural Zimbabwe. As alluded to above, the discussion is premised on interventions by non-state actors commonly known as non-governmental organisations (NGOs). The chapter asserts that in as much as interventions by external development agents have made inroads in building resilience among rural communities, at times the approach is fraught with contradictions and epistemic pitfalls as more often than not the interventions fail to recognise the communities' indigenous ways of knowing and survival strategies. Rural communities, like sheep being taken to the altar are enticed to join projects by external development agents with for example offers of agricultural inputs. It is acknowledged in this chapter that in the midst of these interventions, some enterprising smallholders are making huge strides in building resilience to a changing climatic environment. These are farmers who have realised that 'new situations demand new magic' to borrow a phrase from Evans-Pritchard (cited in Comaroff and Comaroff 1999: 279). However, our observations over the years have been that, in most cases, at the end of interventions by non-state actors, the latter appear to create no exit strategy for rural communities leading to the collapse or demise of the projects. A million dollar question therefore remains: 'Who benefits from these supposedly gestures of good-will-interventions?' Thus at one level, this chapter seeks to examine smallholder – non state-actor nexus in rural Zimbabwe, particularly the Zvishavane Rural Area. At another level, the chapter is an attempt to establish a situated understanding of the interaction of [Western-based] science and the local communities in order to rework the misconception that science is global and therefore bad/local knowledge is good binaries that have become the hallmark of debates on environmental change and development, especially in the rural areas in many parts of Zimbabwe.

Understanding Non-State Actors (NSAs)

The term NSA can be used to refer to "any entity that is not the state... in some contexts the term is used to refer to benign civil society groups working for human rights" (Clapham, undated). According to Umlimwengu (2007: 3-4):

> NSAs cover, but are not limited to, non-governmental organisations (NGOs) and may generally be subsumed under civil society organisations (CSOs) although it is important to note that an important attribute distinguishes some NSAs from the concept of civil society. In much of the literature on the subject, these three concepts (NGOs, CSOs, and NSAs) are often used interchangeably with the concomitant that such interchangeability may sometimes engender.

For purposes of this study, NSAs will be considered as NGOs. This is in view of the realization that the term NSAs has become very much in vogue in the past few decades as many actors including researchers, activists, mediators have sought to comprehend "interventions that fall without the purview of the state" (Umlimwengu 2007: 3). NSAs sprung to prominence in the developing world in the 1980s in the wake of a void left by the impact of neoliberal economic reforms, the structural adjustment programmes (SAPs) at the behest of the Breton Woods institutions – the World Bank (WB) and the International Monetary Fund (IMF). Umlimwengu (2007: 5) argues that "SAPs meant disengagements of most African governments from economic activity as well as from their role as providers of social services such as health and education". This disengagement by African governments was a perfect Godsend which NSAs grabbed with both hands. NSAs are now a common feature in mostly rural Africa and Zimbabwe is no exception.

NSAs interventions in Zimbabwe's rural communities: A case of Zvishavane Rural

Rural Zimbabwe has witnessed a plethora of NSAs implementing a host of interventions meant to cushion communities from the adverse effects of a changing climatic environment. Specifically, this paper will mainly deal with interventions by NSAs in rural Zvishavane and its environs.

Zimbabwe is divided into five agro-ecological regions based on agricultural potential. Zvishavane is in regions IV and V. Agro-ecological region IV is a semi-extensive farming region characterized by low rainfall (450-650 mm). It is subject to periodic seasonal droughts and very dry spells during the dry season. The region is suitable for cattle ranching and drought resistant crop production. Natural region V is characterized by low and erratic rainfall below 600mm.This region is considered only suitable for cattle ranching and wildlife production. Zimbabwe's rural areas comprise about 42 % of the country and support 70% of the population (Andrieni 1993; Makombe *et al*, 2003). The mainstay of the Zimbabwean economy is agriculture. Rural communities mainly depend on rain fed agriculture. They depend on small scale agricultural livelihoods that are susceptible to drought, have few assets and virtually nothing to fall back on when disasters such as drought and famine strike. Thus potentially, rural communities are the hardest hit in the event of a failed harvest as a result of drought.

Some NSAs operating in rural Zvishavane, those we refer in this paper as 'the sheep in sheep's clothing' as they are commonly viewed by rural communities as genuine are implementing projects like chicken farming in rural Zvishavane. The chicken projects are benefiting smallholder farmers living with HIV/AIDS who have been affected by rainfall variability. These farmers are also given seed to grow smaller grains which do well in semi-arid Zvishavane and many have consolidated food security by realising huge harvests. The NSAs involved in these projects also arrange for forums whereby they invite people from neighbouring countries such as Malawi and Zambia to come and share their experiences. These NSAs are spearheading water harvesting as a way of adapting to climate. They use the model of a celebrated smallholder farmer-

Mr. Zephaniah Phiri Maseko of ward 6 in Zvishavane. Mr. Phiri Maseko is a world renowned water harvester who harvests water that cascades down the dwalas next to his homestead (Wilson 2010; Lancaster 2008). Many farmers in the region have now devised water harvesting techniques suitable for their own environments and are benefiting handsomely by engaging in market gardening. They mainly sell their produce in the sprawling urban Zvishavane.

At worst some of these interventions appear to be a feel good exercise with no intentions to benefit the affected people as evidenced by the way they collapse as soon as the donor organisation withdraws. There appears to be no exit strategy on the part of the NSAs as the smallholder farmers involved in the project are left to fend for themselves, and with no adequate financial backup. Consequently, many smallholders abandon the project to pursue strategies they deem vital for their survival. In reality the rural communities are attracted to NSAs projects by offer of agricultural inputs (Research Notes 2012). However, some of the projects have 'good intentions' (to use our respondents' words). Conservation agriculture (CA) as introduced by some NSAs has been implemented in some rural areas with a varying degree of success. Giller *et al* (2009) acknowledge this when they note that CA:

> Aims to address the problems of soil degradation resulting from agricultural practices that deplete the organic matter and nutrient content of the soil and moreover, it purports to address the problem of intensive labour requirements in smallholder agriculture...Zero tillage, together with crop residue management (mulches) and crop rotation are the pillars of CA as it is now actively promoted by a growing number of research and extension programmes, supported by major international initiatives (pp. 24).

However, if our findings are anything to go by, our observations in Zvishavane reveal that CA appears to run at counter purposes with the aspirations of the majority of smallholder farmers in as far as crop residue mulches are concerned. Smallholders mainly use the mulches to feed livestock. Thus cattle take precedence over CA in terms of use of crop residues. Besides, zero-tillage is very labour intensive and can only be done by smallholders who are in good health. With the AIDS pandemic wreaking havoc among rural communities, CA might not offer an escape route from famine. Besides, CA's over-reliance on inorganic fertiliser means that in the long run the soil will be destroyed. Excessive use of inorganic fertiliser also runs in the face of organic farming which is promoted as a prerequisite for healthy living. All this undermines the positive potentialities associated with CA. Realising this lacunae, Giller *et al* (2009) concluded that:

> But in the face of immediate problems of poverty, food insecurity and poor agricultural productivity, soil degradation may be readily relegated down their list of priorities. How can resource-constrained farmers be expected to adopt practices that in the long-term may improve production, but in the short term realise no net benefits, or even net losses? (pp. 31).

In some instances, NSAs embark on projects to economically empower rural communities. Mangoma (2011) gives an example of the New Gato Water Project (NGWP) in the neighbouring Shurugwi District whose intentions were very noble but collapsed after the withdrawal of the donor. However, she asserts that even though the water project collapsed, there is evidence of successes that cannot be ignored. These include, but not limited to technology transfer. Nevertheless, it is worth noting that in as much as there was technology transfer as a result of the aforementioned project, there was no exit strategy in place to ensure its continuation. Such interventions are flawed to say the least.

Interventions by non-state actors in the Third World are mainly premised on Western epistemologies and ontologies which privilege science leading to the sub-alterrnisation of local knowledges. Leach and Mearns (1996: 451) allude to the same point when they argue:

> In virtually any discipline particular methods come to acquire credibility and authority and it can be the heritance of such methods – as much as the actual messages they generate – that explains the persistence of some received ideas. By defining

what is acceptable as evidence, certain privileged methods also act to exclude other sorts of data. It is in this way that certain questions remain unasked, and certain types of evidence are ignored or dismissed as invalid.

Such methods as scientific enquiry stick to disciplinary orthodoxy like a bad breath. It is our contention therefore that, science, in the hands of the state and civil society has become a straightjacket in which rural communities have to fit in matters of a changing climatic environment. Both the state and non-state actors are complicit in preaching as gospel truth the precepts of science. Such misplaced views of environmental change often find purchase among state environmental agents, non-state actors, media (both in the developing and developed world) and constitute "the lie of the land" (Leach and Mearns 1996: 2). Thus, this leads to crafting of legislation whose major objective is to halt what is perceived as the legion of doom. The rural farmers are labelled agents of environmental destruction and have to contend with overwhelming supposedly gestures of 'goodwill' from non-governmental organisations meant to help 'right' the 'environmental catastrophe'. Leach and Mearns (1996: 440) argue further that:

> The driving force behind much environmental policy in Africa is a set of powerful, widely perceived images of environmental change. They include overgrazing and the 'desertification' of dry lands, the widespread existence of a 'wood fuel crisis', the rapid and recent removal of once-pristine forests, soil erosion, and the mining of natural resources caused by rapidly growing populations. So self-evident do these phenomena appear that their prevalence is generally regarded as common knowledge among development professionals in African governments, international donor agencies and non-governmental organisations [(NGOs)]. They have acquired the status of conventional wisdom: an integral part of the lexicon of development. Yet as shown by accumulating research […], these images may be deeply misleading.

Such 'crisis narratives' influences are driven by science's 'snapshot' methods and act as a justification for the intervention of non-state actors. More often than not, solutions are mainly a 'one size fits all'. They prescribe for example the same intervention in areas with different rainfall amounts and different soils. But people have always adapted to rainfall variability since time immemorial. It takes a deep appreciation of the local dynamics of one's environment to be able to adapt. In fact as the adage goes, "necessity is the mother of invention". Understanding how different rural communities cope in response to climate change is critical for sustainable and equitable policy and food security. Also the persistence of these dominant epistemologies means that they give precedence of certain agricultural techniques they consider to be scientific at the expense of 'others' that are labelled as superstitious and relegated to the periphery (Mawere 2011a; Mawere 2011b). Such "blind spots" as Tiffen (1996) would say, are very pervasive and they fail to 'see' such tried and tested soil and water conservation techniques as those of Mr Phiri Maseko.

Brockington and Homewood (1996) cited in Leach and Mearns posit that another "methodological blind spot" has been to erroneously assume conditions at a specific stage to be "representative of an enduring state of affairs". In view of this observation, Brockington and Homewood (1996) argue that colonial authorities in East Africa interpreted the low levels of population at the beginning of the twentieth century as the norm; unknown to them was that the population had been reduced by war and disease at the end of the nineteenth century. According to Leach and Mearns (1996) such misconceptions as this were used by colonial authorities to justify such misplaced claims that the human population had exceeded the carrying capacity in the twentieth century. Environmental degradation in rural areas was blamed on high population growth by colonial authorities (see also Iliffe 1990). In reality environmental degradation can be partly blamed on colonial environmental policies (Mukamuri 1995; Mawere 2013).

One other way in which external development agents justify their interventions in rural areas is labelling (Wood 1985 cited in Leach and Mearns 1996). This is in reference to "the way in which people conceived as objects of policy are defined in convenient images" (Wood 1985: 1). Naming is very powerful; it reverberates and sometimes perpetuates the danger of a single story (to use Adiche 2009). According to Leach and Mearns "target groups" are identified and labels are put on them. Such labels from examples we encountered in the field during our research in Zvishavane rural include "peasant farmers", "rural poor", "land invaders", "people living with HIV and AIDS" etc. "These are categories we live-by," one of the respondents remarked. This is the tonic that spurs NSAs into life. They use this 'dire' situation to legitimise their activities mostly in the rural areas. Their activities are ostensibly meant to avert 'human catastrophe' obtaining in the rural areas. As we observed in Zvishavane, some of them dangle a carrot in the form of inputs (inorganic fertiliser, seed) and at times a grand prize for the winner of competitions the NSAs will be running. The hapless villagers like sheep being taken to the altar often succumb to these enticements of the NSAs, when deep down their hearts they really don't support the projects. As a matter of consequence, duration of most of these projects is short to an extent that the successes of their results are not easily noticeable or realised. The question that lingers in the minds of many, therefore, is "Are NSAs wolves in sheep's clothing or sheep in sheep's clothing?" In a polemical critique of NGOs in Africa, Amutabi (2006: xiv) argues:

... that NGOs are not neutral or innocent bystanders in the great development drama unfolding in Africa but integral to the neo-colonial and neo-liberal projects of western imperialism that have done so much to disempower populations and distort development across the continent and in the global South more generally.

Drawing from Amutabi's assertion above as well as our findings in Zvishavane, there is a point at which it can be argued that some of the NSAs do not work in the same moral conceptual framework as the smallholder farmers. They bring along their ontological and epistemological ideals premised on modernity and this appears to work at counter-purposes with the aspirations of the rural communities resulting in a slow uptake of their innovations. Moreover, the donor factor perpetuated by NSAs creates a dependency syndrome that curtails any form of imagination or creativity. Granted that human creativity is as old as the hills, categorising people as the "rural poor" for example is counter-productive.

Some interventions are imported from outside Zimbabwe, for example one from Tanzania termed *Fanya Juu*. This was implemented in rural Zvishavane, Zimbabwe. *Fanya Juu* is a Swahili term which means to throw opposite side (provide source here). This entailed constructing contours meant to 'throw' water away. They were not as deep as those of Mr Phiri Maseko and were labour intensive. *Fanya Juu* as an agricultural practice was rejected by most of the rural farmers in Zvishavane and therefore it suffered a still birth. This should not be interpreted as arguing all NSAs bring no benefit to rural communities in Zvishavane or elsewhere. The argument is to their credit, some local NSAs working outside the box have been promoting the cultivation of small grains like sorghum and the programme ran from 2010 to 2012. The response was encouraging in the sense that about 300 farmers in one of the wards where Mr Phiri Maseko lives grew small grains. One of Mr Phiri's adopters, who lives in Mazvihwa area of Zvishavane harvested about 42 bags of sorghum in the 2011 to 2012 farming season (Personal communication 24 June 2012). Traditionally, dating back to many centuries ago, farmers have always grown small grains like sorghum and millet thus successfully adapting to climate variability (see also Mawere, Mukombe and Mabeza 2013) Maize was introduced by the Portuguese in about 1500 thereby greatly weakening people's capacity to adapt to climate variability because it was introduced as a cash crop. The cash crop economy appeared to have guillotined rural communities' capacity to feed themselves.

Conclusion

Some of the NSAs pass to be pigeonholed as sheep in sheep's clothing by virtue of the fact that they have made strides in empowering local communities. Others are viewed as wolves in sheep's clothing as measured by their interventions that leave rural communities worse off. They fail to acknowledge that local communities are important decision-makers in adaptation. National policymakers appear not eager to empower the rural people to facilitate adaptation processes that take traditional knowledge into account. In view of our findings with smallholder farmers in Zvishavane, we conclude that policies should recognise the diversity of local innovations and create a facilitating environment for effective local adaptation. Such recognition will go miles in enhancing community development in rural areas. Yet such a development is only possible if firstly, attempts are made at understanding environmental frames of stakeholders in the adaptation process, and secondly, attempts are made to reconcile these counter-frames through stakeholder negotiation at the science-publics nexus.

References

Adreini, M. 1993. The Management of Bani Irrigation Systems in Zimbabwe. PhD thesis. Ithaca, NY: Cornell University.

Amutabi, N. M. 2006. The NGO Factor in Africa: The Case of Arrested Development in Kenya, Taylor and Francis Group, Kenya.

Brockington, D. and Homewood, K. 1996. 'Wildlife, pastoralists and science: Debates concerning Mkomazi Game Reserve, Tanzania', In M. Leach and R Mearns (eds), *The Lie of the Land: Challenging Received Wisdom on the African Environment*, Oxford: James Currey pp. 90 – 104.

Cavendish, W. 2001. Rural livelihoods and non-timber forest products, In De Jong, W. and Campell, B. (Eds). *The role of non-timber forest products in socio-economic development*, CABI Publishing: Wallingford.

Chambers R. 1983. *Rural development: Putting the last first,* Longman, New York.

Chambers, R. and Conway, G. 1992. Sustainable rural livelihoods: Practical concepts for the 21st century, *Discussion Paper 296*, Institute of Development Studies.

Chimamanda, A. N. 2009. *The Danger of a Single Story,* talk filmed in July 2009, online:

www.ted.com/taks/chimamanda_adichie_the_danger_of_a_sin gle_story_.html (16 March 2013).

Clapham, A. (n.y). *Non-State Actors.International Human Rights Law*, 2nd Edition. Moeckli, D. Oxford University Press.

Comaroff, J and Comaroff, L. 1999. Occult Economies and the violence of abstraction: Notes from the South African post colony, *American Ethnologist*, 26 (2): 279-303.

Dovie, B. D., Shackleton, C. M., and Witkowski, E. T. F. 2001. Involving local people: Reviewing participatory approaches for inventorying the resource base, harvesting and utilisation of non-wood forest products, In *Harvesting of non-wood forest products: Proceedings of FAO/ECE/ILO International Seminar*, Ministry of Forestry, Turkey, pp. 175-187.

Ellis, F. 1998. Household strategies and rural diversification, *Journal of Development Studies*, 35 (1): 1-38.

Giller, K. E. 2009. Conservation Agriculture and smallholder farming in Africa: The heretic's view, *Field Crops Research*, 114 (2009) 23 – 34.

Lancester, B. 2008. Case study: Drought resistant farming in Africa. *The Ecologist*, November (Accessed December 2012), www.theecologist.org/how_to_make_a_difference/food_and_ gardening/360257/case_study_drought_resistant_farming_in_a frica.html.

Iliffe, J. 1990. *Famine in Zimbabwe, 1890 – 1960*, Mambo Press: Zimbabwe.

Leach, M and Mearns. R. 1996. 'Environmental Change and Policy', In Leach, M and R. Mearns (Eds), *The Lie of the Land: Challenging Received Wisdom on the African Environment*, Oxford: James Currey.

Makombe, G, Meinzen-Dick, R, Davies S. P. and Sampath R.K. 2001. An Evaluation of Bani (Dambo) Systems in Zimbabwe, *Canadian Journal of Agricultural Economics*, (49): 203-216.

Mangoma, J. F. 2011. *The Effects on Local Livelihoods of a Wetland Development Scheme in a Zimbabwean Village: An ethnographic field study*, PhD Thesis, University of Cape Town, South Africa.

Marongwe, N. 2004.'Traditional authority in community-based natural resource management (CBNRM): The case of Chief Marange in Zimbabwe', In Dzingirai, V and Breen, C. *Confronting the crisis in community conservation – Case studies from*

Southern Africa, Centre for Environment, Agriculture and Development, University of KwaZulu-Natal.

Mawere, M., Mukombe, C., and Mabeza, C. 2013. *Memoirs of an Unsung Legend – Nemeso,* Langaa RPCIG Publishers: Bamenda.

Mawere, M. 2011a. Possibilities for Cultivating African Indigenous Knowledge Systems (IKSs): Lessons from Selected Cases of Witchcraft in Zimbabwe, *Journal of Gender, Peace and Development,* 1 (3): 091-100.

Mawere, M. 2011b. *African belief and knowledge systems: A critical perspective,* Langaa RPCIG Publishers: Bamenda.

Mawere, M. 2013. A critical review of environmental conservation in Zimbabwe, *Africa Spectrum,* 48 (2): 85- 97.

Mukamuri, B. 1995. *Making sense of forestry: A political and contextual study of forestry practices in south central Zimbabwe,* Published PhD thesis, University of Tampere: Finland.

Tiffen, M. 1996. Land and Capital: Blind spots in the study of the "resource poor" farmer, In *The Lie of the Land: Challenging Received Wisdom on the African Environment,* Oxford: James Currey.

Ulimwengu, J. 2007. The Role of Non-State Actors, *A Paper Presented at the 7th African Governance Forum,* Ouagadougou, Burkina Faso, 24-26 October 2007.

Wilson, K. B. 2010. *Overview of Zephaniah Phiri's Book of Life,* On the Occasion of his Lifetime   Achievement Award, Speech given at the University of Zimbabwe (24 August 2010).

Chapter 8

Religion and the Restoration of Health in Africa: A Case Study of the Traditional Akan People of Ghana

Samuel Awuah-Nyamekye

Introduction

Sound health, no doubt, is the soul of every human society, for no human society can thrive if her people are afflicted with ill-health. For this reason, the Akan of Ghana prioritise matters that border on sound health. But among the Akan as is the case in traditional African societies, the line between their secular and religious activities is indistinguishable (Parrinder, 1961; Mbiti, 1969; Opoku, 1978.) This makes the hold of religion on the Akan and, for that matter,traditional Africans, very strong.

In the worldview of the traditional Akan[2] of Ghana, *apotee* or *apomuden* (health or well-being) is not only understood as the absence of diseases and afflictions or misfortunes but also, it includes the presence of good relationship between humans and the spirit beings on one hand and good interpersonal relationship on the other, for the Akan one cannot claim there is good health or well-being while the people in the community are at each other's throat. That is, a good mental framework is inclusive of health in the Akan milieu (Opoku, 1978, Kwame Gyekye, 1996; Awuah-Nyamekye, 211). This mind-set is very common among many African cultures (Gwyneth,. 1994; Makinde 1988:6). This worldview thus, gives direction to the Akan in all their activities including health and its restoration. This also explains the reason why usually the etiology of almost all diseases has supernatural underpinnings (Field, 1961; Foster, 1976). It must, however, be emphasised that in

---

[2] By traditional Akan people, I mean those Akan who generally still keep and live to the customs and traditions of their forebears, particularly their indigenous spirituality (African Traditional Religion) in spite of the influence of impinging religions such as Christianity and Islam

spite of the supernatural etiology of ill-health among the Akan, they also at some point acknowledge the 'Germ Theory' or the 'naturalistic' causes of illneses as Foster (1976)puts it.

Notwithstanding this reality, and paradoxically, the Akan still find it very difficult to de-couple spirituality and therapeutic practices. It is against this background that this chapter argues that among the traditional Akan, religion and medicine are inseparable realities. Literature on health care delivery in Ghana is quite extensive but those on how the local concepts of illness may affect people's choices of health care model are scarce. The discussion is focused on the following themes: Akan conception of medicine, the nexus between religion and medicine, etiological explanation of illness among the Akan and the Akan medical practitioner and the 'Germ Theory' and the prospects of indigenous/traditional medicine in Ghana today.

Methodology

This study has benefited from my earlier research on traditional medicine in Africa particularly in Ghana and personal observation and teaching experience in a course *Religion and Medicine in Africa* in the Department of Religion and Human Values of the University of Cape Coast for the past ten years. I relied on a variety of qualitative research tools, ranging from focus group discussions (FGD), and individual interviews to document analysis. I interviewed a variety of interlocutors who include traditional African Priests, Traditional Birth Attendants (TBAs), orthodox medical practitioners and traditional medical practitioners.

Who are the Akan?

The Akan constitute the largest ethnic group in Ghana. They constitute close to half of the population of Ghana. The 2010 Population census of Ghana put the percentage of the Akan in Ghana at 47.5%. They are mainly found in the middle and the southern part of Ghana. They speak the Akan language. The Akan are culturally homogenous and by and large, matrilineal. Akan are also found in the south-eastern portion of the Republic of Ivory Coast or La Cote d'Iviore (Warren 1986:7; Odame Beeko, 2005)[3].

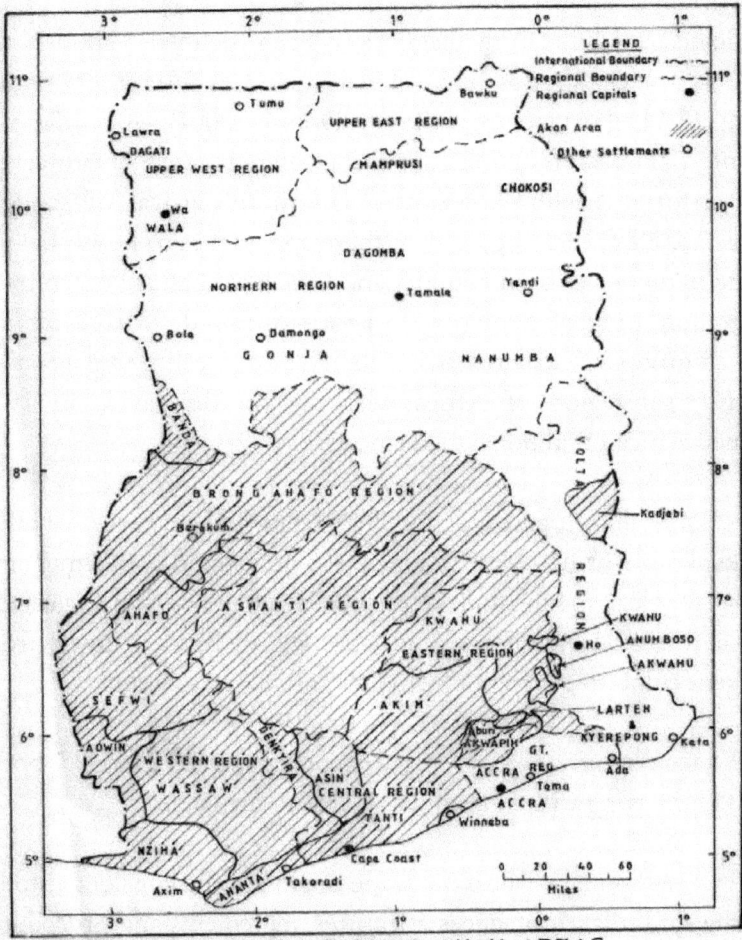

MAP OF GHANA SHOWING AKAN AREAS

SOURCE : Author, 2009

---

[3] For more details on the Akan see: Warren, Dennis M. 1986. The Akan of Ghana: An overview of Ethnographic Literature. Pointer Limited; Beeko, Odame Eric. 2005. Creative Processes in Akan Musical Cultures: Innovation Within Tradition. A Ph.D. dissertation, University of Pittsburgh; Adu Boahen, A. in *Colloque Inter- Universitaire Ghana- Cote-D' Ivoire : Les Populations* , in *Colloque Inter- Universitaire Ghana- Cote-D' Ivoire : Les Populations Communes De La Cote D'Ivoire Et du Ghana, Bondoukou, 4 - 9 Janvier*, 1974, pp. 66-81Pobee, J.S. 1979.*Toward an African Theology*. Abingdon/Nashville.

Medicine among the Akan

Medicine, as practised by the Akan of Ghana, is part of what has become known today as traditional or indigenous African medicine. Traditional medicine has been defined variously by various interest groups and scholars, such as WHO, Parrinder, 1961; Field, 1961; Opoku, 1978; Domfe, 2007). According to Domfe (2007:42), traditional medicine refers to ways of protecting and restoring health that existed before the arrival of modern medicine. He further argues that 'these approaches to health belong to the traditions of each country, and have been handed down from generation to generation'(ibid.). Evans-Anfom (1984:11) reports that a group of experts from the World Health Organization (WHO) sub-region of Africa who met in Brazzaville in 1976 defined African traditional medicine as:

> The sum total of all the knowledge and practices, whether explicable or not, used in diagnosis, prevention and elimination of physical, mental and social imbalance and relying exclusively on practical experience and observation handed down from generation to generation, whether verbally or in writing.

Evans-Anfom (1984:11) again reports the same world body, WHO, as having viewed traditional African medicine as:

> Traditional African medicine might also be considered to be the sum total of practices, measures, ingredients and procedures of all kinds, whether material or not, from which time immemorial had enabled the African to guide against diseases, to alleviate his sufferings and to cure himself.

A careful analysis of the two definitions from WHO shows that they are underpinned with Euro-American categories as the ensuing discussion will show.

In the Euro-American societies, the word medicine has a limited usage. It is any drug or substance, which is taken to cure an illness. For the Akan, however, the word 'medicine' has shades of meaning (see Twumasi 1979; Reynolds 1996.) For instance, it is literally translated in Akan as '*aduro.*' Literally, the word *aduro* may have the same meaning as the West understands medicine to be. However, for the traditional Akan, 'medicine' goes beyond the physical substances that are used to treat diseases (Twumasi, 1975; Opoku, 1978; Awuah-Nyamekye, 2011). Generally, medicine is understood as involving all the indigenous techniques for restoring and maintaining health, which have been developed and used over the years. These techniques are heavily influenced by their cultural and religious beliefs, and are passed on from generation to generation until the advent of the modern conventional methods of restoring and maintaining health (Reynolds, 1996, Awuah-Nyamekye, 2011, Mawere, 2011). The Akan also view medicine in its broader sense as any power that can have a supernatural influence over other powers. In this case then, witchcraft, magic and sorcery are integral parts of medicine in the traditional Akan sense (see Awuah-Nyamekye, 2008, Mawere, 2011). Medicine may also be understood to be any means used to ply the supernatural realm for information, which otherwise could be hidden from ordinary eyes. This explains the reason why in Akan traditional societies, those who practice medicine are mainly those believed to have the ability to communicate with the spiritual world.

Today, this kind of medicine is known among the Akan of Ghana as *Abibiduro,* which literally means 'African Peoples' medicine.' The term was designed by scholars, particularly social anthropologist to differentiate between the African way of treating illnesses from that of the Euro-American societies when colonialism and its attendant Westernisation was introduced to the Africa.

Who is a traditional medical practitioner?

Again, just as it is not easy to arrive at one acceptable definition of traditional medicine (Evans-Anfom, 1986) so also it is with traditional medical practitioner or healer as the concept is looked at from different perspectives. According to the WHO a traditional healer is:

A person who is recognized by the community in which he lives as competent to provide health care by using vegetable, animal and mineral substances, and certain other methods based on the social, cultural and religious background as well as on the knowledge, attitudes, and beliefs that are prevalent in the community regarding physical, mental and social well-being, and the causation of disease and disability (cited in Evans-Anfom, 1986:12).

The above decription of traditional healer can be described as comprehensive, however, in the worldview of the people under study, the role of religion in the practice of medicine is emphasised. Nana Agyemang, a well known tradtional healer in the Berekum area describes a traditional healer in the following words:

> Traditional medicine man/woman (healers) is a person who usually through the aid of the spiritual powers supported with training, and experience has gained a deep knowledge of herbs of all kinds and other necessary materials and their permutations for the purposes of treating those who are afflicted with disease of all kinds in his or her society. Such individual's expertise covers many areas such as mental problems, bone setting, midwifery, skins rashes and other diseases that affect humans (Nana Agyemang, personal communication, January 18, 2013).

Nana Agyemang further explains that the ability to ply into the spirtual world is a necessary ingredient for any successful traditional healer since many diseases in the Akan society are believed to have spitirual undertone. What this implies is that a healer, can be exposed to attack from the source(s) of the ailment if he/she (healer) is not spiritually fortified. That is, as a healer you must know how to protect yourself and that of your client(s) from spiritual attacks. Karim *et al*'s (1994) study among the Zulus of South Africa reveals a similar finding (see also Mawere, 2011). It is against this background that Twumasi (1988) defines traditional medicine as 'a practice in which there is no conceptual separation between natural and supernatural entities. It entails a holistic method utilising medico-religious acts and concepts' (Twuamasi, 1988:9 cited in Setswe, 1999: 57). This explains why religion is an important aspect of Akan medical culture. In the follwing paragraphs, I discuss how religion and medicine move together among the Akan.

The nexus between Religion and Medicine

I have already pointed out that religion plays a vital role in the life of the Akan.. This explains why religion has been one of the key elements in the process and restoration of health among the people under study. The specific elements of religion that often feature in health delivery system among the Akan include: God, divinites, ancestors, and other spirit beings such as *Mmotia* (dwarfs or fairy of the forest). The role of religion in the restoration of health in traditional African societies has been underscored by other studies (Osborne 2003; Foster, 1976; Hammond-Tooke,1989). Osborne (2003) for instance, observes that indigenous African healing stems from ancient, fundamental, philosophical and religious beliefs... and that their concerns about bodily well-being cannot be separated from their spiritual beliefs.

Among the Akan, and indeed, as it is the case among other traditional African peoples, God for instance, is viewed as the ultimate source of all human needs. Medicine for instance, in Akan worldview, is viewed as a gift from God and dispensed through the agency of the divinities (Twumasi, 1975; Awuah-Nyamekye, 2011:72). In traditional Akan society, God is recognised as the giver and healer of all ailments, and hence, the saying: '*Onyame ma wo yare a, oma wo aduru*' 'If God gave you sickness he also gave you medicine' (Rattray, 1923:142). It is thus common to hear traditional Akan medical practitioners always telling their clients when consulted that 'if God permits you will be well.'

The other religious entities that feature actively in the restoration of health among the Akan are the deities. The evidence of the role deities play in health delivery among the Akan can be seen in the names of these deities borne by people in traditional Akan societies. The most common Akan names that are compounded with names of deities include: Asirifi, *Apee, Boɔ, Kune Kru, Mframa* and *Nyamaa* and many others. River deities are also important source of restoring health among the Akan people such that it is very common to find people throughout Akan society

187

bearing names such as *Asubɔnten, Bosomtwe, Komɔɔ, Densu, Densua, Pra,Praba, Tano,Tanoa* —all bodies of water in the Akan land. These names result from either the parents of the children involved consulted these river deities before the conception of the children or the deity involved healed the child of a serious ailment of some sort.

Furthermore, it is very common in Akan society to see people consulting the deities for the treatment of diseases of all kinds. *Tan Kwasi*, the state god of Berekum Traditional Area for instance, is noted for her prowess in handling infertility problems. Other studies elsewhere in Africa also reveal that deities play a role in medicine. Opoku (1978) also reports that *Osanyin* Yoruba god and *Agwu* of the Ibo of Nigeria, are recognised as the guardians of medicine, and are believed to call or possess people to become medicine men and women.

Other spiritual entities that are believed to have a role to play in the practice of medicine in the traditional Akan society are the ancestors. Quite a number of the traditional medicine men/women I interviewed claimed that they received their calls through their grandparents in dreams. It is interesting to note that it is not only among the Akan that Ancestors play a role in medical practice. According to Idowu (1973), *Elesije* an important figure in *Ile-Ife* society in Nigeria is viewed as the first doctor and the ancestral genius of medicine who is always invoked in the treatment of diseases among the people of *Ile-Ife* in Nigeria. Four of my informants claimed that they became medical practitioners through abduction by *Mmotia* (dwarfs or fairy of the forest).

My field work and personal observations as well as teaching experience show that the training process of the traditional medical practitioners indicate an affinity between religion and medicine among the people under study. This is because the category of people who dominate in the practice of medicine in traditional Akan societies and, indeed, all traditional societies in Ghana are mainly ritual specialists such as diviners, priests, prophets, mediums, and magicians. Most of these traditional medical practitioners usually claim they acquire their knowledge through: dreams, visions, voices, and abduction by dwarfs, possession, inheritance, apprenticeship and other means (Opoku, 1978; Awuah-Nyamekye,

2011). To illustrate this, I present below an account of one of my key interlocutors who became a priest/diviner and, consequently, traditional medical practitioner[4]

I became *Benyaade Ɔkomfoɔ* when my maternal uncle died. Immediately after he died, I was sent through a series of rituals. I was made to bath with a concoction in a brass pan (*yaawa*) in the morning, afternoon and the evening for three consecutive days. The concoction was prepared with the following herbs: *guakro (Ageratum conyzoides), atanogya, mee (Ocinum canum), nunum (Ocinum viride)* and *piaa (Hyptis brevipes)*. There was another herb known as *awenade (Akotopotsin)*, which was put into my bath water to be used seven times daily for three days. After this ritual bath, the juices of another set of herbs were dropped on my eyes. These were *asinsan (Cynodon dactylon) and nkrangyedua (Jatropha carcass)*.Then sacred emblem was put on my head for six hours daily for three consecutive days. On the third day, there was a splash on my eyes. I began to shiver profusely. I fell down and became dumb. *Asinsan*, one of the herbs, which were dropped on my eyes, was mixed with other herbs and put into my mouth and I was sent to the outskirts of the village. An egg was given to me. I threw it against at a tree and mentioned the name of my dead uncle, *Ɔkomfoɔ* Adum and greeted him three times: *Ɔkomfoɔ_Adum makye oo!, Ɔkomfoɔ Adum makye oo Ɔkomfoɔ Adum makye oo!* This means: Priest *Adum* good morning Priest *Adum* good morning Priest *Adum* good morning. This was explained to mean that I have successfully gone through the training. Customarily, it was said that the trainee-priest should be able to mention the name of an ancestor of the family and greet him or her when he or she is regaining his or her speech. But if he should mention the name of a person who is living, that person, it is believed, will soon pass away. After these rituals, I could understand the language of my deity *Benyade*. I was told the training should have lasted for three years but since I had served as an attendant under my uncle for more than six years, I was formally trained for three months. This was how I became a diviner/medicine man (Awuah-Nyamekye, 2011:75).

---

[4] This is because in traditional societies, all traditional priests are medical practitioners since medicine is an important aspect of the curriculum that a traditional priest goes through during his or her training:

Even the way the ingredients of the medicine are collected and prepared—performance of certain rituals before plucking some herbs and the healing processes involved--point to the connection between religion and medicine. Mawere and Andile study among indigenous South Africans in this volume confirms the affinity between religion and medicine thus: 'In South Africa, traditional healers are mainly indigenous Africans with spiritual gifts to treat various conditions (ailments/diseases) including resolving many other health related problems.' In the words of Twumasi (1975: 35) 'the distinction between physical cure and magico-religious cure is not usually made since the diagnosis and the treatment of illness are deeply embedded in the utilisation of the supernatural.'

Another important aspect of medicine that can be used to demonstrate the close affinity between religion and the practice of medicine in the study area as has been hinted earlier, is the causative agents of illnesses.

The Akan etiology of illness

The general worldview of the Akan regarding the causes of illnesses could be put under three broad categories—(a)Supernatural, (b) human causes and (c) natural causes or what is referred to now as 'germ theory'. Even in the case of the human causes, it is believed that the human agent(s) make(s) use of the supernatural to cause the illness. That is why the supernatural or the 'personalitic'[5] causes seem to be dominant among the Akan (see Turner 1967; Mutungi 1977; Mawere 2011). The interaction with my key interlocutors revealed the following as the principal means through which illnesses, afflictions or misfortunes resulting from supernatural origins can occur:

    i.   Neglecting one's religious duties
   ii.   Breaking of taboos

---

[5] According to Foster (1976: 775) 'personalistic' etiology of illness is the belief that illnesses are principally caused by the 'active purposeful intervention of an agent, human (witch, sorcerer), non-human (ghost, ancestor, evil spirit), or supernatural (deity or powerful being)'.

iii. Engaging in evil activities

iv. Activities of witches and sorcerers

Neglecting one's religious duties

Nana Fosua (personal communication, January 4,. 2013) contends that the Akan culture can be described as a 'religious culture' and thus religious activities, particularly religious duties cannot be ignored in the day to day activities of the Akan. Therefore, any traditional Akan that thinks otherwise does so at his or her own peril. Specifically, she emphasises that there is no way an Akan can refuse to give due recognition to the ancestors and the gods. Hence, due recognition is given to *Nananom nsamanfoɔ* (Ancestors) among the Akan. This she says manifests itself in the sacrifices and libation that take place on sacred days such as *Adea*[6], and annual festivals that centre around the *blackstools*[7] in the stool rooms and gods in the various Akan communities. What this means is that if a person falls sick and the sickness deifies medical treatment, one plausible ways to explain it is to suspect that the person may have neglected his or her religious duty. The suspicion becomes stronger if the individual concerned is a community leader or an *Abusuapanyin* (family head). This is because one of the main duties of an *Abusuapanyin* is to see to feeding of *Nananom nsamanfoɔ* by way of offering them sacrifices on behalf of other family members.

Breaking of taboos

---

[6] *Adae* in Akan language simply means the sleeping place of the ancestors. But now the concept refers to a sacred day (and in fact, a festival among the Akan) on which the Akan remember their ancestors by offering them food and drink of all kinds. For more details on *Adea* see Opoku, 1978: 39-43.

[7] Among the Akan, every chief is supposed to have a stool, known as *asɛsɛdwa*, which is usually made from *sɛsɛdua* plant (*Funtumia* sp.). It is this stool that is blackened and placed in a special room called *nkondwafieso* ['stool room'] after the death of a chief. Therefore, all the important rituals connected with the ancestors centre around these stools. In fact, the stool is the symbol of a chief's office. Any chief whose stool is not blackened and placed among those of his or her predecessors is not a recognised chief among the Akan (Nana Kwabena Wusu, personal communication, 12 October 2011, at Nana Takyiwaa's palace in Senase).

The institution of *taboos* has been a commonplace practice in many African societies since time immemorial. A *taboo,* according to my informants, is any act that is strictly prohibited in the Akan society infraction of which attracts the wrath of the either the ancestors or the gods of the community concerned. Mawere and Kadenge (2010:29) have given a comprehensive description of what taboos are. They contend that taboos serve: [a]s codes of conduct/commandments and indigenous knowledge systems (IKS) and beliefs that helped in preserving the natural environment, peace, order and the integrity of African societal structures. The word "taboo" is a derivation from the Polynesian term *tabu,* which simply means "forbidden." According to Sarpong (1974: 51), it may be applied to any form of prohibition. The Akan word for taboo is *mmusuo.* Among the Akan, the breaking of certain categories of taboos such as committing murder or suicide, seducing someone's wife are considered as sin. (Awuah-Nyamekye, 2012). In the view of Ɔkomfoɔ Tawia (personal communication, September, 13, 2013), an infraction of a taboo constitutes a sin, and always attracts divine wrath until the spiritual entity involved is propitiated through confession and the performance of the necessary sacrifice(s).

Engaging in evil activities

The Akan believe in retribution, hence, the saying that *ɔkromfoɔ bi ara wu wo nensa ano.* This literally means 'Every thief dies at his/her own hand.' That is, the evil doer dies in his or her own iniquities. For this reason, many Akan use curses as means to cause afflictions of all forms to those who steal their properties especially valuable property like gold ornaments, clothes and others items considered precious. Rivers *Koraa* in Berekum, *Antoa Nyamaa* in Antoa, *Pata Angyeɛ* in Tarkwa in the Brong-Ahafo. Ashanti and Western Regions of Ghana respectively are noted for their ability to retrieve stolen items for their owners through affliction they cause to the perpetrators (the thieves) .Men who chase other people's wives can also suffer through curses. Among the Akan, *sipe*—the harbouring of anger, bitterness and resentment against others for no justifiable cause—is another source of inviting troubles for oneself.

Activities of witches and sorcerers

As I have already explained, traditional/indigenous medical practitioner as a necessity must be spiritually fortified. This means that one should have a good knowledge of how to manipulate the forces of nature to protect either oneself or one's clients—This is the knowledge of counter magic. That is, traditional medical practitioner has the capacity to deploy medicine either for a good or bad purpose (sorcery). However, among the Akan, it is only the good use of medicine that is acceptable, for it is that which makes life liveable. For this reason, sorcerers (*adutofoɔ*) and witches (*abayifoɔ*) are viewed as enemies of society. Because of this, when illness befalls one in the Akan society, the activities of sorcerers become one of the suspected causes. Activities of witches and sorcerers are feared in the Akan societies so much so that the people have a saying that: *Mensuro nea obɛkum me se nea onya me a ɔbɛsɛe me.* This is literally translated as 'I am not afraid of the one who will kill me than one who will destroy me.' Nana Adjei (personal communication) explains further that the destruction (*ɔsɛe*) here may refer to tarnishing one's image but when the Akan utters such words, the emphasis is more on those who use witchcraft or sorcery to cause affliction to people. Mawere's (2011) study of makes similar findings.

I should however point out that although witchcraft (*bayie*) is generally abhorred in indigenous Akan society, the Akan, however, make a distinguish between what they referred to as *bayi pa* (good witchcraft) and *bayi bɔne* (bad witchcraft) or sorcery--simply the use of one's medicine or spiritual power (s) to cause harm to others (Awuah-Nyamekye, 2008). They have no problem with those who use their witchcraft power for good purposes such as healing the sick, protecting children and property and other desirable things in society in general. On the hand, it is *bayi bɔne* (bad witchcraft) or sorcery that is seriously abhorred in Akan society due to the harm that is associated with it. This means that and as Mawere (2011:093) points out, 'a qualitative difference between witchcraft and sorcery is normally drawn' in indigenous African societies. Mawere (2011: 100), thus, complicates 'the view that witchcraft is a metaphysical practice that can only be deployed to cause harm and despondency in society'. Among the Akan, however, the problem is that it is believed that it is more likely for those who have the capacity to use the craft to abuse it such as using it for personal gains or to cause discomfort to unsuspecting peoples that is why witchcraft is generally abhorred among the Akan.

The Akan generally believe that the human person is a compound of both material (physical) and immaterial (spiritual) and such, the two must be in harmony or else illness will occur (see Osei 1976). Therefore, whenever there is ill health, it must be tackled at both the physical and the spiritual levels. The logical implication from this worldview (etiology of illness) of the Akan is that the effective means to deal with ailments emanating from spiritual source lies in the same source. That is, through spiritual means. This is the reason why divination mostly precedes traditional medication, while rituals like prayer; libation and sacrifice usually feature in the traditional healing process. This is meant to appeal to or appease the supernatural agent(s) responsible for the sickness.

The Akan medical practitioner and the 'Germ Theory'

It is important to point out that in spite of the close affinity between religion and medicine among the Akan as discussed above, they are also aware of the differences between what may be termed as psychologically motivated diseases and or naturally motivated diseases—known conventionally as 'Germ Theory'. The Germ theory, according to Encyclopaedia Britannica, states that in medicine, 'certain diseases are caused by the invasion of the body by microorganisms, organisms too small to be seen except through a microscope.' This theory was proposed and developed in the mid-16th century. Its widespread credence was credited to Louis Pasteur (The French chemist and microbiologist), Joseph Lister (the English surgeon) and Robert Koch (the German physician) (http//www.britannica.com/EBchecked/topic/230610/germ theory). It is this concept of the causes of diseases that Foster (1976) refers to as 'naturalistic' or the scientific aspect of healthcare. What is being emphasised here is that, as pointed out by Ɔkomfoɔ Agyemang (personal communication, October 20, 2012), 'we know that if one fails to keep personal hygiene one can get sick out of that and also we are aware of environmentally polluted-related diseases such; Asthma, Cholera, Diarrhoea, Dysentery, Typhoid and many others. In these cases, we do not resort to magico-religious rituals when restoring health.' My interaction with some indigenous Akan medicine men and women in the area also revealed that they are even aware of what modern medicine refers to as *placebo*.[8] In addition, despite the fact that many herbs or cures for ailments are obtained from the supernatural source, they also know that the knowledge of many cures particularly herbs could be acquired through close observation of nature and practical experiences. In some instances, healing techniques or the application of certain herbs has become common knowledge due to their usage over time such that there is no need to consult a specialist when such herbs are being applied. Herbs such as '*akyeampong* weed' (*Chromolaena odorata*) for stopping excessive bleeding and the leaves of the *nim* tree *(Azadirachta Indica)* for curing fever are common knowledge among the Akan (Opoku, 1978; Awuah-Nyamekye, 2011). Opoku (1978: 154) for instance, has listed other practical means of acquiring and applying traditional medicine in Ghana.

Paradoxically, in spite of this knowledge of the Akan people, they hardly separate pure medicine from metaphysics. This confirms Idowu's (1973:201) view that '...unconsecrated medicine has no meaning for Africans.' In the words of Mbiti (1989:165), 'modern hospitals may deal with the physical side of diseases, but there is the religious dimension of suffering which they do not handle...' Merging traditional medicine with modern medicine can be termed 'integrated' approach to healing in the African traditional societies. Consequently one can argue that one cannot say for certain that a traditional medical system among the Akan and, for that matter, among other traditional societies in Ghana and probably beyond will, in the near future, completely do away with religion since their traditional understanding of illnesses and other forms of afflictions are explained in spiritual terms. It is, therefore, not a surprise that despite the widespread criticism of the practice of sending sick people to the religious centres instead of

---

[8] something prescribed for a patient that contains no medicine, but is given for the positive psychological effect it may have because the patient believes that he or she is receiving treatment, Microsoft Encarta.2007. © 1993-2006. Microsoft Corporation.

conventional medical facilities, people still keep on sending their sick relatives to the religious centres in Ghana. This has implication for health care policy-makers since it has been found out that the worldview of a people plays a fundamental role in their health matters and as such

The prospects of indigenous/traditional medicine in Ghana today

Traditional medicine is confronted with a lot of challenges. For instance, the foregoing discussion points out clearly that the indigenous religion--African Traditional Religion--of the people is the bedrock of traditional medicine, but this is a religion that has been subjected to serious attack since Christianity was introduced to Ghana as part of the colonial project. Followers of Christianity denounced (and continue to denounce) traditional African religion. African Traditional Religion is labelled as false religion and superstition. What this means is that the very foundation of traditional medicine is under serious siege. Some Churches even suspend their members for soliciting traditional medicine because traditional medicine is mostly associated with traditional priests and rituals such as libation and sacrifices that usually accompany the practice.

The introduction of scientific or orthodox medicine is another major challenge to traditional medicine. The introduction of orthodox medicine has brought about a serious competition between these two modes of restoring health in traditional Akan society and, for that matter, in traditional Ghanaian societies. Orthodox medicine seems to have gained the upper hand in this competition due to favourable support that it gets from the successive governments of Ghana (Twumasi, 1975). Twumasi (1975) reports that as far back as 1878, the then colonial government of Ghana passed a legislation in favour of orthodox medicine which led to an aggressive campaign to liquidate traditional medicine in the country. Although, there has been a shift from being aggressive to traditional medicine in the country in the recent years, for instance, successive governments have recognised the importance of traditional medicine. In 1975 for instance, the Centre for Scientific Research into Plant Medicine (CSRPM) was established. A unit under the CSRPM was set up as a follow up to coordinate traditional medicine in the country. This has metamorphosed into what is now known in Ghana today now 'Traditional and Alternative Medicine Directorate'. In 1992, the government set up the Food and Drugs Board (FDB) to certify the sale of traditional medicine products to the public. TMPC Act, Act 575 was enacted in 2000 to establish Traditional Medicine Council. This Council was tasked to register all Traditional Medical Practitioners in the country. The above moves are definitely positive but the big issue is that the traditional medical practitioners are not backed by law as it is the case for the orthodox medical practitioners. Closely connected to the above is that the traditional healers are not permitted to issue medical certificates to their clients for excuse duty to employers. The lack of the political will of successive governments of Ghana according to an experienced traditional medical practitioner (personal communication, 12 February 2013) is due to the pressure from the orthodox medical practitioners in the country who always approach traditional medicine with suspicion. This claimed appears to be true as Evans-Anfom (1986), a Western trained medical practitioner in Ghana once admitted that it is not easy for medical practitioner trained in the scientific method to treat the subject of traditional medicine entirely objectively and without bias.

One major criticism that is often levelled against traditional medicine is the way it is prepared. It is argued that the stuffs are usually prepared in an unhygienic condition. (see Evans-Anfom. 1986;Twumasi, 1975. Again, there is the problem of dosage and side effect. At times, the dosage is too much. This obviously will not appeal to buyers.

The infiltration of quack traditional medical practitioners into the practice has also been a serious challenge to traditional medicine practice in Ghana. The consequence has been that people now tend to perceive traditional medicine with scepticism. Many of my informants complained about buying fake traditional medicine from people who claimed to be traditional medicine men/ women. Most of them claimed they bought the medicine in vehicles while travelling. Fake practitioners are cashing in from unsuspecting public. This has been so because even though there is a body in

197

place to register traditional medical practitioner throughout the country, the monitoring has not been the best as admitted by Nana Kusi, an experienced Herbalist (personal communication, May 2012).

Another major factor that impedes the development of traditional medicine is the rapid destruction of the country forests by bushfire and activities of illegal timber contractors. Herbs, bark or roots of plants and parts of some animals are the key ingredients of traditional medicine but in Ghana today over 80 percent of the forest cover has been destroyed (Tamakloe, 2008). This has affected the easy access to the major ingredient of traditional medicine.

Formidable as the above challenges appear to be, it is difficult for one to say that the prospects of traditional medicine is bleak. This is because in spite of these onslaught against the use of traditional medicne, it remains popular among many Ghanaians today due to its easier accessibility and affordability especially in the rural communities (Twumasi, 1975; Domfeh, 2007; Kgoatla, 1997) Athough there are a lot of moderrn facilities for health delivery in the urban centres, a respectable number of urban dwellers still resort to traditional medicne due to high prices associated with treatments at these modern facilities.

The *sankofa* ideology[9] that is being preached throughout the conutry in some ways re-orient people's mind against neglecting their culture. Some now argue that the way forward for national development is to go back to the country's cultural heritage. One significasnt impact of the *sankofa* ideology is the recognition that traditional religion has received over the years. As of now, African Tradtional Religion is taught in most of the major theologicasl instituitions including the Trinity College, which trains pastors for Methodist, Presbyterain and the Anglican Churches in Ghana. All the major Roman Catholics Seminaries in Ghana offer courses in African Traditional Religion. The religion is taught at all levels of education including PhD in Ghana and in some Euro-American universities. What this means is that people's attitude towards the religion will/is changing in favour of African Traditional Religion.

---

[9] *Sankofa* means going back for it. That going back for the cultural heritage of Ghana but with an appraisal with the view to identifying those cultural practices that fit into current realities.

This means people's opposition to it (the religion) being associated with traditional medicne will also change accordingly.

One positive development is that today, some herbal medicines for treating various kinds of diseaeses are certified by Food and Drug Board and can found be in Pharmaceutical shops throughout the country. The certification implies that the issue of unhygienic condition perceived to be associated with traditional medicine has been dealt with. Such traditional medicines include, Malaherb, Living Bitters--for treating malaria, and creams such as Akobalm, Mercy cream, Angels cream, Messia Ontiment—for treating skin diseases of all kinds--and many others. Herbalists (another name for the traditional medical practitioner in Ghana) also sell their medications in moving vehicles all over the country. There some clinics in Ghana which deal mainly in tradtional medicines. Some of which include, Taweed, Aponkye clinic in Accra, the national capital.

The coming together of all the traditional medical practitioners under one umbrella—Ghana Fedreation of Traditional Medicine Practitioners(GHAFTRAM)--is a healthy sign for the development of tradional medicine. This means the problem of fake practitioner may be reduced and at the same time, members can now champion their concerns through one recognised body. Recently during the inaugulation of the Greater Accra Branch of the association, the Nana Kwadwo Obiri, the National Organiser of GHAFTRAM took the opportunity to appeal to the govermnent to involve their members on the education being given to health workers on the *Ebola* epidemics for according to him ' our members are usually the first point of contact when there is the outbreak of any disease' (culled from Daily Graphic, 17th October edition).

All these point to the fact that traditional medicine will be with the Akan, and Ghanaians in general for a very long time if not forever.

Conclusion

In this chapter, I have emphasised that religion permeates the entire life of the traditional Akan people and, for that matter, the phenomenon of religion may be described as an irreducible element in the way of life of the Akan. This explains the reason why religion is a key factor in Akan therapeutics practices. However, in spite of the strong influence of traditional religion on Akan medical practice, there is still room for what has become known today as the 'Germ Theory'. That is, traditional Akan therapeutics or medical culture does not only consist of personalistic but naturalistic as well, although the personalistic dimension is more prominent in this people's medical culture. The discussion has pointed out that *apotee* or *apomuden* (health or well-being) is broadly understood in traditional Akan milieu, to include the presence of good relationship between humans and the spiritual beings as well as good human-human relationship and good mental framework. It has also been pointed out that traditional medicine is confronted with many challenges but the people have not abandoned it due to practical reasons. Furthermore, the discussion has emphasised that the worldview, particularly the faith of a people plays a role in their health matters and as such, if a healthcare delivery system is to succeed in Ghana then, the worldview of the people must be taken into consideration when designing a healthcare delivery model in the country.

References

Awuah-Nyamekye, Samuel. 2012. Sasa: Its implications for flora fauna conservation in Ghana.
Nature and Culture, 7(1):1–15.
Awuah-Nyamekye, Samuel. 2012. Religion and Development: African Traditional Religion's
Perspective, *Journal Religious Studies and Theology,* 31(1):75-90.
Awuah-Nyamekye, Samuel. 2011. Religion: The Gateway to Traditional Medicine: A case Study of Berekum Traditional

Society of Ghana. *Waves An English speaking world Journal: Civilisation- Literature – Linguistic* (13): 70-79.

Awuah-Nyamekye, Samuel. 2008. Magic: Its Nature and Meaning in the Akan Society of Ghana. *Orita, Ibadan Journal of Religious Studies* XL/1 (June): 25-46.

Boahen, A. Adu. 1974. *Colloque Inter- Universitaire Ghana- Cote-D' Ivoire : Les Populations Communes De La Cote D'Ivoire Et du Ghana, Bondoukou, 4 - 9 Janvier.* pp._66-81*Daily Graphic*, 17th October edition.

Domfeh, K.A. 2007.Indigenous Knowledge Systems and the Need for Policy and Institutional Reforms. Tribes and Tribals, Special Volume No. 1:.41-52.

Field, M. .J. 1961. *Religion and Medicine of the Ga People (reprinted).* Accra: Presbyterian Book Depot.

Germ Theory. *The Encyclopaedia Britannica* http://www.britannica.com/EBchecked/topic/230610/germ-theory

Gwyneth Davies. 1994. The Medical Culture of the Ovambo of Southern Angola and Northern Namibia. PhD Diss., University of Kent at Canterbury.

Hammond-Tooke, D. 1989 *Rituals and Medicines, Indigenous Healing in South Africa.* Johannesburg: A. D. Donker:

Idowu, E. Bolaji. 1973. *African Traditional Religion: A Definition.* London: SCM Press Ltd.

Janzen, J. 1981. The Need for a Taxonomy of Health in the Study of African Therapeutics. *Social Science and Medicine* vol. 15B.

Karim .S.S.. *et al.* 1994. Bridging the gap. Potential for a health care partnership between African

traditional healer and biomedical personnel in South Africa. *South African Medical Journal.* Pinelands: MAS.

Kgoatla, P. 1997.The use of traditional medicines by teenage mothers in Soshanguve.*Health SA Gesondheid*, 2 (3): 27-31.

Makinde, M. Akin 1988. *African Philosophy, Culture, and Traditional Medicine* Ohio: Centre for International Studies Ohio University.

Mawere, M . 2011. 'Possibilities for Cultivating African Indigenous Knowledge Systems (IKSs): Lessons from Selected Cases of Witchcraft in Zimbabwe', *Journal of Gender, Peace and Development*, 1 (3): 091-100.

Mawere, M. and Kadenge,. M. 2010. *Zvierwa* as African Indigenous Knowledge System: Epistemological and Ethical Implications of Selected Shona Taboos. *INDILA Journal of Africa Indigenous Knowledge,* 9 (1): 29-44.

Morrison, E. Mark. 2007. The Politics of Medical Syncretism in the Ghanaian National Healthcare System. Thesis, McAnulty College and Graduate School of Liberal Arts Duquesne University.

Mutungi, O.K. 1977. *The Legal aspects of Witchcraft in east Africa with particular reference to Kenya,* Nairobi: East African Literature Bureau.

Opoku, Kofi Asare .1978. *West African Traditional Religion.* Accra, Bangkok, Hong Kong: FEP International Private Limited.

Osborne, Oliver. 2003. 'Health-Care Systems in Post-Colonial Africa'. The Microsoft Encarta Reference Library, 2003.

Osei, Yaw .1975. The Fundamental Basis of African Traditional Medicine, *Ethno medicine and Social Medicine in Tropical Africa,* ed. S. Paul, 35-55. Hamburg.

Parrinder, E.Geoffrey.1961. *West African Religion: A study of the Beliefs and Practices of Akan, Ewe, Yoruba, Ibo and Kindred peoples.* London: Epworth Press.

Pobee, J.S.1979.*Toward an African Theology.* Abingdon/Nasshville.

Rattray, R.S. 1923. *Ashanti.*Oxford: Oxford University Press.

Reynolds, P. 1996. *Traditional Healers and Childhood in Zimbabwe.* Ohio: Ohio University Press.

Tamakloe, William. 2008. State of Ghana's Environment-Challenges of Compliance and Enforcement, 2008. (Accessed 10 May 2013).

http://www.inece.org/indicators/proceedings/04h_ghana.pdf.

Sarpong, Peter Kwasi. 1974. *Ghana in Retrospect: Some Aspects of Ghanaian Culture.* Tema: Ghana Publishing Corporation.

Setswe, G. 1999. The role of traditional healers and primary health care in South Africa. Health SA G esondheid, 4(2):56-60.

Turner, Victor .1967. *The Forest of Symbols* .Cornell Uni. Press.

Twumasi, P.A. 1975. *Medical Systems in Ghana: A Study in Medical Sociology.* Accra: Ghana Publishing Corporation.

Twumasi, P.A. 1979. 'Ashanti Traditional Medicine and its Relation to Present-day Psychiatry', *African Therapeutic Systems,* ed. Z. A. Ademuwagun *et al* .Crossroads Press: ASA.

Vanderpool, HY,. Levin, J. S. 1990. 'Religion and Medicine: How are they Related?' *Journal of Religion and Health, 29: 9.*

Chapter 9

Indigenous Knowledge and the Management of Ecological Resources for Africa's Development

Elias Asiama

Introduction

Nations have developed to levels where we begin to realise the detrimental effects of the very development we thought would be a solution to human problems. "Washing the baby and throwing away the bath water and the baby is not a wise thing to do" so a Guan proverb goes. Before the advent of Western and American styles and forms of development, many civilizations had come and gone. The indigenous people of the African continent, the Inca of Latin America, the Ancient Oriental civilisations like: the Chinese, Indian, Indonesian, Japanese have strong evidence of alternative approaches to promoting development that is much more nature-friendly emanating from these cultures.

There is no doubt that tropical Africa has been interrupted, destabilised, and framed -up by powers that be over many centuries through atrocious practices like: colonisation, slave-trade, and other forms of exploitations. While there might have been some good purposes for such actions, there are some that were unpardonable and a shame to humanity. It is time for Africa and for the purposes of this chapter I will focus on Ghana, a classic example of a country that serves as an epitome for Africa. Africa still has a good number of her indigenous people whose total or semi transformation from Indigenous life to Modern /Western life styles is evident. The main aim of this chapter is to recover indigenous knowledge for development purposes: - i.e. promoting indigenous medicine and to document indigenous knowledge and values for posterity.

This chapter critically analyses the factors that have affected the African continent from developing its systems for particularly economic emancipation and take-off and also to encourage the youth of Africa to take interest in African values, personality and development. The recovery of the African cultural heritage for the development of the continent and the retrieval of the knowledge of useful indigenous medicine for contemporary use in Ghana and beyond constitute the major focus of the chapter.

For the continent to rise above its developmental challenges, African leaders may reconsider their development objectives to include the following:

1. Find practical ways to salvage the African continent from poverty in the midst of overabundance; e.g. Africa abounds in numerous mineral resources like gold, diamonds, oil to mention few, yet the general populace still lives in abject poverty.

2. To re-educate the African youths in converting simple ecological resources into economic wealth; e.g. most African youths are alienated from the indigenous technologies that sustained their forebears till the advent of the European. Soap making e.g. Alata samina, textile-e.g. kente and kyenkyen clothes, basketry and various metal works, traditional medicines including bone – setting etc., were all known among the various ethnic groups of Ghana (i.e. the Gold Coast) before the coming of the European, but all these have not been consciously nurtured, protected, and promoted till date hence the loss of these skills. To achieve balanced and holistic development, the recovery of indigenous knowledge becomes very important today especially in the area of finding alternative medicine, collaboration between our formal and informal education sectors might be the solution.

3. One of Africa's greatest deficits is the lack of record keeping, documentation and preservation of indigenous knowledge and values for posterity. To solve this, a massive revamp of our educational policies, methodologies and content must be consciously undertaken.

In this chapter, I will use the Buem for example to buttress the argument that indigenous people have all it takes to make life meaningful, happy and dignifying. After all what are we after on this planet? What we need is rather virtues, policies, systems and spaces that will enhance peaceful and symbiotic co-existence.

While formal education prepares us for a living, it is rather estranging that the kind of education most colonized African states inherited rather serve as a mental slavery apparatus. What this means is that, the formal education was tailored to make the colonized African state subservient to the colonial masters. Therefore for almost over four hundred years of colonial rule the Gold Coast for example had its "original will" and "focus", above all its personality affected. Whilst one may argue that colonialism and slave trade eras are long gone, and that modern African should not blame European powers anymore, the fact still remains that the harm and damage have already been done.

Counting the cost may not be necessary but knowing the causes of the burdens of the African helps to tackle the challenges. Education that does not meet the needs and expectations of a people needs to be critically analysed. It means Educationists have an onerous responsibility to fashion out both content and philosophy that prepares the African to be able to appropriate the resources available to them on the continent for the improvement of their living standard. This means exploring, developing, repackaging and managing the resources available to a people within a geographical region to meet their needs.

In the case of medicine, the African flora and fauna has a lot to offer but sadly enough the African factor has been down played rather vehemently during independent Africa eras. Rather the Western, the American, Oriental allopathic medicines are hailed and promoted over and above indigenous medicines. The solution lies rather in a methodology and an attempt by which indigenous knowledge and local resources are integrated into fighting health challenges on the continent. In Buem, as in many other African indigenous societies, plant medicine is well known but this has been suppressed. It is now time for younger generations, scholars with formal educational backgrounds to consciously spell out programmes for the recovery, documentation, preservation and conservation of the indigenous knowledge, skills, values and practices for posterity.

Apart from traditional medicine the indigenous people however have other very useful resources that have also suffered oppression and extinction. The knowledge of indigenous menus, textiles, arts and crafts are examples. Among the Northern Volta ethnic groups, brown rice and pea nut (groundnut) are cultivated and processed for local consumption. Of late this is becoming a thing of the past. This is because younger generations find the cultivation as a tedious and less paying job. Also the introduction of imported long grained but polished white rice have invaded local market thus strangulating indigenous vocations and markets. As a result of our truncated nature of education, we have misplaced our values and have taken to unbeneficial values to the extent that even the food we eat must be imported. White rice offers nothing nutritionally apart from carbohydrate and sugar which when over eaten leads to non-communicable diseases like obesity, hypertension, cholesterol, high sugar level and finally diabetes. There is the need to step up education on diet. What we have as people for example our locally produced foods like brown rice, plantain, ayoyo, yellow yams i.e. nkanfo etc. must be encouraged for consumption.

The wanton cultural rejection by our own people leaves much to be desired. In recent times our rejection of the African culture, fashion or textiles and even crafts is on the increase. African governments, stakeholders and policy makers need a massive reorientation and conscientisation on the importance of promoting self-confidence, high appreciation in what we have as a people and a consistent program for the everyday application and use of products, knowledge and values emanating from the African continent itself. Let us, through this chapter, rather consider how the African continent could pick up the pieces and stitch together the continent beyond where it has reached. The future of the continent lies much more in our ability to transform the numerous resources it possesses into tangible and intangible products.

The values, norms and ethics of the African specifically Ghana, have been totally eroded by the influx of Western cultures and the so-called civilisation. Social values like humility, respect, greeting the elderly, going on errands, saying 'please' when talking to the elderly, helping the elderly with their luggage, wearing of decent clothes inter alia have been washed away by the coming of the Europeans.

Its rippling effects are what we are seeing today as teenage pregnancy, low life expectancy rate, the theft and robbery menace (Danso, Justin, 1999).

In modern Ghanaian lifestyle, it could be observed that the Western culture have dominated our indigenous values and hence posing the challenge of total loss of identity as a people in the future and for that matter the need for conscious efforts in restoring significant indigenous Ghanaian values like our food, clothing, festivals, culture etc. The Ghanaian traditional value in present day is practically way ward as far as tradition is concerned. Africa and Ghana for that matter is known for her rich culture and tradition and this identity needs to be preserved. The act of human right is perceived to have been a major contributing factor of the adulteration of tradition to some extent thus in the instances of the belief of human sacrifice during some festival's celebration. However, this must be addressed to ensure that festivals portray the Ghanaian identity and is passed on to the younger generations for posterity in the most positive manner. Ghananians in the perspective of communication, have forgotten about their roots and oral traditions ever since the European came with their documented stuff and wrote some of our languages for us. Though quite good in keeping our cultures, notwithstanding, it has diverted the African's attention to copy blindly. We now even talk to our parents in 'jargons' and other disrespectful ways.

Before the coming of the Europeans, our oral traditions though outmoded, served as the largest repertoire of knowledge. It was through that means that we transmitted the knowledge of weaving, basketry, pottery, sculpture and other craftsmanship skills and trade. These knowledge base, made us so skilful. Today, about ninety-nine percent of us have resorted to the book-worm attitude of the west and thrown away the practical and skills that could have spelt our uniqueness and brought us prestige. It is therefore not surprising that, the whites had stolen that outstanding part of us and made it theirs. An epitome is that of the Kente which California of America claims ownership over.

African cuisine has something unique to offer. However, very little effort has been in the conscious promotion of local menus in Ghana. The best Ghanaian dishes have almost been displaced and

European and other 'exotic' menus promoted above the indigenous meals. The African philosophies are deeply rooted in their oral traditions like the drum language, proverbs, traditional stories and wise sayings that lace the palace or court language of the indigenous people. Lyrics of indigenous songs are deep and reflective of the thought patterns of the people. There is still much to be gleaned from these sources for Africa's development and stakeholders must consciously explore this asset.

The pre-colonial Africa is to be considered and the remnants of their cultural heritage carefully retrieved for posterity. The indigenous vocations of our forebears, the belief systems, the medicinal plant knowledge, the food multiplication, conservation, and preservation techniques are all to be understudied for contemporary use. Colonialism had its impact on the African and its toll has continued to affect the African till date.

List of some of the over abundant resources:
1. Land/Rich soils,
2. Rivers/water bodies,
3. Mountains,
4. Fauna – (animals) and Flora,
5. Large human populations,
6. Existence of sunlight,
7. Cultural capital: Africa's cultural diversity.

The fact that Africa abounds in these seven listed resources points to the possibility of the continent's potential of wakening up from her long sleep into an economic giant. Each African state has something of unique economic value that could be managed to make life most dignifying and worth-living.

Politically, African governments should find creative and more humanitarian approaches and methodologies to relate to each other more pro-actively. North Africa, South Africa, East and West Africa, Central Africa, should seek to collaborate, relate and shoulder each other's burdens more practically and objectively than never before. There surely is a way forward for African nations should there be the conscious deliberation on how African nations could solve their economic challenges using the very resources at their disposal.

■ *The Land factor*

Examining each country and its land and agronomical potentials for agricultural or economic gains is not only a common sense approach but also a very practical path to solving the nation's developmental problems. Tropical Africa is primarily an agro-based continent and governments of this continent would surely succeed only when appropriate ways of tapping and managing these resources are factored and fully supported to initiating a green revolution.

Taking Ghana for example, there is the challenge of poor land management and also the lack of interest on the part of the youth in getting into agriculture as their mainstay and life career. This is the greatest challenge every developing nation should consciously fight against and or find lasting solutions to. The vast uncultivated lands of this country are unimaginable and seem not to be seen as wastage and a dent on the economy and peoples of Ghana.

Apart from land, Ghana is blessed with big rivers that drain the land thus creating good conditions for irrigational canals for agricultural purposes. However, this has not been seriously considered let alone factored into our national development agenda. If the river banks are dredged and small canals dug out into the neighbouring farmlands, much could be achieved for dry season gardening. The potential is quite huge should such projects be given a trial in this country.

■ *Unexploited water transport*

Water transport is another potential we could put our big river to. This has equally not considered apart from the minimal investments made on the Volta. Other smaller rivers could be developed at the Assembly levels to facilitate water transport using canoes. The Hohoe Dayi River could be explored and experimented for networking between Hohoe and Kpandu even if not all year through, during the high peak seasons. This has never crossed the minds of local people, neither occurred to District level development promoters.

■ *Beautiful landscape*

Ghana is a country with various landscapes ranging from low lying or flat lands from along the Coastal belts to towards inland terrains that rise high to several thousands of feet above sea levels; especially along the eastern borders between Ghana and Togoland. These are regions with the highest mountain peak found in Ghana: Mt Afadzato. Others are: Dutukpene, Gemi, Kutuatu to mention a few. These are hills that could be harnessed for power generation. The Akwapem ridge, the Kwahu ridge, the Gambaga scalp, and the various inselbergs dotted in our plains are a catchy site for the promotion of Eco-tourism and other recreational and educational purposes.

■ *Under-rated forest resources*

Ghana's forest is key to the promotion of a powerful pharmaceutical industry but this has not been seriously tackled by government. The useful medicinal plants in our forest reserves could go a long way to promoting a good health facility and package for the people of Ghana and beyond. The Forestry Commission may have to critically consider this sector and consciously include a department to promote medical forestry. This will not only be an innovation, but a positive boost to forest management, resource development, and higher consciousness in forest conservation. Private individuals should be educated on the medicinal /pharmaceutical benefits of plants and be encouraged to create: lungs and banks of medicinal plants in every district assembly for posterity.

■ *The Fauna and flora reserves*

A conscious protection of the various animals, rodents, reptiles, birds, ants, insects etc. found in specific ecological zones are powerful resources that must be encouraged. These are aspects that our Game and Wildlife Institutions may have to step up and win many of our future generations to their side. "Ecology- and by ecology I understand the study of the reciprocal relations of all forms of life, one with the other, and with their environments- is not for the scientific agriculturalist alone; its light must guide the path of the farmer ,administrator, and the statesman" (Dr. Kwame

Nkrumah, 1959). The flora we have on the African continent alone is a huge resource we have under-rated till date.

African governments should consciously undertake serious projects to promote the creation of 'zoological banks' where various animals and birds are raised in greater numbers for both economic and aesthetic purposes. African nations have a great asset yet to be tapped. The intensification of the breeding of wildlife for export, local markets, and for aesthetic investments purposes might be a way out for African economies. National parks, gardens, and consciously created recreational spaces are not only for beautification objectives, but could also contribute income generation in Africa. A second thought may have to be given to these forms of investments by national governments on the African soil because that is what we have relative advantage on.

■ *The large human populace*

Africa has a large human populace. This is not necessarily a burden or challenge as some allude. The large populations should rather be trained to serve as qualified work force, human force for various sectors of our economy. Primarily, the large African populace could be a force to reckon with for Agricultural purposes. Households could be transformed into powerful cooperatives and labour force for the realization of economic and financial stability. The numerous crises, strife and war that are prevalent on the continent could be eradicated if the people are taught to realize the significance and benefits of recognising each other and fostering productivity together.

The African tropical forest is in fact never to be under-rated as a major source of foreign income generation. The main challenge is the constructive management of the natural resources. The depletion of our natural resources is rather at an alarming and frightening rate in recent times. This calls for a concerted effort to stem up the conservation and protection of these wonderful resources. Conscious nurseries for Africa's most endangered tree species should be put in place to mitigate the over exploitation of the natural resources and its consequential negative impact on human life. The awareness -creation on such interventions are indispensable for the future of the continent.

■ *The abundance of the tropical sunlight*

The phototropic benefits of the sunlight in Africa reflect its rich vegetation ranging from: the tropical rain-forest, deciduous forest, savannah, derived savannah, Sahel vegetation and finally the Sahara desert.

Before the advent of the white man to the West African shores, the West African people had their own ways of living. They had the sense of political leadership and their political order still evidenced in their kingship and chieftains that have survived to date. Furthermore, they had valued systematic ways of passing on knowledge and information to their younger generations and amongst themselves. They had their philosophies and belief systems that sustained them.

Ghana like many other African countries is endowed with very rich culture and tradition. The traditional culture of Ghana stressed a strong relationship with the environment, and in the past, a culturally acceptable environmental management resulted from strictures and taboos related to water bodies, land, and deep forest. Though there are some cultural practices that are peculiar to some towns and villages, in general they have so many things in common and served the same important purpose of conserving nature. This, to a large extent helped saved the environment and our ancestors rarely died of pollution related ailments. With the advent of Christianity, Islam, civilization and its accompanying technology in Ghana, however, many of these beliefs, taboos, customs and traditions have been relegated to the background and are regarded by many as fetish and useless, though they played a key role in environmental protection.

Among the Akan community which forms the majority ethnic group in Ghana, water bodies are associated with the gods or abosom and are used in accordance with strictures and rules that are relayed to the local folks by fetish priests who are the mouthpiece of the gods. Customary laws mandate users to keep lakes and rivers pure because they are regard as the dwelling place of the gods (abosom). The abosom were highly revered and feared in the past and even they are still accorded that respect by some Ghanaians. It is believed that, these gods are highly endowed with divine powers and will strike defaulters dead instantly with no mercy or give a second chance.

In the past, our ancestors used a very astute way to protect the water bodies and avoided many water related diseases. Those part of the river used for bathing, swimming, or for watering crops and washing domestic animals were found downstream in relation to those used as a sources of drinking water. In an effort to minimize water pollution from household waste and to reduce the quick spread of water-borne diseases, communities were often situated more than half a mile radius from rivers and lakes. Since the distance makes the drawing of drinking water a heinous task, water conservation was a common tradition. People feared the gods and hence adhered strictly to these directives and preserved the water bodies better than what pertains in contemporary Ghana. Apart from the general regulations, there are specific prohibitions or taboos to prevent the use of metal implement in lakes and rivers, to ban fishing at specific times of the year, and to disallow laundering of clothes on certain days. In addition to taboos, special communal labours were organized for the clearing of weeds and debris along river banks and for deepening sources of drinking water.

These customary regulations worked very well in the olden days and are still common in the countryside. However, it tends to break down where population mobility has led to coexistence of groups with varying customs. Difficulties arise also where previously small communities grow into one another, bringing together groups of different religious beliefs, and where towns have sprung up along certain parts of the river. In order to mitigate these drawbacks, there is the need for us as a country to device more pragmatic policies that will integrate our traditions and customs that promotes environmental sustainability with that of modern Ghanaian beliefs to achieve the ultimate goal.

In the past, the deep forests were also regarded as a place of abode of the gods and the dead ancestors. Such places were highly revered and worshiped. Farming, hunting, felling of trees for fire wood and many other activities were forbidden in those forests. It was a taboo for anyone to fell trees or farm in such restricted forests. This indisputably helped preserved the forest vegetation and biodiversity which our current generation is destroying now.

Our forefathers were very conscious and protected our natural resources in what one may described as unscientific, but in effect, we inherited rich forest which was stocked with great medicinal sources and precious minerals. If our ancestors who did not know anything about schooling and technology were able to conserve the environment in such a laudable fashion, what are we doing as contemporary generation with formal education and technological advancement? I believe the time to combine technology and tradition to save our perishing natural resources is now.

Among almost all the ethnic groups along the coast of Ghana, it is forbidden to go fishing on Tuesday. The sea is believed to be a goddess and worshiped by these communities. It is believed that, Tuesdays are days which the goddess has time with her children which were mostly fishes. In order not to disturb the goddess and her children it was a great taboo for anyone to go fishing that very day. Though this may sound unscientific, many who disobeyed these directives and went on fishing on those days were drowned and had no help from anyone. It was also forbidden to go fishing at certain periods of the year among many of the fishing communities. From the scientific point of view these free period enhanced fish reproduction and also protected fingerlings from being caught. It was also forbidden to eat certain type of fish, even if they were caught by the fishermen they were freed because they were regarded as beloved children of the goddess.

Current scientific investigation has shown that such fishes have low productivity rate and immense harvesting may cause their extinction. Our ancestors had no scientific knowledge when they passed some of these rules, yet they were able to preserve the lives of these vulnerable fishes.

Ethnic groups that are located in the forest zones of Ghana forbid hunting and farming in the forest on some days and some periods of the year. It is also a taboo for a hunter to kill an animal and refuse to eat. It is even a worse offence for a farmer or hunter to kill game that is young, pregnant or fending for their young ones. It is believed that Asase Yaa, goddess of the earth will punish the defaulter. It was also believed that such a person might also not have children or lose his children if he kills a pregnant or young game. The reverence given to some of these traditional believes is

216

gradually loosing grounds in Ghana with the advent of foreign religion and formal education. This has led to the extinction of many animals and endangering of so many others.

I believe that there is the need to revisit the past and integrate the good parts of our traditions and customs with modern ones and to safeguard Ghana's natural recourses and promote environmental sustainability. There is an African proverb that says that 'a man who does not know where he is coming from does not know where he is going to'. (Acheampong E.K Nov, 2010).

It could be said that Africa as a whole was evolving its own civilization up until the Western Cultures intruded and destabilized these. This chapter seeks to examine some of the factors that have affected the African continent and her development in general, using Ghana's (Gold Coast) experience as a case study. The people of Ghana practiced or had the following before the advent of the white-man on the African soil. However, these very indispensable fabrics of the African were those that were targeted if not negatively attacked and affected.

While there might have been some good purposes for such actions, there are some that were unpardonable and a shame to humanity. Let us through this chapter rather consider how the African continent could pick up the pieces left and stitch together for the benefit of the continent and beyond where it has reached.

Pre-colonial Gold Coast (4th BC – 1471 AD)

The Gold Coast was populated by several ethnic groups that co-existed within the West African sub-region. There were indigenous boundaries, indigenous political systems, indigenous religious practices, indigenous forms of educating the individual, indigenous Agricultural practices, indigenous medicines, indigenous industries, indigenous Architecture, indigenous menus, and indigenous arts, textiles and astrology, to mention a few.

Colonial Ghana (The Gold Coast) (1471-1957) 496 years

The physical edifices like the castles, forts and fortresses dotted along the shores of present day Ghana serve as evidence for the European presence and dominance on the coastlines of the then Gold Coast.

217

Taking a close look at the roughly (400) four hundred kilometres coastline stretching from Cape Three Points through to Keta reveals the number of castles that represent the various European nations that tried to colonize the Gold Coast.

Colonialization had various influences on the country. The worse form of the influence is what Slave trade brought to humanity. The atrocious business persisted on over many centuries between the Americas, Europe and many parts of the world. The Colonial eras were laced or followed up by an active Missionary enterprise that saw the Roman Catholic, Anglican, Presbyterian, Methodist, Zion Churches seriously evangelizing along the Coastlines of (Ghana) and later into the hinterland areas of the Gold Coast.

It is obvious that Western Education has had some impact on the African. This could be said to either be positive or negative impact. In this chapter some concrete examples will be spelt out to support various stance of the author.

Partition or Demarcation of Africa

The demarcation of the African land has been very beneficial to Africans. Due to the boundaries we now have more definite boundaries at the regional, national and local levels thus preventing possible conflicts. Adversely, ethnic groups have been separated by this act causing discomfort in our boarder communities. This is witnessed in the numerous unrest along the West African neighbouring cities. Examples are Cameroon-Nigeria, Ghana-Cote D'ivoire, Ghana-Togo.

Colonial Impact on Education

Educationally, the white colonial masters gave us formal education which has helped us to document some of our historical events, traditions and customs. We are now literates which has helped us to also develop our own local languages into writing. An example is that the Bible has now been translated into some local languages like Twi, Ewe, Dabgani and others.

Although these have benefited us greatly, it has also made us lose some of our cultural values, language and morals. Most Ghanaians for instance consider English Language as superior to our local languages. Some parents force their children to speak English instead their mother tongues at home. Also, Western lifestyles or ways of doing things have now been adopted by some Ghanaians to the neglect of our local languages and culture, thus creating a cultural alienation.

Colonial Impact On Health

The European contact with Africa and Ghana in particular brought about the establishment hospitals and clinics. They also trained African personnel to take care of the health needs of the individuals. Also certain equipment such as the x-ray machine were introduced thus helping to better the health delivery services.

In as much as these equipment like: the x-ray, scanning machines are concerned, they have helped us, however, they also cause certain side effects as a result of the radiation. However, these modern approaches have weakened participation in traditional ways of healing by use of our herbal medicines. These are now regarded as barbaric and outmoded. People such as herbalist have no much recognition in the society. The Western medicine also comes along with various side effects because they are chemically prepared. It is hoped that people will be able to decide for themselves as to whether to patronise Western or indigenous medicine or combine.

Western Technological Advancement

The introduction of advanced technologies from the West have also made living comfortable to some extent for Ghanaians. Mobile phone has made information to be transmitted easily within the shortest minute. Aeroplanes, cars, ships and others have made travelling and life easier for the Ghanaian.

Aside that, there is also the tendency of misappropriating technologies. There are those who abuse the privacy of others, internet fraud, people are framed up, cloned and wrong pieces of information are sent to people. Again certain classified information (secrets) that are not supposed to be released easily before a formal disclosure are laid across through the mobile. Internet or electronic technology in the communication has also caused a degree academic dishonesty- i.e. some students make use of these but would not acknowledge the sources.

Modern technology has its bad effects on the climate, climate change and its concomitant underpinnings. The effects of the fumes of cars and other machines cannot be ruled out from the negative. The Missionaries and the Ghanaian values/culture: The Missionary Churches introduced formal education thus establishing schools, hospitals and other trade/vocational institutions across the length and breadth of the then Gold Coast. The question is: Has the coming of the European to Africa south of the Sahara been a blessing or curse? I argue in view of this question that the future of the continent lies much more in our ability to transform the numerous resources it possesses into tangible and intangible products. Cultural heritage is the legacy of physical artefacts and intangible attributes of a group or society that are inherited from past generations, maintained in the present and bestowed for the benefit of future generations. Cultural heritage includes tangible culture (such as buildings, monuments, landscapes, books, works of art, and artefacts), intangible culture (such as folklore, traditions, language, and knowledge), and natural heritage (including culturally significant landscapes, and biodiversity).

The deliberate act of keeping cultural heritage from the present for the future is known as preservation (American English) or conservation (British English), though these terms may have more specific or technical meaning in the same contexts in the other dialect. Cultural heritage is unique, irreplaceable and beautiful which places the responsibility of preservation on the current generation. Smaller objects such as artworks and other cultural masterpieces are collected in museums and art galleries (Bell 1979). Grass roots organizations and political groups, such as the international body UNESCO, have been successful at gaining the necessary support to preserve the heritage of many nations for the future generations to cherish.

Traditional knowledge (TK), indigenous knowledge (IK), traditional ecological knowledge (TEK) and local knowledge generally refer to knowledge systems embedded in the cultural traditions of regional, indigenous, or local communities. Traditional knowledge includes types of knowledge about traditional technologies of subsistence (e.g. tools and techniques for hunting or agriculture), midwifery, ethno botany and ecological knowledge, celestial navigation, ethno-astronomy, the climate etc. (Morin-Labatut and Akhtar, 1992). These kinds of knowledge are crucial for the subsistence and survival and are generally based on accumulations of empirical observation and interaction with the environment. Indigenous knowledge (IK) is the local knowledge – knowledge that is unique to a given culture or society. IK contrasts with the international knowledge system generated by universities, research institutions and private firms. It is the basis for local-level decision making in agriculture, health care, food preparation, education, natural-resource management, and a host of other activities in rural communities (Warren 1991).

In many cases, traditional knowledge has been orally passed for generations from person to person. Some forms of traditional knowledge are expressed through stories, legends, folklore, rituals, songs, and even laws. Other forms of traditional knowledge are expressed through different means. Indigenous knowledge has been defined as a cumulative body of knowledge, know-how, practices and representations maintained and developed by peoples with extended histories of interaction with the natural environment. These sophisticated sets of understandings, interpretations and meanings are part and parcel of a cultural complex that encompasses language, naming and classification systems, resource use practices, ritual, spirituality and worldview (See Waren 1991).

According to Grenier (1998), traditional knowledge typically distinguishes one community from another. For some communities, traditional knowledge takes on a personal and spiritual meaning. Traditional knowledge can also reflect a community's interests. Some communities depend on their traditional knowledge for survival. This is particularly true of traditional environmental knowledge, which refers to a particular form of place-based knowledge of the diversity and interactions among plant and animal species, landforms, watercourses, and other qualities of the biophysical environment in a given place (Grenier 1998). An example of a society with a wealth of TEK is the South American Kayapo people, who have developed an extensive classification system of ecological zones of the Amazonian tropical savannah (i.e., campo / cerrado) to better manage the land.

Some social scientists conceptualise knowledge within a naturalistic framework, and emphasize the graduation of recent knowledge into knowledge acquired over many generations. These accounts use terms like "adaptively acquired knowledge", "socially constructed knowledge", and other terms that emphasise the social aspects of knowledge (Tabor and Hutchinson 1994). Local knowledge and traditional knowledge may be thought of as distinguished by the length of time they have existed – decades to centuries versus millennia. A large number of scholarly studies in the naturalistic tradition demonstrate that traditional knowledge is not a natural category, and may reflect power struggles and relationships for land, resources and social control rather than adherence to a claimed ancestry or heritage.

Traditional knowledge, on the other hand, may be perceived very differently by indigenous and local communities themselves. The knowledge of indigenous and local communities is often embedded in a cosmology, and the distinction between "intangible" knowledge and physical things is often blurred. Indigenous peoples often say that "our knowledge is holistic, and cannot be separated from our lands and resources". Traditional knowledge in these cosmologies is inextricably bound to ancestors, and ancestral lands. Knowledge may not be acquired by naturalistic trial and error, but through direct revelation through conversations with "the creator", spirits, or ancestors. As Chamberlin (2003) writes of a Gitxsan elder from British Columbia confronted by a government land claim: "If this is your land", he asked, "where are your stories?"

Indigenous and local communities often do not have strong traditions of ownership over knowledge that resembles the modern forms of private ownership. Many have clear traditions of custodianship over knowledge, and customary law may guide who may use different kinds of knowledge at particular times and places, and obligations that accompany the use of knowledge. From their perspective, misappropriation and misuse of knowledge may be offensive to traditions, and may have spiritual and physical repercussions in their cosmological systems. Subsequently, indigenous and local communities argue that others' use of their traditional knowledge warrants respect and sensitivity. Critics of 'traditional knowledge', however, maintain that such demands for 'respect' are really an attempt to prevent unsubstantiated beliefs from being subjected to the same scrutiny as other knowledge claims. This has particular significance for environmental management because the spiritual component of 'traditional knowledge' can be used to justify any activity, including the unsustainable harvesting of resources.

The potency of indigenous knowledge

In the emerging global knowledge economy a country's ability to build and mobilise knowledge capital, is equally essential for sustainable development as the availability of physical and financial capital. (World Bank 1997) The basic component of any country's knowledge system is its indigenous knowledge. It encompasses the skills, experiences and insights of people, applied to maintain or improve their livelihood.

Significant contributions to global knowledge have originated from indigenous people, for instance in medicine and veterinary medicine with their intimate understanding of their environments. Indigenous knowledge is developed and adapted continuously to gradually changing environments and passed down from generation to generation and closely interwoven with people's cultural values. Indigenous knowledge is also the social capital of the poor, their main asset to invest in the struggle for survival, to produce food, to provide for shelter or to achieve control of their own lives. Medicinal properties of the neem tree (*Azadirachta indica*), which, among others, is researching traditional pastoralists as guardians of biological diversity.

Today, many indigenous knowledge systems are at risk of becoming extinct because of rapidly changing natural environments and fast pacing economic, political, and cultural changes on a global scale (Ellen and Harris 1996). Practices vanish, as they become inappropriate for new challenges or because they adapt too slowly. However, many practices disappear only because of the intrusion of foreign technologies or development concepts that promise short-term gains or solutions to problems without being capable of sustaining them. The tragedy of the impending disappearance of indigenous knowledge is most obvious to those who have developed it and make a living through it. But the implication for others can be detrimental as well, when skills, technologies, artefacts, problem solving strategies and expertise are lost.

Indigenous knowledge is part of the lives of the rural poor; their livelihood depends almost entirely on specific skills and knowledge essential for their survival. Yet, it is not yet fully utilised in the development process. In Africa, Ghana to be precise, conventional approaches imply that development processes always require technology transfers from locations that are perceived as more advanced.

Higher yielding sorghum varieties were introduced in Ethiopia to increase food security and income for farmers and rural communities. When weather and other conditions were favourable, the modern varieties proved a success. However, in some areas complete crop failures were observed, whereas local varieties, with a higher variance of traits, were less susceptible to the frequent droughts. The loss of an entire crop was considered by the farming community as more than offset by the lower, average yields of the local variety that performed also under more extreme conditions. An approach, that had included the local experience of farmers, might have resulted in a balanced mix of local and introduced varieties, to reduce the risk for the producers.

Introduced varieties and commercially marketed seeds are replacing local varieties – along with them, the concomitant local knowledge disappears. For many years, the international community is establishing – with considerable effort – gene banks to preserve the genetic information of local varieties or indigenous species. However, the seeds and clones do not carry the instructions how to grow them. This knowledge needs to be captured, preserved and transferred as well. Indigenous knowledge is relevant on three levels for the development process:

■ It is, obviously, most important for the local community in which the bearers of such knowledge live and produce.

■ Development agents (CBOs, NGOs, governments, donors, local leaders, and private sector initiatives) need to recognize it, value it and appreciate it in their interaction with the local communities. Before incorporating it in their approaches, they need to understand it – and critically validate it against the usefulness for their intended objectives.

■ Lastly, indigenous knowledge forms part of the global knowledge. In this context, it has a value and relevance in itself. Indigenous knowledge can be preserved, transferred, or adopted and adapted elsewhere.

The development process interacts with indigenous knowledge. When designing or implementing development programs or projects, three scenarios can be observed: The development strategy either relies entirely or substantially on indigenous knowledge, overrides indigenous knowledge or, incorporates indigenous knowledge. Planners and implementers need to decide which path to follow. Rational conclusions are based on determining whether indigenous knowledge would contribute to solve existing problems and achieving the intended objectives. In most cases, a careful amalgamation of indigenous and foreign knowledge would be most promising, leaving the choice, the rate and the degree of adoption and adaptation to the clients. Foreign knowledge does not necessarily mean modern technology, it includes also indigenous practices developed and applied under similar conditions elsewhere. These techniques are then likely to be adopted faster and applied more successfully. To foster such a transfer a sound understanding of indigenous knowledge is needed. This requires means for the capture and validation, as well as for the eventual exchange, transfer and dissemination of indigenous knowledge.

Findings, suggestions and recommendations

In 21st century, Ghana's indigenous knowledge is being abandoned in the name of modernity. Old ways of doing things are now being neglected in favour of the so called "modernity", most school curricula have now stopped teaching indigenous knowledge and have now embraced Westernised ways of doing things which should not be so. It is easy for one to say that our youth are now being less African each passing year because of the impact of Westernization. There is a saying that: 'old things are gold', when Ghanaian indigenous knowledge is consciously integrated into modern ways of doing things it will go a long way in the development of our country than what is happening now in Ghana. Medicinal plants abound in Ghana and so are also a relatively good percentage of the populace knowledgeable of how these plants could be processed in medicines for the treatment of various diseases. However, it is also becoming clear that many are not interested in the medicines produced by local expertise.

From my study, one realizes that indigenous knowledge and practices offer fertile grounds for new processes, products, and perspectives. To totally cut away from indigenous values, practices and avoiding their critical examination for the benefit of posterity only opens the door to self-destruction and loss of national orientation, identity and direction. There is the need for efforts, structures, systems, policies and expertise to be put in place to ensure the passing on of skills, knowledge, and experience to younger generations if Ghana must see any true development.

Attractive packages to draw a large following of the youth into Agriculture should be thought of and carried out. The direct benefits of farming (i.e. Agriculture) should be made open to the younger generations of Africa in order to encourage them take farming seriously as a profession and life-long career. Certain concrete evidence made known to the youth will definitely convince them to enter into farming as their mainstay. If for example the younger generation gets to know that a hectare of cocoa plantation can pay him or her better than locking oneself up in the banking business where one is made front-desk personnel.

From my study, it is clear that Africa has all it takes to rise into a great continent and also to eradicate poverty, disease, and war. The challenge is how to educate, conscientise, and make the African aware of the potentials they have as a people, and also to assist them improve upon their confidence levels.

Another challenge that needs to be overcome is that of appreciating what one has. Africans have more than enough but still remain unappreciative of what they have and go cap in hand begging for assistance even where they could have been the donors. The younger generations are to learn to be appreciative of what we have as Africans. The African cultures, languages, menus, clothing etc. are to be promoted. The documentation of the cultural heritage and resources found across Africa for posterity may have to be undertaken without delay.

Conclusion

To conclude, this chapter has laid bare some thorny but very indispensable facts about what Africa needs to do in order to remain truly African yet Global in thinking and in attitude. It is clearly argued that Africa's resources are more than enough to help salvage its economy and improve the living standards of its populace. The health and welfare needs of Africa are all in reality available on the continent. The pharmaceutical and nutritional needs of the continent are equally also available on the continent. To process and translate our resources into products or tangible materials for the benefit of the general populace is what needs to be tackled.

References

Acheampong, E.K. 2010. *The Role of Ghanaian Culture and Tradition in Environmental Sustainability*, Heinemann.

Bell, M. 1979. The exploitation of indigenous knowledge or the indigenous exploitation of knowledge. Whose use of what foe what? *Institute of Development Studies, 10(2): 44-50.*

Ellen, R. and Harris, H. 1996. *Concepts of indigenous environmental knowledge in scientific and development studies literature – A critical assessment,* Draft paper East-West Environmental Linkages Network Workshop 3, Canterbury.

Elias Kwaku Asiama, 2003. *Buem Oral History and Cultural Practices, Multi-Media Central Café, University of Ghana Legon.*

Elias Kwaku Asiama, 2010. *Re-Inventing Tradition – Buem as Study, School of Communication Studies.*

Grenier, L. 1998. *Working with Indigenous Knowledge – A Guide for Researchers,* IDRC, Ottawa.

Danquah, J. B. 1968. *The Akan Doctrine of God,* Frank Cass & Co. LTD Thomas Nelson (Printers) LTD., London.

John Mbiti, 1969. *African Religion and Philosophy,* (2nd edition) Heinemann, London.

Kofi Asare Opoku, 1978. *West Africa Tradition Religion,* FEP International Private Limited.

Larson, J. 1998. *Perspectives on indigenous knowledge systems in South Africa,* Washington D.C World Bank Discussion paper No.3.

Mathias, E. 1995. Framework for enhancing the use of indigenous knowledge, *Indigenous Knowledge Monitor Vol. 3, (2)* August, 1995.

Mundy, P. and L. Comton. 1991. Indigenous Communication and Indigenous Knowledge, *Development Communication Report 74 (3): 1-3.*

Rajasekaran, B. and D. M. Warren, 1990. *The Role of Indigenous Knowledge System in Drought Relief Activities,* Report: Drought Disaster Workshop, United States Agency for International Development, USAID, Washington.

Tabor, J. A., Hutchinson, C.F. 1994. Using Indigenous Knowledge, Remote Sensing and GIS for Sustainable Development, *Indigenous Knowledge Monitor Vol. 2, (1) April 1994*

Warren, D. M. 1991. *The Role of Indigenous Knowledge in Facilitating the Agricultural Extension Process,* Paper presented at International Workshop on Agricultural Knowledge system and the Role of Extension. Bad Boll, Germany, May 21-24.

World Bank, 1997. Knowledge and Skills for the Information Age, The First Meeting of the Mediterranean Development Forum; Mediterranean Development Forum, URL:http://www.worldbank.org/html/fpd/technet/mdf/obje ctiv.htm.

Chapter 10

The Role of Indigenous Shona Cultural Beliefs and Practices in the Conservation of the Environment

Liveson Tatira

No matter how advanced *technologically people may seem to be, they cannot reproduce nature. Plants, animals and water all of which man depend on cannot be artificially reproduced on purely technological basis (Agazzi 1994).*

Introduction

This chapter focuses on the role of indigenous Shona cultural beliefs and practices in conserving the environment. It explores and investigates the importance of such beliefs and practices in conserving the environment. The chapter argues that the Shona beliefs and practices help to enforce environmentally friendly behaviour. It is through the beliefs and practices that the Shona people are discouraged from destroying their environment. There are a wide range of taboos, among other things, which are meant to conserve trees, animals, both domestic and wild, land, bodies of water and birds, to mention but just a few.

In view of the above, this chapter addresses itself to the role of indigenous Shona cultural beliefs and practices in the conservation of the environment. Indigenous knowledge is pivotal to sustainable resource use and development contrary to the view that considers it as primitive and an obstacle to development. The same view is supported by many scholars, among them, Awuah-Nyamekye (2012); Awuah-Nyamekye (2014); Mawere (2014b); Gyekye (1996); Hadebe (1998); Hapenyengwi – Chemhuru (1998) and Tatira (2000). It is believed that issues expressed here are true to most if not all African societies. The chapter advances the argument that the conservation of the environment becomes effective because it is not human-policed but is perceived to be supernaturally enforced. Among the Shona people, supernatural enforcement becomes a way of life rather than a mere human externally cohesive force.

The environmental problems

The environmental problems have engaged the attention of people such as philosophers, clergymen, humanists, politicians, and scientists. There is no other time humanity has felt threatened by the environmental problems than in the recent years. People all over the World are crying over the imminent destruction of the ozone layer. The ozone layer has been greatly affected by the atmospheric pollution. Back in Africa, there are threats of the ever encroaching deserts, the wanton destruction of forests, droughts, siltation, and ever widening gullies. The present environmental problems demand that African people should revisit and reassess their engagement with their physical environment. It is high time that Africans reengaged their beliefs, and cultural practices, especially, those that have something to do with the conservation of the physical environment.

This chapter puts special emphasis on the beliefs of Africans, Shona people in particular, not because the Shona people are the only human group with such beliefs, but because the writer has direct experience, since he belongs to the Shona ethnic group. The Shona people had certain beliefs and practices which ensured the conservation of their environment. This relates with Johnson (1992) and Menzies (2006) who argue that indigenous environmental knowledge includes close observations about the surrounding environment, and a system of self-management that govern resource use. Through such observation about the environment, the Shona people developed their indigenous knowledge, which is capsuled in their cultural beliefs.

The Shona indigenous environmental knowledge refers to the knowledge on how to conserve environment that the Shona people inherited from past generations. Such knowledge is transmitted through oral means, mostly in concrete terms rather than in written and abstract means. Taboos play a central role in prohibiting certain behaviour towards the environment (Tatira 2000; Mawere and

Kadenge 2010; Awuah-Nyamekye 2014). This mode of transmission ensures that every member of the society becomes an active participant in conserving the environment because of its clarity as each prohibition spells clearly the consequence that follows if an individual transgresses. Before we get into the details of the indigenous environmental knowledge, it is pertinent at this point to give the definition of environment and culture. Environment can be interpreted in two senses as it can refer in one sense to the total physical surroundings or in another sense to include social, which is non-physical, condition. Therefore, the concept of environment can be concrete as well as abstract. When we refer to the abstract environment, we are referring to the non-physical environment such as the political, social or economic environment. In this chapter we will only be concerned with the concrete concept, which includes the physical environment such as trees, land, mountains and bodies of water to mention a few.

In order to meaningfully discuss the environment, we should take cognizance that culture has a profound bearing on the environment. Generally, culture refers to the people's way of life. It is a sum total of people's beliefs and practices. The beliefs and practices influence people's behaviour towards their environment.

Bude (1991) observes that culture and environment cannot be separated. He sees the two as influencing each other. His argument is that culture is normally part of environment whereas the environment of a given society might be a product of that society's culture. The Shona culture as will be discussed, shortly, is environmentally conservative. The Shona culture as shall be discussed has an in-built mechanism that discourages the destruction of the environment. It is legitimate to argue that most of the present environmental problems are not Shona, neither are they African, by design but European. We say so because the Shona since time immemorial have always taken the environment as sacred (Tatira, 2000). Nyamekye (2012) has observed the same phenomenon among the Akan of Ghana. It should also be noted that the present storm of animal rights and proposition of land ethics and even arguments by Christopher Stove that trees should stand, (De George 1994) were all inherent in Shona culture.

The Western concept of the environment

Kant, a western philosopher, believed that animals and indeed the rest of creation exist for man. The attitude is in line with the Western conception of nature. The Western concept of nature is that it is there for humans to interrogate, subdue, dominate and manipulate (De George 1994; Mawere 2005). This means that man should subdue the vicious wild animals, the hostile weather, and the bad climatic conditions. The whole physical and air space should be under the control of man and should be used for his benefit. Aristotle, the ancient philosopher quoted in Oruka by Hapanyengwi-Chemhuru (1998:37) aptly summarises the Western concept of the environment as follows:

> Plants exist [for the sake of animals while] animals [exist] for the sake of man, the game for use as food, the wild, if not all, at least the greater part of them, for food and for the provision of cloth and various instruments. Now if nature makes nothing incomplete, and nothing in vain, the inference must be that she has made all animals for the sake of man.

This concept of environment may obviously lead to exploitative non-responsibility or rather irresponsibility stance towards the environment. The Western view of natural environment is exploitative in nature and by intention. The physical environment, which includes water, trees, land, mountains and other natural resources, are viewed with irreverence. Natural resources are normally plundered for capital gains.

Mountains are precious if they have granite boulders, which can be crushed into quarry stones. Quarry stones and quarry dust are sold to various urban centres while behind, the environment suffers. If such mountains are spared from the cruelty of the grinding machines, they will not escape the camera of the commercial photographer. The photographs will normally be sold in curio shops both at home and abroad. This proves to the fact that the Western conception of nature is purely monetary oriented and nothing else. Chiwome (2000:68) on a related but different note, commenting on the concept of commercialisation notes:

232

Demaland has since been mapped and added to the list of sources of 'pure adventure' that Zimbabwe offers to tourists. It joins other expropriated areas like Matopo National Park. Zambezi Valley, Victoria Falls, Nyanga and Hwange National Parks…Tourists agencies have played a significant role in commoditising historical and cultural knowledge.

According to the Western view of life, trees are valuable if they can be fashioned into furniture or if they meet other uses demanded by the ever-expanding industry. Many overloaded lorries are a common sight in Zimbabwe highways. They move slowly destroying behind the tarmac as well as polluting the environment with columns of dark smoke they emit as they almost grind to a halt under the burden of heavy loads. All such lorries head to "centres of development". The so-called development, which in real sense, is counter-development because it accounts for the permanent destruction of the environment.

Land is valued for its mineral content or for its crop production capacity, while water is harnessed as a commodity to be chemically treated and sold at a profit to urbanites or used to irrigate cash crops. Natural resources as explained above are viewed in terms of economic gains. It, therefore, means that as long as such natural resources can be turned into liquid cash, the environment would continue to suffer at the hands of exploiters who would want to sustain their coffers.

African concept of the environment: A focus on the indigenous Shona of Zimbabwe

While the Westerners treat the environment as a phenomenon meant to serve and satisfy the needs of the people, the traditional Africans and in particular the Shona people view the natural environment with reverence. The indigenous Shona cultural beliefs hold that the natural environment and men are in co-existence. Between nature and man there is no master of the other and natural resources are revered. Man sees himself as a steward. He keeps the environment on behalf of the ancestors. The ancestors are the owners of the natural environment and are believed to guard the environment jealously against those who want to destroy it. The belief, among the Shona, that they have inherited the natural environment from their ancestors and that they are expected to keep it in good shape leads the Shona to desist from the exploitative attitude towards nature.

To a traditional Shona person, land and implicitly all nature, deserves reverence and that nature has intrinsic value. Land should not be tempered with lest one angers the departed (ancestral spirits), who are the guardians of land (Bourdillon, 1976). The ancestors' post-human home is the land, on which they are buried. This land should be protected from exploitation. Land is important in the Shona culture because it is land which gives identity and humanity to an individual. It is land, which unites the living and the dead. The union between man and land is evidenced by the practice where traditionally a Shona newly born baby has his/her umbilical cord buried in the soil. The practice symbolically unites and introduces the living baby to the departed ancestors. Therefore, from birth, the Shona child has a cultural bond with the land and it is the same land upon which one is buried when one completes one's journey on earth. The same land sustains most of the Shona people through production of staple crops like maize, finger millet and sorghum. Therefore, land is an important resource to the Shona people.

Some people might argue that production of food on land is a potentially destructive activity but a closer look at how the Shona produce food might help to avoid such arguments. The Shona people practice mixed crop farming whereby different crops are grown on the same piece of land. It is a common practice among the Shona people to grow leafy legumes among the maize (Kunnie, 2000). The practice among other things helps to cover the bare surface from direct raindrops thus minimising soil erosion. The Shona people who farm on sloppy landscape make terraces to prevent soil erosion (Mapara 2009; Mawere 2014a).

From my experience as a Shona person, I have observed the other cultural practice that makes the Shona people revere land. This is witnessed when they rejoice after spilling something on the ground. The loss becomes an occasion to celebrate since the Shona say *zvadyiwa nevadzimu* (It has been drunk by ancestral spirits). From

234

this belief, *vadzimu* (ancestral spirits) are all over, under the ground, not only restricted in their graves, so land and indeed the whole environment should not be tempered with lest one provokes the *vadzimu* (ancestral spirits). In the rural areas, no one has title to land, the chief is the custodian of the land. He keeps the land on behalf of the *vadzimu* (ancestral spirits). The chief regulates land use and one of his roles is to protect it from being abused by his subjects (Gelfand, 1976) and (Bourdillon, 1976).

Trees, traditionally, were generally viewed as sources of medicine, food, shade and shelter for alien spirits (Bourdillon 1976). Alien spirits are believed to be spirits of dead people who after death proper rituals were not performed for them. Because of the absence of such rituals, alien spirits are believed to wander from place to place having big trees as their shelter (Bourdillon, 1976 and Hens, 2006). Cutting of certain trees was totally prohibited. Fruit trees were not supposed to be cut because they were considered to be sources of food during times of hunger.

Muchakata tree (*Parina curatellifolia*), apart from being a fruit tree, it had a special function among the Shona people. *Muchakata* tree (*Parina curatellifolia*) was believed to be the only tree where hunting rituals could be performed as well as other crisis resolution rituals like appealing to the ancestral spirits of the land when one is at the point of starving. An individual who cut a *Muchakata* tree (*Parina curatellifolia*) was liable to a heavy fine from the chief. It can be seen that the *Muchakata* tree (*Parina curatellifolia*), in the Shona worldview, was not merely a botanical entity but a source of food and more importantly a shrine. Under such trees, rituals such as sacrifices and prayers to the ancestral spirits were performed. In some cases, even to the present day such rituals are carried under such trees in the rural areas.

The same phenomenon of using trees as shrines is also practiced in Ghana. Hens (2006: 23) notes that in parts of Ghana, people perform rituals under the following trees: Oduma (*Chlorophora excelsa*); African Mahogany (*Kaya invorensis*); Shear butter (*Butyrospermun parkii*) and the Dawadawa (*Parkia clappertoniana*). In Chile, the *Araucaria Araucana* tree is regarded as sacred by the Mapuche people (Herrmann, 2006).

The Shona cultural beliefs ensured the protection of some trees, especially big leafy trees. The Shona were prohibited from cutting down such trees because it was believed that alien spirits resided in such leafy trees. If an individual cut such a leafy tree, it meant the alien spirit would not have a place to reside. This meant that the alien spirit would follow one who had cut the tree in search of its new home. In order to avoid being followed and subsequent torment by the alien spirit, the Shona people avoided cutting down such trees. This belief and fear of the alien spirit helped the Shona people in conserving the environment. Through such a belief, it can be seen that it protected a large number of trees, which were not protected under fruit and medicinal trees thus conserving the environment. It is, therefore, clear that the mentioned trees are protected from being cut down unnecessarily by people. The practice helps in conserving the environment. Such beliefs still exist among some Shona people, especially those who stay in rural areas.

Trees were cut, yes for shelter and for other domestic uses but the chief regulated such practice so that it was kept under control. Such cutting of trees did not in any way constitute wanton destruction of trees. Shona people were also prohibited from cutting at random popular medicine trees. A popular medicine tree provides medicine, which is known, to almost every mature member of society. On the conservation of medicinal trees, Hadebe (1998: 121) notes:

> Medicinal practitioners were controlled in exploitation of trees, shrubs and whatever natural resources they used for medicinal purposes. For instance one would dig roots from a certain side of a tree, usually to the east or west. That ensured the survival of the tree.

The secretive nature of the operation of the medical practitioner, which requires that the exposed parts of the tree should be covered after the removal of some roots ensured, among other things, that the tree was not, exposed to adverse environmental conditions therefore no life threatened (Hadebe, 1998).

Trees, which are seasonally inhabited by edible insects, which are sources of food, were also not supposed to be cut down (Mawere 2013). Examples of such trees are *Mukarati (Burkea Africana)* inhabited by *harati* (edible insects) and *Mushuku/muzhanje (Uapaca kirkiana)* normally inhibited by *harurwa* (edible insects). Droppings from some animals like *mhembwe (buck)*, *nungu* (porcupine), *zhou* (elephant), and *shuro* (hare) were used for medicinal purposes. Some of such animals like the porcupine and the elephant though, they were sources of meat, were protected from extinction because of their medicinal value. They were protected because they were/are totem animals for some members of the group. Such group members did not prey upon them thus reducing the number of people who killed them.

Other rare species like the pangolin were not allowed to be eaten by every member of the society. Only chiefs were allowed to eat such animals. This meant that a pangolin was a prey to a few individuals in a particular society since there are few chiefs among the Shona people. The practice was meant to leave the slower-moving animal to multiply without serious human threat (Tatira, 2000).

The institution of totems also helped in conserving some animals. All the Shona people have totems. These totems define the Shona peoples' circle of relatives. A greater number of totems are taken from animals. The totem animal is not supposed to be killed or eaten by the members who belong to that particular totem. This view is also supported by Awuah-Nyamakye (2012) when he describes totems of the Akan people of Ghana. Among the Akan people, plants can also be totems but among the Shona there are no plant totems. The practice of totems helps to conserve many animals. All these cultural beliefs were effective indigenous strategies for ensuring the sustainable use of local natural resources. The practice, though it did not protect everything in the environment, it managed to conserve the environment. In any case not everything in the environment needs human protection to survive.

Conclusion

This chapter has discussed the role of indigenous Shona cultural beliefs and practices in the conservation of the environment. The chapter has argued that the environmental problems we are facing today are a worldwide problem but its origin is largely not African. Africans, the Shona in particular, had their cultural beliefs and practices, which ensured the conservation of the environment. The Shona concept of the environment is conservative, not exploitative. Through their belief system, the Shona people revere animals, trees and other things within their environment. The plundering of the environment is often interpreted as an insult to the ancestral spirits who would punish the plunderer. The belief in such a non-physical retributive force helps in the conservation of the environment.

It is our sincere belief, therefore, that the present environmental problems demand that the Shona people vigorously reengage their fundamental practices when engaging with their environment. It is through the use of their indigenous knowledge that the environment can be conserved.

References

Agazzi, E. 1994. "Philosophy, Humanity, and Environment", in Oruka, H. O. (ed.) *Philosophy, Humanity, and Ecology: Philosophy of Nature and Environmental Ethics*, Acts Press, African Centre for Technology: Nairobi.

Awuah-Nyamekye, S. 2012. Totemism, Akyeneboa and Plant Ethics, *Philosophy, Activism: Nature*, (9): 5-10.

Awuah-Nyamekye, S. 2014. 'Indigenous Ways of Creating Environmental Awareness: A Case Study from Berekum Traditional Area, Ghana', In *the Journal of the Study of Religion, Nature and Culture* vol. 8 number1, March 2014, p46-63.

Barbour, I, G. (ed.) 1972. *Earth might be fair: Reflections on Ethics, Religion and Ecology*, Prentice-Hall International: London.

Bourdillon, M.F.C. 1976. *The Shona People*, Mambo Press: Gweru.

Bude, U. (ed.) 1991. *Culture and Environment in Primary Education*, Zed: Bonn.

Chiwome, E.M. and Mguni, Z. 2000. 'It May Really Exist-The Two-Toed Tribe of the Zambezi'': Myths Versus Indigenous Knowledge and Technology,' In Chiwome, *et al Indigenous Knowledge and Technology in African and Diasporan Communities: Multi-Disciplinary Approaches*, California State University: USA.

Gelfand, M. 1976. *The Genuine Shona: Survival Values of an African Culture*, Gweru: Mambo Press.

Kunnie, J. 2000. 'Developing indigenous Knowledge and Technological Systems', In Chiwome, E. M. Mguni, Z. and Furusa, M. (eds). *Indigenous Knowledge and Technology in African and Diasporan Communities Multi-Disciplinary Approaches*, California State University: USA.

De George, R. T. 1994. 'Modern Science Environment Ethics and the Anthropocentric Predicament,' In Oruka, H. O. (ed.) *Philosophy, Humanity, and Ecology: Philosophy of Nature and Environmental Ethics*, Acts Press, African Centre for Technology Studies: Nairobi.

Hadebe, S. 1998. 'The Traditional Ndebele Practice of Ukuzila and Environmental Conservation,' In Chiwome, M. and Gambahaya, Z. (ed) (1998). *Culture and Development*, Mond Books: Harare.

Hapanyengwi-Chemhuru, 1998. Culture and Environment: The present Crisis in Development,' In Chiwome, M. and Gambahaya, Z. (eds.) *Culture and Development*, Mond Books: Harare.

Hens, L. 2006. 'Indigenous Knowledge and Biodiversity Conservation and Management in Ghana,' *Journal of Human Ecology*, 20 (1) pp21-30.

Herrmann, T. M. 2006. 'Indigenous Knowledge and Management of Araucaria Arucana Forest in the Chile Andes: Implications for Native Forest Conservation', In the *Journal of Biodiversity and Conservation*, (0960-3115), 15 (2): 647-662.

Johnson, M. (ed.) 1992. Lore: *Capturing Traditional Environmental Knowledge*, Dene Cultural Institute International Development Centre: Ottawa.

Mapara, J. 2009. Indigenous Knowledge Systems in Zimbabwe, *Journal of Pan African Studies*, September, 2009, vl3 no1 p37-56.

Mawere, M. 2005. Life After bodily Death: Myth or Reality? *Zambezia Journal of Humanities,* University of Zimbabwe, Vol.32 (1&2) 26-31.

Mawere, M. 2013. A critical review of environmental conservation in Zimbabwe, *Africa Spectrum,* 48 (2): 85- 97.

Mawere, M. 2014a. *Environmental Conservation through Ubuntu and Other Emerging Perspectives,* Langaa RPCIG Publishers: Cameroon.

Mawere, M. 2014b. *Culture, Indigenous Knowledge and Development in Africa: Reviving Interconnections for Sustainable Development,* Langaa RPCIG Publishers: Cameroon.

Mawere, M and Kadenge, M. 2010. *Zvierwa* as African Indigenous Knowledge System: Epistemological and Ethical Implications of Selected Shona Taboos, *INDILA Journal of Africa Indigenous Knowledge,* 9(1):29-44.

Menzies, C. R. (ed.) 2000. *Traditional Ecological Knowledge and Natural Resource Management,* University of Nebraska: Lincoln and London.

Tatira, L. 2000. "The role of *Zviera* in Socialisation" in Chiome E.M et al. 2000. *Indigenous Knowledge and Technology in African and Diasporan Communities,* Mond Press: Harare.

_____ 2000. *Zviera ZvaVaShona,* Mambo Press: Gweru.

Chapter 11

Indigenous Knowledge Systems and Dispute Resolutions: The Yorùbá Example

Hezekiah Olufemi Adeosun

Introduction

Yorùbá, like every other society has a history behind its knowledge resources which guides its development resource. This is greatly explicated in its oral literature; like proverbs, folktales, Ifá corpus, songs, and festivals. This chapter aims at investigating the Yorùba indigenous knowledge systems in conflict resolution process. Twenty proverbs are copiously selected for analysis out of the fifty proverbs collected. The proverbs are selected based on the thematic pre-occupation of the study and analysed with the Nativist Model of Postcolonial theory. The model suggests that the people and race that had been colonised by the West, at a time in history, should dig deep into their culture and tradition, and make use of their indigenous languages for their literary discourse. The chapter reveals, among other things, that proverb as an indigenous knowledge system among the Yorùbá serves as a potent tool in resolving disputes. It has worked for the people in the past to curtail disputes and crises, which brought about a peaceful society. The chapter, therefore, recommends that adoption of indigenous knowledge system as proverbs in resolving contemporary issues relating to dispute and conflict will be of immense contribution to bringing sanity to the society. The two major concepts that are central to this chapter are indigenous knowledge and conflict resolution. It is wise to unpack these concepts before we delve into a deeper discussion of them.

Indigenous Knowledge Systems

Indigenous knowledge, according to Melchias (2001) cited in Eyong (2014:121), refers to "what indigenous people know and do, and what they have known and done for generations – practices that evolved through trial and error and proved flexible enough to cope with change". Eyong (2014:121-122) explains that this definition draws one's attention to the colonial racist idea that indigenous knowledge is a monopoly of *trials and error* while modern knowledge is *science* characterised by *experimentation*. Hence, while the former is presumed clogged, concrete, and inaccurate, the latter is painted as intangible, weighty, right, and imbued with universal reasoning.

Indigenous knowledge systems, as is the case with modern knowledge, were also developed by experimentations though these experiments were not documented and the knowledge systems were legitimised and fortified under suitable institutional frameworks, culture and practices. They have been passed on to other generations through oral tradition and have enabled indigenous people to survive, manage their natural resources and the ecosystems surrounding them. Unfortunately, these knowledge systems are fast eroding due to the lasting effects of colonialism, commercialisation, globalisation and modernisation, lack of efficient codification, breakdown of the traditional family structure and function (the institution that helps in the socialization of tacit knowledge).

Mapara (2009:140) describes indigenous knowledge systems as a body of knowledge, or bodies of knowledge of the indigenous people of particular geographical areas that they have survived on for a very long time. They are knowledge forms that have failed to die despite the racial and colonial onslaught that they have suffered at the hands of Western imperialism and arrogance. Altieri (1995:114) also notes that "indigenous knowledge systems are forms of knowledge that have originated locally and naturally". Mapara (2009:140 citing Altieri 1995:114) explains that these knowledge forms are known by other names, and among them are indigenous ways of knowing (Nyota and Mapara 2008), traditional knowledge, indigenous technical knowledge, rural knowledge as well as ethno-science (or people's science). The use of proverbs is an example of ethno-knowledge that has been used to ensure social harmony and peace within the Yoruba communities.

Shizha (2013:2) describes Africa as a salad bowl of indigenous people who were formerly colonised but do not share a common ancestry or a common culture. Shizha posits that "the culture of indigenous Africans is characterised by cultural heterogeneity (cultural diversity) rather than cultural homogeneity (cultural uniformity). Africans do not share a common culture, but have cultures that are particularistic and based on high levels of cultural and linguistic diversity". Ocholla (2007:2) shares same view with Shizha (2013:2) when he declares that indigenous knowledge is embedded in the culture/tradition/ideology/language and religion of a particular community and is therefore not universal and difficult to globalise. It is mostly rural, commonly practiced among poor communities and is therefore not suitable in multicultural, urban and economically provided communities. From the foregoing, indigenous knowledge system is culture-based that is owned and controlled by a group of people in a community. Warren (1991:1) states that:

> Indigenous knowledge is the local knowledge – knowledge
> that is unique to a given culture or society. Indigenous
> knowledge contrasts with the international knowledge system
> generated by universities, research institutions and private firms.
> It is the basis for local-level decision making in agriculture,
> health care, food preparation, education, natural-resource
> management, and a host of other activities in rural
> communities.

Similarly, Ocholla (2007:1) postulates that indigenous knowledge (i.e., local/traditional/folk knowledge, ethno science) is a dynamic archive of the sum total of knowledge, skills and attitudes belonging to and practiced by a community over generations, and is expressed in the form of action, objects and sign language for sharing. Examples of these knowledge systems among the Yoruba of Nigeria are festivals, storytelling, proverbs, folk-songs, dances, traditional medicine, art and craft, community/family trade, etc.

243

Shizha (2013:4) quoting Flavier, de Jesus, Navarro and Warren (1995:479) assert that "indigenous knowledge is the information base for a society, which facilitates communication and decision-making. Indigenous information systems are dynamic and are continually influenced by internal creativity and experimentation as well as by contact with external systems".

What can be inferred from these different definitions is that indigenous knowledge systems have utility value in indigenous society. They are experiential and address diverse and complex aspects of indigenous peoples and their livelihoods. In the process of generating indigenous knowledge systems, indigenous people take into account their cosmos, spirituality, ontological realities, land, socio-cultural environment and historical contexts. Indigenous knowledge systems are transmitted, maintained and retained within specific cultural sites for education and sustainable development (Shizha 2013:4). Indigenous knowledge systems have high credibility because they are familiar to the people and are controlled locally (Adeosun, 2010:8). For this reason, dispute or conflict arising among the indigenous people are effectively resolved through indigenous knowledge systems as proverbs.

Conflict and Conflict Resolution

Conflict means contradiction arising from differences in interest, ideas, ideologies, orientations, perceptions and tendencies. These contradictions exist at all levels of the society: individual, group, institution and nation, as well as in interpersonal and international relations. Conflict, therefore, is an integral part of the society, which could be brought about by myriad of factors. A conflict is a situation when the interest, needs, goals or values of involved parties interfere with one another. Different stakeholders may have different priorities; conflicts may involve team members, departments, projects, organisation and client, boss and subordinate, organisation needs versus personal needs (www.personalityexplorer.com/conflictManage).

There are however divergent views on conflict. To some, conflict connotes negativism, while to others it connotes positivism. For Part and Borge (1921:272) as reported by Michael and

Iwokwagh (2006:246), "conflict is designed to resolve divergent dualism and achieved some kind of unity, even if it be through the annihilation of one of the conflicting parties". There are situations where different people with different goals and needs have come to conflict. Such situations often result to intense personal animosity. Michael and Iwokwagh (2006:246) further explains that Lund Berbe (1939:275), Wilson and Kolb (1947:114) both see conflict from a negative perspective. For them, "conflicts are negative totally as dysfunctional or disjunctive process and the breakdown of communication". On the contrary, however, Deutsuch (1973:156) cited in Michael and Iwokwagh (2006:246) argues that "although conflict generally exists where incompatible activities occur, and may result in a win or lose situation, the resolution, transformation and management of conflict may produce a win-win situation". The fact that conflict exists, however, is not necessarily a bad thing. As long as it is resolved effectively, it can lead to personal and professional growth. In many cases, effective conflict resolution can make the difference between positive and negative outcomes. If conflict is not handled effectively, the result can be damaging.

There are many different approaches to respond to conflict situations. Kenneth Thomas and Ralph Kilmann (1970) identify five main styles/approaches of dealing with conflict that vary in their degrees of cooperativeness and assertiveness. They argue that people typically have a preferred conflict resolution style. However, they also note that different styles are most useful in different situations. Hence, they develop the Thomas-Kilmann Conflict Mode Instrument (TKI) (1970) which helps one to identify which style/approach one tends towards when conflict arises. The five styles which I explain in some detail below are: competitive, collaborative, compromising, accommodating, and avoiding.

Competitive

People who tend towards a competitive style take a firm stand, and know what they want. They usually operate from a position of power, drawn from things like position, rank, expertise, or persuasive ability. This style can be useful when there is an emergency and a decision needs to be made fast; when the decision is unpopular; or when defending against someone who is trying to exploit the situation selfishly. However, it can leave people feeling bruised, unsatisfied and resentful when used in less urgent situations.

Collaborative

People tending towards a collaborative style try to meet the needs of all people involved. These people can be highly assertive but unlike the competitor, they cooperate effectively and acknowledge that everyone is important. This style is useful when one needs to bring together a variety of viewpoints to get the best solution; when there have been previous conflicts in the group; or when the situation is too important for a simple trade-off.

Compromising

People who prefer a compromising style try to find a solution that will, at least, partially satisfy everyone. Everyone is expected to give up something, and the compromiser him/herself also expects to relinquish something. Compromise is useful when the cost of conflict is higher than the cost of losing ground, when equal strength opponents are at a standstill and when there is a deadline looming.

Accommodating

This style indicates a willingness to meet the needs of others at the expense of the person's own needs. The accommodator often knows when to give in to others, but can be persuaded to surrender a position even when it is not warranted. This person is not assertive but is highly cooperative. Accommodation is appropriate when the issues matter more to the other party or when peace is more valuable than winning.

Avoiding

People tending towards this style seek to evade the conflict entirely. This style is typified by delegating controversial decisions, accepting default decisions, and not wanting to hurt anyone's feelings. It can be appropriate when victory is impossible, when the controversy is trivial, or when someone else is in a better position to solve the problem. However, in many situations this is a weak and ineffective approach to take (www. mindtools.com/pages/article/newLDR-81.htm).

Once the different styles are understood, one can use them to think about the most appropriate approach or mixture of approaches for the situation one finds oneself. Conflict is often seen as a threat to peace and depicted as if it is totally negative. However, depending on how it is handled, conflict can either be constructive or destructive. Be that as it may, conflict in this chapter is seen in the positive light as Yoruba proverb is used in resolving conflicts.

The Yorùbá People

The Yorùbá have several traditions about how they began life. One of the traditions says that it was at Ilé-Ifẹ, which the Yorùbá regard as the birthplace of their nation, that mankind was first created. Another tradition tells the story of a great ancestor and hero called Odùduwà. He is said to have come from far in the east and settled at Ilé-Ifẹ, and it was from here that his descendant went out to rule the various branches of the Yorùbá. One of his sons, for example, is said to have become the first *Aláàfin* of Ọyọ, as well as being the father of the first *Ọba* of Benin, while another was the first *Onísábẹ* of Sábẹ; his eldest daughter is remembered as the mother of the first *Alákétu* of Kétu (in modern Dahomey), while another daughter gave birth to the *Olówu* of Òwu (Davidson 1981:118-119).

Yorùbá people are found today in the South Western States of Nigeria namely; Ogun, Lagos, Ọyọ, Ọṣun, Èkìtì, Ondo, and part of Kwara and Kogi States. According to Falola (2012:20), the massive expansion of the Yorùbá occurred in the context of the Atlantic World, the four continents united by the Atlantic Ocean. The Yorùbá were among the African slaves drawn from Central and West Africa and tragically relocated to the Americas. As the enslaved, they were funnelled to the Atlantic. After the abolition of the Atlantic slave trade, secondary migrations occurred as freed slaves returned to West Africa, and thousands migrated within various countries in the Atlantic World. Falola states that the slave trade violently took the Yorùbá to several places in the Americas: Brazil, Cuba, Uruguay, Argentina, Haiti, Venezuela, Trinidad and

247

Tobago, and the United States. The Yorùbá extended themselves in West Africa and gained tremendous influence in various parts, notably along the coastal areas.

The Yorùbá originally were traditional worshippers. They, however, believe in the existence of an Almighty God, who they term *Ọlọrun* (Lord of Heaven). They acknowledge Him, Maker of heaven and earth, but too exalted to concern Himself directly with men and their affairs, hence they admit the existence of many gods as intermediaries, and these they term *Orìṣas* (Johnson 1976:26). Politically, the government of Yorùbá proper was an absolute monarchy; the king (*Ọba*) was more dreaded than even the gods. The office was (and still) hereditary in the same family, but not necessarily from father to son. The word "king" as generally used in this country includes all more or less distinguished chiefs, who stand at the head of a clan, or one who is the ruler of an important district or province, especially those who can trace their descent from the founder, or from one of the great leaders or heroes who settled with him in the country (Johnson 1976:40-41).

Preservation of Peace among the Yoruba

Long before the establishment of British rule in Yoruba land, the people had reached the stage where redress for injuries, suffered directly or indirectly, was out of the hands of the individual and his kindred. Fadipe (1970:223) observes that the Yoruba are interested not only in retributive and reparatory justice but also in what may be called peace-making justice. In peace-making justice the aim is to intervene and arbitrate in quarrels and misunderstandings which impair kinship or social solidarity or are likely to deteriorate into an actual breach of the peace. Peace-making justice is little if at all developed in Western societies. Among the Yoruba, it is considerably well-developed, although its machinery is in private hands rather than in those of the public authorities. In this form of justice more than in others while the apportionment of praise and blame is the desideratum, it sometimes requires to be tempered by the necessity to conciliate according to the prejudices and customs current in Yoruba society (Fadipe 1970:223). Thus conceptions of seniority, or of the superiority of husband to wife, chiefs and subjects, parents and children or even of man to woman, are often taken into account in adjudicating in disputes of this class. As to the nature of such disputes, they generally involve breaches of codes of conduct, behaviour and usages such as cannot be taken direct cognisance of by the authorities because they do not constitute any material injury to the aggrieved person. The settlement of quarrels of this nature rarely goes before the public authorities unless the parties concerned are themselves members of the administration, or unless curses are invoked and the matter cannot be settled informally (Fadipe 1970:224).

Fadipe posits further that it is the duty of every Yoruba to mediate physically between two persons engaged in a fight by separating them unless the disparity in size of the combatants and him/herself renders it out of question. The actual settlement of such a dispute very rarely, in pre-colonial days, got to the notice of the authorities unless some serious physical injuries had been inflicted. If the person who separated the combatants was old enough and had the time for it, the two might state their cases to him or her and get it settled. If more serious, the matter was settled in the compound, if both disputants were of the same compound. If they belonged to two different compounds in the same ward of the town, and the two heads of the compounds were not on hostile terms, steps were taken to have the case heard and settled between the two heads. Owing to the partial decentralisation of the judicial machinery among the Yoruba, the administration of public justice may be said to begin at home (according to the nature of the case and the relationship of the parties involved) and to end with the highest state authorities as the highest tribunal as well as the highest court of appeal. Generally speaking, the justice that had to be administered in pre-colonial days was in accordance not with any written code of laws but with a body of customs, usages (such as proverbs), and codes of manners. The only sense in which 'law' can be used in connection with the administration of justice among the Yoruba is that of a usage that has long been established and sanctioned by custom (Fadipe 1970:224).

Theoretical Framework for this study

The framework adopted for this study is the nativist model of postcolonial theory. The postcolonial theory is as area of cultural and critical theory that has been used in the study of literary texts. It focuses largely on the way in which literature by the colonisers distorts the experience and realities of the colonised, and inscribes the inferiority of the colonised while at the same time promoting the superiority of the coloniser. The postcolonial theory is also about the colonised and formerly colonised announcing their presence and identity as well as reclaiming their past that was lost or distorted because of being othered by colonialism (Mapara 2009:141).

However, the focus of the nativist model of postcolonial theory, according to Adeyemi (2003:114), is "to re-invent and reconstitute the traditions that the Colonial Master had tried to destroy. Nativism is an astute celebration of cultural and political nationalism, a 'look back' of the periphery to its 'traditional civilisation' as a way of subverting the Centre's cultural, textual and epistemological dominance". The nativist model of postcolonial theory calls for going back to the root, to identify the original culture and use it to champion a definite identity for the African society. Nativism recommends the African literature as a prosaic experience germane to the peculiar African situation. It advocates the inscription of traditional African communalism in the delineation of characterisation, features of orality such as proverbs, folktales, riddles, songs, poetry-incantations and other stylistic devices such as repetition, irony, metaphor, simile, hyperbole, etc. (Adeyemi, 2003:117-118). With one's understanding of the nativist model which is the bedrock this study rests on, the next section shall be the analysis of selected proverbs which focus on conflict resolution.

Methodology and Presentation of Data

The proverbs used as data for this study were gathered from the author's home town, Ifọ, Ogun State, Nigeria. The method adopted in data gathering was participant observation. The author, being a

Yorùbá native speaker and one of the elders in his family compound has participated in series of dispute resolution activities. This has given him an ample opportunity in gathering his data over a period of time. The twenty proverbs selected for this study out of the fifty proverbs gathered are as follow:

(1) Agbè ní í jẹ ẹgbin omi, àgbàlagbà ní í jẹ ìyà ọ̀ràn

A gourd absorbs dirt in the water, an elder suffers the guilt of a case)   .

(2) Agbẹjọ ẹnìkan dá, àgbà òṣìkà ni.

(One who listens only to a side of two disputants is a wicked elder).

(3) Àìsí ẹnìkẹta lẹni méjì n ja àjàkú.

(Absence of a third party makes two people fight endlessly).

(4) A kì í tó níí bá gbé, kí á má tó níí bá sọrọ.

(What qualifies one to live with others, makes one qualify to advise one another).

(5) Àìfi ẹsọ ké ìbòòsí ni kò jẹ káráyé bá ni jó o.

(Inability to raise an alarm with ease makes no one dance along).

(6) A kì í rojọ wíwò ká jàre.

(One does not accuse others of eyeing one and wins a case).

(7) À n jà bí i ká kú kọ.

(Fighting each other does not mean one wants the other dead).

(8) Aṣọhùn ẹhìnkùlé n ba ara rẹ nínú jẹ, ohun tó wu ni làá sọ nínú ilé ẹni.

(An eavesdropper poisons his mind, one is at liberty to say whatever one likes in one's house).

(9) Bí a bá kìlọ fólè, ká kìlọ fóníṣu ẹbá ọnà.

(If a thief is warned, owner of tuber of yams at the road side should equally be warned).

(10) Bí a bá yọ ipin lójú, a fi í han ojú kí ojú lè mọ pé òun n ṣe ọbùn.

(If dirt is removed from an eye, one shows the dirt to the eye for it to know that it is dirty).

(11) Bí a kò bá torí iṣu jẹ epo, à ó torí epo jẹ iṣu.

(If palmoil is not eaten because of yam, yam must be eaten because of palmoil).

(12) Bí a ní kí á jẹ èkuru kó tán láwo, a kì í tún gbọn ọwọ rẹ sí àwo.

(If one desires to eat all the grains in the plate, one does not return the remnants in one's hand to the plate).

(13) *Bí igí bá dúró, tí ènìyàn dúró bí a bá ní kí á bẹ igi, a ó bẹ ènìyàn mọ ọn.*

(If a tree stands closely by a human being, and one attempts to cut the tree, the human being may be affected).

(14) *Bí ènìyàn bá n yọ ilẹ dà, ohun búburú a máa yọ ọ ṣe.*

(If one betrays, evil things are bound to befall the betrayer.

(15) *Bí ènìyàn búburú bá n kọjá tí a dijú, títí ènìyàn rere yóò fi kọjá, a kò níí mọ.* (If one closes one's eyes for a bad person to pass by, one may not know when a good person will pass by).

(16) *Bí etí kò gbọ yìnkìn, inú kì í bàjẹ.*

(If ears do not hear bad thing, one's mind is not poisoned).

(17) *Bí ẹlẹjọ bá mọ ẹjọ rẹ lẹbi, kì í pẹ ní ìkúnlẹ.*

(If one realises that one is guilty of an offence, one does not need to stay long on one's kneels begging).

(18) *Bí ilé kò bá kan ilé kì í jó àjóràn.*

(If residential houses are not constructed close to one another, disaster will be curtailed in case of fire outbreak).

(19) *Àròkàn-àròkàn ní í fa ẹkún àsunìdákẹ.*

(A prolonged brooding breeds unending sobbing).

(20) *Bí a kò bá gbàgbé ọrọ àná, a kò ní í rẹni bá ṣeré.*

(If one does not forget the incident of previous day, one may not likely see anyone to play with)

Analysis of the selected Proverbs in conflict resolution among the Yoruba

The first proverb, *"Agbè ní í jẹ ẹgbin omi, àgbàlagbà ní í jẹ ìyà ọràn".* (A gourd absorbs dirt in the water, an elder suffers the guilt of a case) explains a scenario where one of the disputants is older than the other or in a case of husband and wife. The mediator, having tried to broker peace between the disputants and discovered that the younger is guilty, he may ask the younger to apologise and conclude the settlement with the proverb by appealing to the elder to forgive the younger. An elder is compared with a gourd which absorbs both clean and dirty water of all sorts, hence elders among the Yoruba are expected to show maturity and patience in all matters. However, if it is the older that is guilty a proverb as *"àgbàlagbà kì í ṣe lángbálángbá"* (An older person is not expected to

252

act childishly) will suffice. The second proverb *"Agbẹjọ ẹnìkan dá, àgbà òṣìkà ni"* (one who listens only to a side of two disputants is a wicked elder) is used to condemn injustice on the part of a mediator who listens to a side and cares not to listen to other side before passing a judgment. That mediator is regarded as a wicked person who is not qualified to be called an elder, because he does not maintain balance between the two fighters. The third proverb, *"Àìsí ẹnìkẹta lẹni méjì n ja àjàkú"* (Absence of a third party makes two people fight endlessly) confirms the need and role of a mediator in dispute resolution. A mediator is expected to be a wise and a respectable person who is respected by the two conflicting groups. He or she should be seen as an umpire who does not take side with any group, he/she should be objective in his/her judgment. As soon as the two sides discover that the judgment is without prejudice, it is likely the quarrel ends there immediately. For instance, if a husband and a wife quarrel with each other for a long time, people around them tend to ask a question that 'does that mean there is no elderly person in their family that can help resolve the matter? Such a scenario brings the proverb *"àìsí ẹnìkẹta lẹni méjì n ja àjàkú"* (absence of a third party makes two people fight endlessly). Going further, the fourth proverb *"a kì í tó nìí bá gbé, kí á má tó nìí bá sọrọ"* (What qualifies one to live with others, makes one qualify to advise one another) also corroborates role of a mediator as explained in the third proverb. If the two conflicting groups refuse to sheath their swords, and all efforts by the mediator proved fruitless, then the mediator may say the proverb to, perhaps, appeal to their senses. Having said the proverb, the two warring groups may think otherwise and decide to respect and honour the mediator.

The proverb, *"àìfi ẹsọ ké ìbòòsí ni kò jẹ káráyé bá ni jó o"* (Inability to raise an alarm with ease makes no one dance along) in the fifth proverb, tells the significance of patience and calmness while presenting a vital issue to others concerned. It is possible one has a genuine case or message to present but the medium or time of presenting it may be faulty, hence the proverb. In Yoruba society, a man is seen as the head of his family while the woman, as his wife, is expected to be under the man's authority. However, if the man is fond of a habit that is detrimental to himself or the family, it is expected that the woman applies wisdom, calmness and patience in explaining to the man the dangers inherent in his actions. With that the man may listen to her and change for the better. On the other hand, if the woman handles the matter forcefully, the man may translate it to be that the woman is attempting to control him which may lead to conflict in the home. When such case arises and someone interferes in order to resolve the matter, he may make the man realise that the woman has not done anything wrong, only that her presentation was not good enough to the man. She ought to have presented her point with love and wisdom.

The sixth proverb *"a kì í rojọ wíwò ká jàre"* (One does not accuse others of eyeing one and wins a case) is better understood in a milieu of two rival women, perhaps, of the same husband or among children. According to Yoruba culture, marrying more than one wife by a man, which is otherwise known as polygyny, is acceptable. Thus, if there is a misunderstanding between the rival wives and in the process of settling the matter by elders in the compound, a rival woman accuses other woman of eyeing her, the proverb would be said condemning the accuser of having no point. The elders may even add that she should also eye her since both of them have eyes to look at any direction they wish. Conflict is seen to be inevitable in every society, therefore, when there is conflict among the Yoruba, it is meant to correct some anomalies so as to continue living harmoniously. Therefore, when there is a misunderstanding between two people and they continue having malice against each other, the proverb number 7 *"à n jà bí i ká kú kọ"* (Fighting each other does not mean one wants the other dead) is used by the mediator to persuade the two disputants. Proverb number 8 *"asọ hùn ẹhìnkùlé n ba ara rẹ nínú jẹ, ohun tó wu ni làá sọ nínú ilé ẹni"* (an eavesdropper poisons his mind, one is at liberty to say whatever one likes in one's house) frowns at the attitude whereby one accuses the other of over-hearing the accused saying some ugly things against one. Since it was not alleged that the accused came directly to one to say such, to the Yoruba, such an allegation is baseless and unfounded. Therefore, that should not be enough to warrant a dispute.

The nineth proverb *"bí a bá kìlọ fólè, ká kìlọ fóníṣu ẹbá ọnà"* (If a thief is warned, owner of tuber of yams at the road side should equally be warned) attempts to maintain balance in peace-making process between two people or groups. Though, the gravity of offence of the former might be so enormous, however, the latter also shares from the blame. This is done to ensure that each party realises where his fault lies and to prevent future occurrence. The same interpretation goes for proverb number 10 which says *"bí a bá yọ ipin lójú, a fi í han ojú kí ojú lè mọ pé òun n ṣe ọbùn."* (If a dirt is removed from an eye, one shows the dirt to the eye for it to know that it is dirty). The proverb simply declares that, as a mediator, one should not be partial in one's judgment. Each disputant should be told where he or she has erred. When a conflict resolution process seems to be unrealised, and the two warring groups become adamant by shifting ground on certain issues, the mediator's integrity is brought to test by saying the proverb in number 11 *"bí a kò bá torí iṣu jẹ epo, à ó torí epo jẹ iṣu"* (If palmoil is not eaten because of yam, yam must be eaten because of palmoil) which translates that if both of them do not respect each other, they should, at least, consider his age or status and listen to him. With this statement, the two disputants may change their earlier hard posture and allow peace to reign. Proverb 12 *"bí a ní kí á jẹ èkuru kó tán láwo, a kì í tú-n gbọn ọwọ rẹ sí àwo"* (If one desires to eat all the grains in the plate, one does not return the remnants in one's hand to the plate) is said by a mediator when two disputants keep on insisting or repeating a matter over and over again without giving the mediator chance to resolve the issue. "Ekuru" (grain) in this context is a burning issue needed to be resolved.

Proverb 13 *"bí igi bá dúró, tí ènìyàn dúró bí a bá ní kí á bẹ igi, a ó bẹ ènìyàn mọ ọn"* (If a tree stands closely by a human being, and one attempts to cut the tree, the human being may be affected) calls for caution and tolerance in the face of provocation so that regret will not be the end result of the crisis. The Yoruba people abhor the act of betrayal and that is why when they are into a relationship, they commit everything within their reach into that relationship. At times, in order to concretise the relationship, they enter into a covenant or swear an oath among themselves. The repercussion of betrayal, according to the Yoruba belief, is great and severe. If for example two people are entering into a business, they swear an oath that none of them will betray the other. This type of agreement brings sincerity, faithfulness and commitment. Hence, the proverb in number 14, *"bí ènìyàn bá n yọ ilẹ̀ dà, ohun búburú a máa yọ ọ ṣe"* (If one betrays, evil things are bound to befall the betrayer). Act of betrayal brings about discord, enmity and conflict. Therefore, to avoid these, the proverb is said to warn the participants in the relationship.

Moreover, the fifteenth proverb *"bí ènìyàn búburú bá n kọjá tí a dijú, títí ènìyàn rere yóò fi kọjá, a kò níí mọ̀"* (If one closes one's eyes for a bad person to pass by, one may not know when a good person will pass by) means that in as much as quarrel among people is inevitable, yet one should have a sense of forgiveness to create a room for better relationship. For someone who does something painful to one today may do something pleasant to one the following day. That is why the Yoruba say this proverb when they are mediating in a conflict. Proverbs 16 and 18 *"bí etí kò gbọ́ yìnkìn, inú kì í bàjẹ́"* (If ears do not hear bad thing, one's mind is not poisoned) and *"bí ilé kò bá kan ilé kì í jó àjóràn"* (If residential houses are not constructed close to one another, disaster will be curtailed in case of fire outbreak) have some similarities with proverb number 8 earlier discussed, warning that one should not listen to hear-say. There are some people that are interested in creating conflict or quarrel between two people that are friends or couple. They move from one person to the other saying that 'Mr. A said this while Mr. B was away'. This kind of move causes conflict between two people and is capable of breaking a home or a relationship. Thus, in the process of resolving conflict between two people, a mediator may say these proverbs to quench the fire of discord already created by mere hear-say. The proverb in number 17 *"bí ẹlẹ́jọ́ bá mọ ẹjọ́ rẹ̀ lẹ́bi, kì í pẹ́ ní ìkúnlẹ̀"*. If one realises that one is guilty of an offence, one does not need to stay long on one's knees begging) quickly settles a minor quarrel between two disputants who may likely be a couple or friends. In this instance, one of the disputants early realises that he is guilty of the offence and urges the mediator to assist him or her in begging the other party. Having realised this, the mediator will join the guilty person in apologising to the other person by saying the proverb. Proverbs number 19 and 20 *"àròkàn-àròkàn ní í fa ẹkún àsunìdákẹ́"* (a prolonged brooding breeds unending sobbing) and *"bí a kò bá gbàgbé ọ̀rọ̀ àná, a kò ní í rẹni bá ṣeré"* (If one does not forget the incident of previous day, one may not likely see anyone to play with) have same connotations. The two proverbs foreground forgiveness as a crucial tool in conflict resolution among the Yoruba. The major concept in conflict resolution is "give and take". This concept cannot be achieved without a spirit of "give and take" on the part of the two disputants. As human beings, there is a tendency one begins to think of pains the other party has inflicted on one in the course of crisis. However, for peace to be brokered, one needs to forget what has happened in the past and forgive each other. This is where the mediator's role is felt. He/She should be able to appeal, persuade and bring his/her wealth of experience to bear in resolving the matter.

Discussion and Recommendations

Having examined roles of proverbs in dispute resolution among the Yorùbá of Nigeria, it is expedient, therefore, to make some recommendations to the individuals, groups, associations and government at all levels. Use of proverbs is mostly restricted to indigenous people living in rural or semi-urban areas in Nigeria. Globalisation and Westernisation which have corrupted the African culture through their progressive technological changes in communication, political and economic power, knowledge and skills, as well as cultural values systems and practices, have negatively affected use of indigenous language (where its indigenous knowledge systems are embedded) among the Yorùbá elites. In view of the foregoing, this chapter adapts the following recommendations from Awóbùlúyì (2014). They are: 1. Government should promote indigenous Nigerian languages for official use in education at all levels, in government and the judiciary at all levels, in law enforcement, commerce and industry, as well as in mass communication; 2. Parents should be enlightened and encouraged to communicate with their children at home in their indigenous languages. Many Western educated Yorùbá parents today seem to consider it a mark of sophistication for them to speak English where they should speak Yorùbá, their native language. They speak only English to their children at home, and wish only English to be also spoken and taught to them at school

257

from the Kindergarten level to the University level; 3. Governments in Yorùbá spoken States should endeavour to restore Yorùbá to its natural status as the host language in all their schools, and make it compulsory for all pupils and students from kindergarten to university level within the Yorùbá community. At present, the time allotted to English on the school timetable is about five times the one grudgingly granted to Yorùbá; and 4. Yorùbá needs also to be declared the official language for all institutions and establishments, both public and private, throughout the Yorùbá community. Yorùbá should be the only medium of written and spoken communication among workers at work, and among the criteria for eligibility for appointment into any institution or establishment within that community should be a high degree of competence in the written and spoken forms of the language. If this is done by the various governments in the Yorùbá spoken states, parents/guardians and their wards will begin for a change to see the study of Yorùbá in schools and colleges as a form of training that assures economic reward and upward mobility. Furthermore, the language will, like English today, gain value and prestige, and there will be no further cause for anyone to denigrate it.

Conclusion

This chapter has examined the Yoruba indigenous knowledge system as exemplified in their proverbs in conflict resolution. Twenty proverbs selected based on their thematic relevance were analysed using nativist model of postcolonial theory. Yoruba use proverbs to remind people of what the society's moral and value codes require of them, hence, the proverbs used in this study postulate the high level of intelligence and wisdom of the Yoruba in resolving conflicts among themselves. Yoruba, in one of their proverbs, believe that *"bí ọọdẹ ò dùn, bí ìgbẹ ni ìgboro n rí"* (if one's home is not pleasant, town (society) will only look like a bush). This means that charity begins at home. In the Yorùbá opinion, if quarrel at family or compound level is not checked, it may develop into a serious crisis in the society. Thus, at every strata of the Yoruba society are levels of peace-making process, starting from the head of a family to the head of the community. This chapter has also recommended that indigenous language which accommodates the indigenous knowledge systems should be encouraged and taught at all level of formal education, which will thereby enhance the knowledge of our youth in applying proverbs in their daily lives.

References

Adeosun, H.O. 2010. Indigenous Languages and Mass Communication Media in Nigeria: The Case of Nigeria. In *Centrepoint: A Journal of Intellectual, Scientific and Cultural Interest* 13.1, pp. 1-13.

Adeyemi, O. 2003. Political Consciousness and the Yoruba Novels. A Study of Works of Owolabi, Yemiitan, Ọlabimtan and Abiọdun. PhD diss., University of Ilorin.

Altieri, M. A. 1995. Agroecology: *The science of sustainable agriculture,* IT publications: London.

Awobuluyi, O. 2014. *Yoruba must not die out,* Faculty lecture, Obafemi Awolowo University: Ile-Ife.

Davidson, B. 1981. *A history of West Africa 1000-1800,* Longman Publishers: UK.

Eyong, C. T. n.d. 'Indigenous Knowledge and Sustainable Development in Africa: Case study on Central Africa', Available at: www.krepublishers.com/06-special volume- journal/S.T (Retrieved: 21 August 2014.

Fadipe, N. A. 1970. *The Sociology of the Yoruba,* University Press: Ibadan.

Falola, T. 2012. *Atlantic Yoruba and the expanding frontiers of Yoruba culture and politics,* University of Ibadan: Ibadan.

Johnson, S. 1976. *The history of the Yorubas,* C.S.S. Bookshops: Lagos.

Mapara, J. 2009. Indigenous knowledge systems in Zimbabwe: Juxtaposing postcolonial theory. In *The Journal of Pan African Studies,* Available at: www.questia.com/library/p62352/the-journal-of-pan-african-studies-online/i2497913/vol-3-no-1-september (Retrieved: 26 November 2014).

Melchias, G. 2001. *Biodiversity and Conservation,* Science Publishers, Inc: Enfield.

Ocholla, D. 2007. 'Marginalized knowledge: An agenda for indigenous knowledge development and integration with other forms of knowledge', Available at: www.worldbank.org/afr/ik/basic.htm (Retrieved: 26 November 2014).

Shizha, E. 2013. 'Reclaiming our indigenous voices: The problem with postcolonial Sub-Saharan African school curriculum', Available at: www.hawaii.edu/sswork/jisd (Retrieved: 26 November 2014).

Thomas, K. and Kilmann, R. 1970. 'Conflict resolution: resolving conflict rationally and effectively', Available at: www.mindtools.com/pages/article/newLDR-81.htm (Retrieved: 26 November 2014).

Warren, D. 1991. Using indigenous knowledge in agricultural development, The World Bank: Washington, DC.

www.personalityexplorer.com/FREEResources/ConflictManage.../ (Retrieved: 26 November 2014).

Chapter 12

The Role and Efficacy of Indigenous Knowledge in Fostering Sustainable Development in Africa: A Case Study of Zimbabwe

Blessing Makunike and Munyaradzi Mawere

Introduction

This chapter discusses the potential and value of using indigenous knowledge as a compliment of_modern 'scientific' techniques to enhance the sustainable management and productive use of land. In recent years, advocacy for community participation in project cycle activities has demonstrated that local level initiatives are an important basis for sustainable advancement in the use of land resource (see also Chambers and Conway 1992; Ellis 1998; Carney 1998; Cavendish 2001). More often than not, it is easier to work with and through existing structures rather than develop new ones to execute project goals and objectives. Indeed past attitudes of scepticism and contempt for local farmers' knowledge have been the cause of many government and aid sponsored failures, and have contributed to mistrust and suspicion of local people towards officialdom (Amutabi 2006; Mawere and Mabeza, this volume).

The problems affecting rural development should no longer be seen to reside in the "traditional" and "old fashioned" cultures of the so-called under-developed people, but rather in the neglect, partial or biased recognition and understanding of the central importance of indigenous knowledge systems. Using information gathered through direct observation and informal interviews with the Manyika people of Mutasa District in Manicaland Province of Zimbabwe, the present chapter seeks to complement the existing and growing body of literature on how indigenous knowledge can foster sustainable development (see for example, Altieri 1995; Tatira 2000; Mawere 2014; Semali and Kincheloe 1999; Ntuli 1999;

Goduka 2000; Veitayaki 2002; World Bank 1998; Duri and Mapara 2007).

While it could be universally agreed that indigenous Knowledge derives from past experiences, is transmitted from one generation to another, evaluated and fine-tuned as people engage in a continuous process of experimentation and innovation, there is no universally agreed upon definition of what it entails. It can also be understood as long standing or historical traditions and ways of doing things which apply to defined spatial, indigenous or local communities. According to Millat-e-Mustafa (2000:27), the term "indigenous" is synonymous with "traditional" or "local", differentiating this knowledge from that which is developed by formal science in institutions such as universities and government research centres. Having been tried and tested over many generations to meet the demands of the 'local people' who use it, indigenous knowledge concentrates on adaptation and experimentation, and is less formal in its social organisation. The fact that indigenous knowledge is tried and tested through time makes it no less than the so-called Western scientific knowledge. In sustainable and participatory approaches to development, it is increasingly being recognised as a resource that should be mobilised to complement scientific knowledge, in the promotion of plans, programmes and projects for rural development.

That there is a link between agriculture, rural development and indigenous knowledge is no longer indisputable (World Bank 1998; Mapara 2009; Mawere 2014; Semali and Kincheloe 1999). There is need to go further and state that strategies for sustainable rural development should be developed from where the communities are rather than from where the so-called "scientists" want them to be. The "top down approach" should give way to dialogue between the different partners in development such as the government, non-state actors, and local communities, the so-called scientists among others. The convergence between farmers' knowledge and that of modern science oriented personnel or the so-called scientists does provide an important entry point for farmer – scientist collaboration in addressing problems of rural development. Scoones and Thompson (2009) argue for the development, promotion and sharing bottom-up farmer centred approaches to technology development for agriculture. Amongst others, they raise the following approaches: participatory plant breeding involving farmers in trait selection and breeding programmes across a range of crops; participatory extension and learning approaches, including Farmers Field Schools for farmer-based learning about integrated pest management or soil fertility; and networks for sharing farmer experimentation and rural innovation as well as new farmer-scientist research partnerships to promote innovation.

Many post-colonial governments in Africa, for example Mozambique and Zimbabwe among others, implemented land reform programmes. These were designed, broadly to correct historical imbalances in land-ownership and at the same time to empower the local communities who derive their livelihoods from land. In Zimbabwe, traditional structures were severely weakened by the colonial government policies (Mukamuri 1995; Madzudzo 2002; Marongwe 2004; Shizha 2012; Mawere 2013a; Makumbe 1998). They were either ignored or at most marginally consulted if only to support and be politically compliant. However, this chapter makes the case that, indigenous people who received land under Zimbabwe's land reform programme represent diverse language and ethnic groups who undoubtedly are a reservoir of untapped indigenous agricultural and natural resource knowledge and experience.

Whilst acknowledging that the role of indigenous knowledge and institutions in Zimbabwe's land reform programme has been largely obscure and highly contentious, we contend that cognisance should be taken of the capacity of this knowledge and institutions to impact on the process given the socio-economic and political conditions. We, thus, make a case for blending 'indigenous' knowledge systems with modern 'scientific' knowledge in the context of land reform. It is important that modern day scientific enquiry should establish dialogue with the time honoured traditional knowledge if local communities are to be part of the national development plan.

The study area

The research that resulted in this chapter was carried out among the Manyika people of the eastern part of Zimbabwe between 2009 and 2010. The Manyika are a Shona people who live in the Eastern region of Zimbabwe. They reside in Manicaland Province, which is one of the 10 administrative provinces of Zimbabwe. The case study was Mutasa District which is 30km from Mutare, the province's administrative capital. The district is in the Highveld and received an average of more than 1000mm annual rainfall which makes it prone to soil erosion. It is however suited for diversified farming activities including livestock raring and cultivation of crops, timber and fruit.

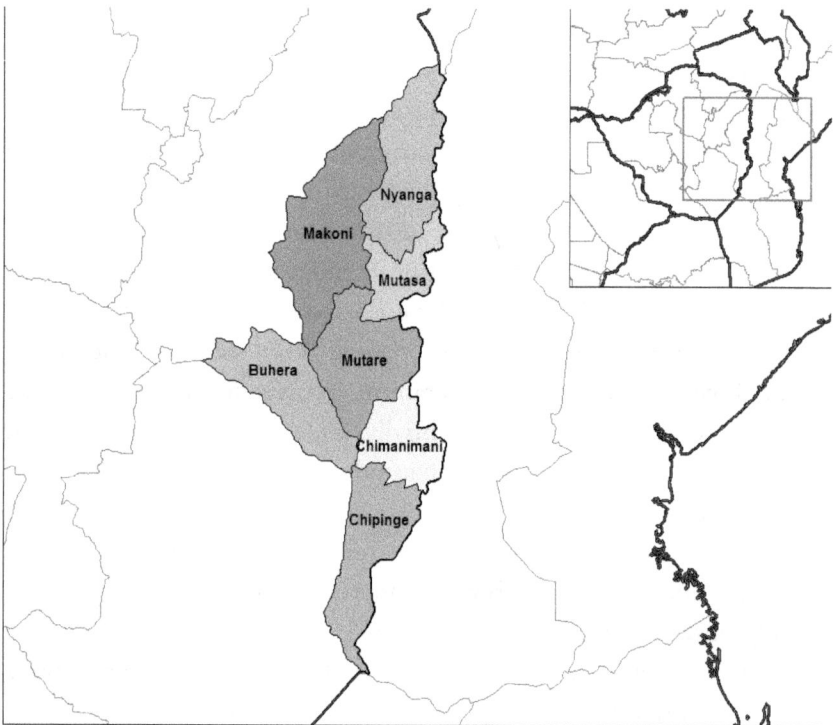

Fig 1: Map showing Mutasa District in Manicaland Province in Zimbabwe
Source: Zimbabwe Archives

Indigenous knowledge and sustainability

According to Miah (2000:23), sustainability can be defined in two ways: either from a resource base focus which emphasises conservation; or from an output focus which emphasises livelihood or development. The resource base focus states that natural resources must not lose their capacity to produce, through depletion or pollution. On the other hand, the output focus states that productivity must not decrease. However, in the context of agriculture, sustainability should refer to the capacity to remain productive while maintaining the resource base. Agricultural production needs to be maintained through application of scientific technical knowledge, but at the same time, environmental degradation needs to be minimised or kept within "acceptable" bounds.

The 1987 World Commission on Environment and Development (WCED), through its infamous Brundtland Report of 1987, observed that sustainable development is development that meets the needs of the present without compromising the ability of future generations to meet their own needs (WCED 1987: 43; IPCCC 2012). This definition comprises two key concepts: the concept of "needs" of the poor or indigenous people to which overriding priority should be given; and the idea of limitations imposed by the state of technology and social organisation on the environment's ability to meet present and future needs.

The wider environment is uncertain and always changing. Therefore, it should be understood that sustainability, in view of development discourse, is the ability of a people to adapt and survive the uncertainties that confront them as they struggle to survive, without compromising future generation's ability to do the same. By the same fact, sustainable development is concerned with improving the quality of human life while living within the carrying capacity of the supporting ecosystem. It follows, therefore, that if humanity is to survive and prosper, it should benefit from indigenous peoples' basic principles of conservation, environmental ethic s and regard for future generations. Due to their harmonious relationships with nature facilitated through traditional institutions and indigenous knowledge systems, indigenous people are the custodians or guardians of the vast habitats which are critical to modern societies for regulating water cycles, maintaining the stability of the climate, and providing valuable medicinal plants and animals.

Sillitoe (2000) observes that efforts to achieve sustainable development in agriculture from which the majority derive their livelihoods should take into account indigenous knowledge in order to reduce reliance on scientific technical knowledge. Over time, indigenous people develop their own location-specific knowledge and practices of agriculture, natural resource management, veterinary and human health care. Indigenous knowledge is dynamic and responds to changes in the environment through experimentation, creativity, innovation as well as through contact with other knowledge systems.

According to Naseem (2000), indigenous farmers have three approaches to experimentation: curiosity experiments, problem solving experiments, and adaptation experiments – all of which are mutually inclusive. That is to say, problems are identified; assumptions about better options are made, followed by the design and implementation of an experiment and assessment of the results and finally widespread communication and adaptation of the solution. This suggests the use of logic which comes close to the western scientific concept, where a direct cause-effect relationship between two variables is assumed.

Kunnie (2000: 34) observes that the above establishes the unequivocal scientific character of indigenous knowledge. Therefore, as opposed to viewing indigenous knowledge systems as primitive and superstitious, modern science is compelled to re-examine its biased and prejudicial disposition towards these systems. The nexus between indigenous knowledge and sustainability is clear. Firstly, indigenous people have the ability to engage in self-sufficiency. Secondly and more importantly, they are able to live in relatively peaceful co-existence with the natural environment, harnessing the forces of nature in a spiritual manner that preserves the potential of natural resources for use by future generations. (Kunnie (2000) argues that among such indigenous societies, there is no predatory and parasitic obsession as is the case with Western European societies that exploit and consume finite natural resources ad infinitum, devastating human communities, destroying vegetation and contaminating water and air systems to the point that climate hostile to human existence.

The consumerist and capitalist culture of the West has destroyed many ecosystems and the ozone layer because of emissions from industry. On the contrary, ecologically sensitive and harmonious modes of cultivation as practised by the indigenous people of Africa, and in particular those of Mutasa in Zimbabwe, are rooted in indigenous knowledge systems which have been applied for a long time. Although at times living on the margins of society, indigenous people are good stewards of nature as everything is imbued with spiritual significance and divinely inspired. Indigenous knowledge systems foster deliberate natural resources management which are in sync with natural cycles in all ecosystems.

Application of indigenous knowledge in resource utilisation: A conceptual framework

Indigenous Knowledge enables households and even individuals to exploit the various natural resources available to them. It also serves as the basis upon which households and individuals make decisions to adopt, adapt, reject or develop new management tools (Simpson, 1999). Local people rely on their detailed environmental and ecological knowledge to make important management decisions at major stages in the cropping cycle. Simpson (1999) further notes that in Mali for example, observations of the weather patterns and constellations, the behaviour of certain plants, animal and bird species, are used in forecasting the change of seasons and making decisions on when to begin land preparation and planting (see for example, Mapara 2009; World Bank 1998; Semali and Kincheloe 1999; Mawere 2014). Similarly in Zimbabwe, when the local people see a certain bird species on the tree tops, they know that it is time to start clearing the fields.

In some parts of Africa such as Zimbabwe, Mozambique, Swaziland and Ghana, among others (Mawere 2014), local farmers also have ways of differentiating between and among the major classes of resources important to their livelihoods; for example, soil types, plant species, animals, etc. Simpson (1999) observes that this leads to widely observed prohibitions concerning the avoidance or socially differentiated use and consumption of specific resources, foods or animals and the more general overarching beliefs in the ebb and flow of seasons, cycles of birth and death and renewal.

267

Occurrences of specific events, such as droughts or illness are often explained in indigenous world views. In many African traditional societies such as that of the Shona people of Zimbabwe, local religious beliefs are often consulted to mediate between the physical and the spiritual world, or rituals are sometimes performed before engaging in certain acts, such as preparing one's field, planting or cutting a tree. However, it is acknowledged that such traditional belief systems and their associated practices are fast eroding in some communities and especially among the young farmers.

With regards to the actual farming, soils are often given names for features in the landscape where they are found, or for specific attributes like their colour or texture and are managed as the farmers sees fit. The soil position in the landscape and its colour (indicative of parent material) are also a very important characteristic used in differentiating soils. In Zimbabwe, the most common indigenous soil classifications are the clays (*dongo* in local Shona language), the sandy loam soils (*senya* in local Shona language), and red or black heavy soils (*gadhi* in local Shona language) (Personal communication 2009). Farmers know that high clay content indicates a high capacity to hold moisture and nutrients as opposed to sandy soil and so they go ahead and plant crops with a high demand for such. Traditional farmers in Zimbabwe, as elsewhere in Africa, are also aware of the fluctuating nature of soil fertility which is depleted through continuous cultivation. They know that it can be restored by crop rotation and fallow.

It should be underscored that indigenous knowledge is an invaluable basis for food security and natural resources management and various other activities that sustain societies in many parts of Africa. In addition, since it is a product of a long process of experimentation, adaptation and innovation, it enables the reproduction of livelihoods. It enables communities to survive. Whereas scientists use formal training to innovate in order to satisfy their professional expectation, local farmers innovate in order to survive and develop themselves and their societies just like Western science does. Therefore, any development initiatives should build upon community based knowledge. It then follows that indigenous knowledge can be harnessed to complement any technological and scientific interventions in society. Development initiatives should interact with, and not override local knowledge.

Variations of indigenous knowledge

The dependence of livelihoods upon local production ensures that indigenous knowledge is local or community specific, yet this should not be interpreted to mean that it (IK) cannot be transferred from one locality to another (Mapara 2009; Mawere 2014; Altieri 1995). Elsewhere (Mawere 2014), one of the co-authors of this chapter has challenged the belief by some scholars (such as Hountdonji 1997, Turnball 2000) who believe that indigenous knowledge is static. According to Millat-e-Mustafa (2000), the understanding of IK as local specific means that the general applicability of IK to other environments or social circumstances can be limited in its application to other contexts. Indigenous knowledge informs decisions which are entirely rational within their own socio-economic contents, but if this context is subjected to external pressure, then the logic informing the decision making may be compromised. It also means therefore that, indigenous knowledge is liable to change in conditions of rapid social and environmental change. For example, if it is transmitted by word of mouth, once forgotten, it may be lost forever.

Simpson (1999:50) adds that the commonly held traditional wisdom and individual understanding also differs in both qualitative and quantitative terms. Individuals participate in a number of different, overlapping and social networks from which they received, and to which they contribute information. The associations influence the type of information to which individuals have access, and also serve to delimit the type of experiences and opportunities through which individuals can observe and interact with others. Friendships and personal affinities also facilitate the exchange of information across socialised lines of communication. In addition, public places like markets, dip tanks and water wells, and activities such as group labour, provide physical and social contexts within which the exchange of information between individuals often takes place.

As noted by Millet-e-Mustafa (2000), there are again many variables affecting the type and degree of knowledge held by various members of the same community as well as their ability to communicate or share this information with others. As such development workers and researchers need to recognise the following main variables:

■ *Gender*

Gender affects the type and amount of knowledge held by and individual, particularly in communities where there is gender division of labour. In most parts of Africa, a lot of agricultural activities are divided along gender lines under the direction of the eldest active male, with the eldest active female coordinating and organising activities assigned to household women (Simpson, 1999). However, the division of labour also depends as much on interpersonal relations and negotiations, as any broader cultural trends and vary from household to household and villages.

By and large, gender based tasks leading to indigenous knowledge differentiation is common where, for example, cultivation of specific food and cash crops, collection of wild fruits and leaves, preparation of food etc. are assigned to different gender and age groups (Simpson, 1999; see also Ellis 1998; Mawere 2013b). Women exchange information and experiences in the course of performing daily chores like fetching water, gathering firewood or while walking from the fields. During winnowing, which is usually done as separate groups (male/female) or where young boys are forbidden, women get the opportunity to freely discuss and share information which sometimes could be forbidden by the male hierarchy.

■ *Age*

While indigenous knowledge of classification of resources may be broadly shared by farmers in a community, individual knowledge of the more detailed attributes of each resource within the classification schemes are largely based upon personal experience (Simpson, 1999). This means that the range of personal experiences involved in managing and using different resources as well as the length of association with the resource is important. Depth of

270

knowledge is rooted in early childhood development as children develop a cognitive map of village lands and associated activities while carrying out daily chores, such as gathering wild fruit and minding livestock. As one gets older, they are expected to become knowledgeable about the history and development of different farming methods and other practices essential for sustaining livelihoods. This experience they may use for their own benefit individually, or as a household.

Sometimes, older and inactive but experienced individuals may give advice to young farmers who may not necessarily be family members. But, again also in the family, the eldest children (both male and female) may be given more detailed agricultural and natural resources instructions and information by the elders so that their share with their brothers and sisters. In this way, age results not only in quantitative knowledge differences, based on levels of experience, but also include elements of qualitative differences, due to the nature and level of detail contained in the information passed on by members of one generation to the next.

■ *Education*

Formal education affects the type of knowledge held and the way an individual expresses that information. The assumption is that the more formally educated an individual is, the more likely he is to be an important source of useful agricultural knowledge. It is also acknowledged that gender affects access to formal education. This is because some ethnic groups in Africa deny the girl child access to education as opposed to boys. The reasoning seems to be that it is a waste of resources to send the girl child to school since after that she will be married off to the benefit of her new family.

Indigenous knowledge and land reform in Zimbabwe

Zimbabwe has been repossessing and redistributing land to its sons and daughters since independence in 1980. Within a period of 25 years, the land redistribution programme transferred 12.3 million hectares of land from the White minority to 203,000 small scale farmers and led to the establishment of 30,000 indigenous black commercial farmers (Pazvakavambwa and Hungwe 2009: 137).

However by the 1990s, land redistribution had stalled due to a combination of many factors including donor fatigue and economic structural adjustment. However, in 1999, government responded to the imperatives of the national land question by launching the second phase of the Land Reform and Resettlement Programme. One of the laudable objectives of this programme was to enable local indigenous people to repossess their land from white owned large scale commercial farming sector.

On this note, we underscore that the indigenous people who received land under the land reform programme represent different language and ethnic groups who undoubtedly are at the same time a reservoir of untapped indigenous agricultural and natural resource knowledge and experience. The land reform programme, thus, in a way could be viewed as a long waiting opportunity for the deployment and validation of the efficacy of indigenous knowledge systems in Zimbabwean communities. Studies by Scoones *et al* (2010) and Hanlon *et al* (2013) confirmed that land which was previously occupied by a single farmer was divided into plots and now being used by a diverse group of people. This diversity in the indigenous smallholder farmers has the advantage of adding new skills and experiences in securing livelihoods and ensuring food security. Therefore, if government recognises that indigenous farmers can contribute to achieving national food self-sufficiency and national development, policy makers and development planners need to consider the following, among others:

■ Local communities' knowledge of animal breeding and production, classification of animal diseases and ethno veterinary medicine,

■ Farmers' perspectives of positive and negative characteristics of varieties of major crops such as rice

■ Indigenous soil classification and management systems

■ Indigenous agricultural and natural resource management systems for aquatic resources, water and soil, domesticated and wild plants, crop varieties, and crop pest management,

■ Indigenous disease classification systems and the use of herbal remedies in the treatment of diseases,

■ Knowledge of relationship between food and nutrition status,

272

- Indigenous knowledge relating to crop production, crop storage, food processing and crop/food marketing,
- Indigenous approaches to innovation and experimentation as responses to locally identified problems (see Warren 1993).

For Zimbabwe, apart from documenting indigenous knowledge systems, there is need for research also on the adaptability of these systems in circumstances involving rapid population increase like the resettlement areas. Indeed the land reform programme significantly altered the agrarian structure by increasing the average land units and gave access to a large number of indigenous people who had been deprived of land rights through historical injustices, particularly colonial subjugation by European settlers.

Although indigenous knowledge systems were not recognised during the colonial period to the extent that they were sadly labelled as unscientific, primitive, illogical, and anti-development, advocacy for community participation in project cycle activities demonstrates that local level initiatives are an important basis for sustainable advancement in the productive use of the land resource. Njie and Muir-Leresche (2000: 10), observe that past attitudes of scepticism and contempt for local farmers' knowledge have been the cause of many government and aid sponsored failures, and have contributed to the mistrust and suspicion of local people towards officialdom. A good entry point for the mobilisation of local communities to develop sustainable systems for greater self-reliance would be proper acknowledgement of the indigenous farmer as the real master of the land.

The dominant development paradigm until recently was the modernisation and transfer-of-technology model which was blind to local knowledge issues. There has now been a shift from "top down" imposition of interventions to a "grassroots" participatory perspective. There is now growing consensus that farmer's own indigenous knowledge should be mobilised in the production of plans and interventions for rural development programmes. This knowledge derives from past experiences, is transmitted from one generation to another, evaluated and fine-tuned, as people engage in a continuous process of experimentation and innovation. It therefore forms an important basis for decision making in both familiar and new circumstances, problems and challenges. In indigenous communities such as those of Zimbabwe, indigenous knowledge is therefore important for sustainable development planning because it has been tried and tested through time to meet the demands of local conditions.

We argue in this chapter that the success of development projects under the land reform programme in Zimbabwe depends to a great extent on participation by local indigenous farmers. This means that agricultural extension staff needs to be familiar with indigenous knowledge so that they are able to understand and communicate with the local people. Development practitioners and local people should work as partners in planning and implementing projects. Quite often, solutions offered by a development project may fail it does not fit with local knowledge. In any case, indigenous knowledge may suggest alternatives. Indigenous knowledge can offer comparatively low-cost approach with potentially high benefits.

In some cases, indigenous knowledge used effectively by one group can also be used to solve issues or challenges faced by another society in a similar agro-ecological environment. For example in Zimbabwe, Kunnie (2000) observes that there are over 500 types of plants found all over most of the country which can be used for medicinal purposes using indigenous knowledge. Mawere (2014) has also identified more than thirty indigenous knowledge systems that can be transferred and used in other communities in Zimbabwe and beyond. The point is that local people have knowledge which should not be viewed as a constraint but rather as a positive resource to promote participatory development. It can either be incorporated into existing efforts to enhance and expand effectiveness, or it can also serve as the basis for new initiatives. Indeed the looking down upon local ways of doing things often yields negative self-esteem among the intended beneficiaries and is at odds with goals of self-sufficiency, sustainability, and participation. An understanding of local knowledge makes for better development programmes, and more effective cross cultural communication.

Besides, indigenous knowledge also provides the basis for local level decision making (also see Warren 1993). Communities have indigenous forum through which group-decision making takes place. Sometimes these forums are elusive and invisible to an outsider. By identifying local decision making forum and understanding their structures and their functions, development planners are able to give indigenous knowledge the chance to contribute to sustainable development. Membership to these forums can be based on a variety of criteria such as age, gender, totem, etc. Often, it is easier to work with and through existing structures rather than develop new ones to carry out project goals and objectives.

It is also important to point out that local communities manage their common property resources through indigenous decision making. No wonder Warren (1993) notes that common property should not be mistaken as free for all. There are structured ownership arrangements within which management rules are developed, group size is known and enforced, incentives exist for co-owners to follow the accepted institutional arrangements and sanctions exist to ensure compliance. Masiiwa (2002: 17) adds that informal socio-legal exist to regulate access, use and benefit rule. For instance, it is expected that people take from nature what they need and leave the rest to nature and others. Resource degradation is sometimes due to the neglect or dissolution of local level institutional arrangements whose very purpose was to promote resource use patterns that were sustainable.

Basing on the foregoing, we argue that there is a case to put time and effort into understanding, recording and utilising indigenous knowledge especially in agriculture and rural development. Warren (1993) suggests that it is critical for agricultural research and extension services to work with parallel indigenous systems. Standard guidelines will then need to be developed which establish ethical codes of practice in the use of indigenous knowledge, based on principles such as informed consent and right to know, intellectual property rights, compensation rights, cultural rights and other generally recognised rights.

Policy makers should also look at how the national education policy in Zimbabwe can incorporate material on the nation's indigenous knowledge into various curricula at universities, colleges and vocational training centres. Further, researchers should also take interest in the use of indigenous communication channels and their application to sustainable development discourse. This is because the success and sustainability of development initiatives hinge on active and meaningful participation of the local indigenous people who are also the intended beneficiaries.

Research methodologies and findings

Regular visits to the countryside gave us the opportunity to pursue a variety of informal and unstructured interviews and discussions with local small scale or household farmers to get information on community practices and indigenous knowledge systems. We also relied on direct observation; by seeing the indigenous knowledge, in the various forms, applied and being applied in their natural setting. Seeing the place where something was done or takes place, helped to increase our understanding of the issues under study. These findings exclude large scale or commercial farmers, who were not the subject of the study. The following issues were noted as part of our findings:

■ *Land classification and management*
Farmers know that the colour and texture of soil and the type of vegetation found there is an indicator of the level of fertility of that particular soil. Red and black clay soils (also known as *chidhaka or gadhi* in the local language), where tall grass and *Musasa* trees (*Brachystegia speciformis*) grow are classified as fertile soils with a high water table. On the other hand sandy soils (also known as *jecha* in the local language), where short grass and thorny bushes grow, are classified as poor soils with little agricultural potential.

Farmers are also aware of the fluctuating nature of soil fertility which is depleted through continuous cultivation. They know that it can be restored by crop rotation involving legumes. Farmers mix soil with ash, or humus and compost manure to improve soil fertility, as well as the soil's water holding capacity. Farmers also dig contours and plant grass or shrubs and fruit trees on ridges as a way of reducing soil erosion.

■ *Predicting and coping with the weather*

Farmers rely on a number of indicators to predict the start of a good or bad rainy and cropping season. The blossoming on the *Musasa* trees (*Brachystegia speciformis*) and noise from frogs in water pools at night are indicators of impending rains. On the other hand, the appearance of certain insects like grasshoppers is viewed as signs of impending droughts.

Thick clouds and lightning are interpreted as signs of impending heavy rains. Farmers respond by moving essential goods, grain and livestock to higher ground in case of floods. They can also read clear skies at night during certain months as well as changes in wind direction to mean impending drought or low rainfall season. It is known that North-Easterly wind brings rain, and if it did not blow from that direction, there was likely to be below normal rainfall. Normally farmers respond by creating a community granary to store grain at the headman or chief's homestead for use by the whole village should the cropping season fail.

■ *Rainwater harvesting*

Local people intercept and collect rainwater from the roofs, and also ground catchment in order to supplement water supplies for both domestic and agricultural purposes. Water collected from roof gutters is normally used for domestic use whereas rainwater collected in ponds is used to irrigate vegetable gardens. Vegetable gardens are situated along rivers and streams to enable easy bucket irrigation from the pools dug in the streams. They are fenced by dead tree branches to keep out grazing animals. Farmers also use dead leaves and maize stocks in the vegetable gardens, as mulching, to reduce direct sun, as a way of conserving soil moisture.

Elsewhere in Zimbabwe, the idea of harvesting rainwater was popularised by a villager (Zephania Phiri) from Zvishavane District in the Midlands province, who in 1987 established the Zvishavane Water Project (for more on Phiri see Mary Witoshynsky 2000; Ken Wilson 2013; Brad Lancaster 1996). A key activity was to dig contour ridges with infiltration pits (swales) along every field to harvest run-off water, as well as planting trees to stabilise the soil and prevent erosion. This was useful to him and other small scale farmers in his community.

■ *Agro-forestry*

Farmers exercise self-sufficiency and reliance on locally available natural resources. They plant multi-purpose trees around their homesteads. These trees are a source of fruits, firewood, and are also an important source of shelter from severe winds and storms. The farmers also plant trees and shrubs around the boarders of gardens and fields, not only to mark boundaries, but to reduce soil erosion, to provide shelter from the sun for the people tilling the land and to trap underground water in order to maintain soil moisture. Farmers also have knowledge of mode of propagation as well as flowering and fruiting times of different "useful" trees and shrubs. They also exercise restraint in the cutting of such useful trees and shrubs. Some trees like the fig-tree are actually considered as sacred and cannot be cut without permission of the headman or chief. This is because rituals are normally performed under the fig-tree, which is considered the favourite by the ancestors.

■ *Cropping*

Not all farmland under the control of a household has equal agricultural potential. Farmers know this and so they carefully select crops and individual varieties to match the soil types and moisture regimes. For example, they plant small grain crops such as rapoko or finger millet (*Eleusine Coracana*) (*Zviyo* in local language) and sorghum (*Sorghum Bicolor*) (*Mapfunde* in local language) on drier pieces of land because their demands for moisture are low. Rapoko is popular because it is an important source of amino acid methionine which lacks in the diets of people who live on starchy staples like maize as is the case in Zimbabwe. The grain is ground to make powder for porridge or fermented to make a drink. Similarly, they plant yams in clay and water logged soils because they demand a lot of moisture. Farmers also practice mixed cropping as a way of preserving soil fertility and soil erosion because of the variety of the root systems of the different crops. Mixed cropping also ensures moisture conservation because the variety of crop leaves reduces direct sunlight and over-heating of the soil surface. During the main cropping season which runs from October to March, they plant maize (staple crop) in rows and sugar beans in between the rows.

278

Beans are a legume which gives the soil nitrogen through *Rhizobium leguminozorum,* which is a nitrogen fixing bacterium.

Rains normally come in mid-October. Farmers know that if the rains come too early or too late, it is an indication that the season has shifted. Farmers have to make decisions on what type or crop to plant which suits the shift in the season. For example, they know when it is now too late to plant maize or too early to plant potatoes.

■ *Pest control*

Farmers alternate crops on the same piece of land as a way of destroying the habitats which support life cycles of pests. The most common indigenous methods of pest control are handpicking pests and pulling out diseased plants which nurture pests. In some cases, ash is applied to seedbeds and vegetable gardens in order to control pests. In the case of livestock, besides using different herbs to control parasites, in extreme cases, they put down the diseased animal and burn the carcase, to avoid spread of contagious diseases such a foot and mouth disease in cattle.

■ *Seed preservation*

For each important crop, like maize, farmers select the healthy ones or those with preferred characteristics for drying and preservation so that they can be used as seed during the next planting season. Earthen pots or calabashes are used to store the seeds. These are carefully kept in the dry corners of the granary. Farmers only buy seed to supplement or after a number of poor cropping seasons since seed can be preserved for more than one season. They are sceptical about new seed varieties produced and recommended by seed houses in the towns and cities because they have their own tried and tested "reliable" varieties. New crop varieties also require different "scientific" preservation methods which famers take long to embrace. I case in point is that SR52 hybrid maize, a high-yielding variety was resisted by farmers because they alleged that it had low germination rates and required chemical fertilisers which they could not afford.

Women are a very important source of indigenous knowledge on seed processing and storage. This is because in the Manyika culture, there is a rough working classification of crops by gender.

Crops such as pumpkins, groundnuts and millet, which meet multiple household needs, are considered women's crops whereas those with less diversified uses like maize are considered men's crops. Because of this, women possess knowledge about various seed types, their tolerance to drought and disease, and suitability to different terrain and soil types.

■ *Livestock rearing*

Livestock is viewed with pride as a sign of wealth. Farmers keep cattle for meat and milk as well as for drought power for ploughing the fields. Livestock and poultry are also a source of fuel and manure. Cow-dung, especially, is used for both cooking and as manure. Cattle are selectively slaughtered for meat during special occasions like traditional ceremonies, and funerals, or as medium of transactions/exchange during marriages. To this extend, farmers use a wide variety of indigenous medicines to cure animal diseases. Ethno-veterinary medicines are cheap, familiar and locally available. Leaves of the soft and woody shrub called *Tephroia Vogelli* (Leguminous plant) are popularly used to treat ticks, roundworms and tapeworms in cattle. Leaves of *Aloe Vera* (*Gavakava* in the local language), *Ozora Reticulata* (*Mugaragunguwo* in local language) are used to treat internal parasites in livestock, and *Strychnos Spinosa* (*Mutamba* in local language) is also used to treat internal parasites and eye problems in cattle (cf. Mawere 2014).

Conclusion

This chapter has discussed indigenous knowledge systems in terms of how they embrace knowledge, innovations and practices of indigenous peoples and local communities. These are therefore local, community-based systems of knowledge which are unique to a given society and which have developed over time. The people have inhabited a particular ecosystem and so they have knowledge about sustainable relationships between themselves, habitat and nature. It is unique because it is often oral based, often revealed through stories and legends and may be difficult to transmit the ideas and concepts to those people who do not share the language, tradition and cultural experience.

The chapter concludes that in Zimbabwe, indigenous knowledge is the basis for local-level decision making in areas of contemporary life including agriculture and natural resource management. It is also inherently dynamic, constantly changing through experimentation and innovation from fresh insight and external stimuli. It is therefore important for government and other stakeholders to recognise that agricultural and natural resource policy initiatives as well as technological advancement should acknowledge the positive influence which indigenous knowledge systems can have.

There is always a potential conflict between those who practice agriculture and those who purport to know it as scientists. Scientists, often with a college qualification, involve themselves in policy planning and introduction of technology. They do this in the name of rural development. Unfortunately, however, they tend to overlook the farmers knowledge and beliefs. Therefore, the Government of Zimbabwe should encourage the identification, collection and documentation of indigenous knowledge before much of it is lost. New and existing policies and strategies of extension agencies including NGOs should emphasise sustainable issues, and the value of the many centuries old indigenous practices.

References

Altieri, M. A. 1995. *Agro-ecology: The science of sustainable agriculture*, 2nd Ed, IT Publications: London.

Amutabi, N. M. 2006. *The NGO Factor in Africa: The Case of Arrested Development in Kenya*, Taylor and Francis Group, Kenya.

Bruce, J.W. and Migot-Adhola, S. E. (eds), 1994, *Searching for land Tenure Security in Africa*, Washington USA, Kendall/Hunt Publishing Company.

Buthelezi, S. (ed.), 2009, *The Land belongs to us: The Land and Agrarian Question in Africa*, Pietermaritzburg, South Africa, Intrepid Press.

Carney, D. 1998. *Sustainable rural livelihoods: What contribution can we make?* Department for International Development, London.

Cavendish, W. 2001. Rural livelihoods and non-timber forest products, In De Jong, W. and Campbell, B. (Eds). *The role of non-*

timber forest products in socio-economic development, CABI Publishing: Wallingford.

Chambers, R. and Conway, G. 1992. Sustainable rural livelihoods: Practical concepts for the 21st Century, *Discussion Paper 296*, Institute of Development Studies.

Cheru, F. 2002. *African Renaissance: Roadmaps to the Challenge of Globalisation*, London and New York, ZED Books.

Chiome, E. M, Mguni, Z and Furusa, M. 2000. *Indigenous Knowledge and Technology in Africa and Diasporan Communities*, Harare, Jongwe Printers.

Cusworth, J. 1992. " Zimbabwe: Issues Arising from the Land Resettlement Programme" 89-101 in Dudley, N. *et al* (eds.), *Land Reform and Sustainable Agriculture*, United Kingdom, Intermediate Technology Publications.

Deng, L. A. 1998. *Rethinking African Development – Towards a Framework for Social Integration and Ecological Harmony*, Asmara, Eritrea, Africa World Press.

Duri, F. and Mapara, J. 2007. Environmental awareness and management in pre-colonial Zimbabwe, *Zimbabwe Journal of Geographical Research*, 1 (2): 98-111.

Ellis, F. 1998. Household strategies and rural diversification, *Journal of Development Studies*, 35 (1): 1-38.

Goduka, I. 2000. Indigenous ways of knowing: Affirming a legacy, pp. 134-145, In Chiwome, E. *et al* (Eds). *Indigenous knowledge and technology in Africa and Diasporan communities: Multi-disciplinary approaches*, Southern African Association for Culture and Development, Harare: Zimbabwe.

Hanlon, J. Manjengwa, J. Smart, T. 2013. *Zimbabwe takes Back its Land*, South Africa, Stylus Publishing, LLC.

Hountondji, P. 1997. (Ed). *Endogenous knowledge: Research trails*, CODESRIA, Senegal.

IPCC. Managing the Risks of Extreme Events and Disasters to Advance Climate Change Adaptation. *A Special Report of Working Groups I and II of the Intergovernmental Panel on Climate Change*. Field C. B, Barros V, Stocker T. F, Qin D, Dokken D. J, Ebi K. L, *et al*, editors. Cambridge: Cambridge University Press; 2012. pp.582.

IUCN, 1997, *Indigenous Peoples and Conservation Initiative – Cases and Action*, International Books, Utrech, Netherlands.

Kunnie, J. 2000. '*Developing Indigenous Knowledge and Technological Systems*, in Chiome, E. M, Mguni,   Z. and Furusa, M. pp. 33-44. *Indigenous Knowledge and Technology in Africa and Diasporan Communities*, Harare, Jongwe Printers.

Lancater, B. 1996.*The man who farms water (Zephania Phiri's swales)*, Lancaster Publication, USA.

Madzudzo, E. 2002. Outcomes of CBNRM programmes: A case study of CAMPFIRE in Bulilimangwe District of Zimbabwe, *Unpublished PhD Thesis*, Wageningen University: The Netherlands.

Makumbe, J. 1998. *Democracy and development in Zimbabwe: Constraints of decentralisation*, SAPES Trust: Harare.

Mararike, C. G, 1999, *Survival Strategies in Rural Zimbabwe*. Mond Books, Harare.

Mapara, J. 2009. Indigenous knowledge systems in Zimbabwe: Juxtaposing postcolonial theory, *Journal of Pan African Studies*, 3 (1): 139-155.

Marongwe, N. 2004. Traditional authority in community-based natural resource management (CBNRM): The case of Chief Marange in Zimbabwe, In Dzingirai, V. and Breen, C. 2004. *Confronting the crisis in community conservation: Case studies from southern Africa, Centre for Environment: Agriculture and Development*, University of KwaZulu Natal, South Africa.

Mawere, M. 2012. *The Struggle of African Indigenous Knowledge Systems In An Age of Globalization – A Case for Children's Traditional Games in South-eastern Zimbabwe*, (2012), Langaa RPCIG Publishers: Cameroon.

Mawere, M. 2013a. A critical review of environmental conservation in Zimbabwe, *Africa Spectrum*, 48 (2): 85- 97.

Mawere, M. 2013b. *Environment and natural resource conservation and management in Mozambique*, Langaa RPCIG Publishers: Cameroon.

Mawere, M. 2014. *Culture, indigenous knowledge and development: Reviving interconnections for sustainable development*, Langaa Research and Publishing Common Initiative Group, Bamenda: Cameroon.

Mawere, M. and Mabeza, C. (this volume). 'Sheep in sheep's clothing or wolves in sheep's clothing?' Interventions by non-state actors in a changing climatic environment in rural Zimbabwe.

Miah, A. M. 2000, *"Indigenous Technical Knowledge: Unexplored Potential for Sustainable Development"* 23-25 in Sillitoe, P (ed) Indigenous Knowledge Development in Bangladesh, Present and Future, University Press Limited, Dakar.

Millat-e-Mustafa, M. 2000, *"Towards Understanding Indigenous Knowledge Systems"* 27-30 in Sillitoe, P (ed) Indigenous Knowledge Development in Bangladesh, Present and Future, University Press Limited, Dakar.

Masiiwa, M. 2002, "Common Property Rights and the Empowerment of Communal Farmers in Zimbabwe: Institutional Legal Frameworks and Policy Challenges under Globailisation"15-30 in Chikowore, G. Manzungu, E. Mishayavanhu, D. And Shoko, D. Managing Common Property in an Age of Globalisation. Zimbabwean Experiences, Harare, Weaver Press,

Moyo, S. 1995, *The land Question in Zimbabwe*, Harare, SAPES Books.

Pazvakavambwa, S. and Hungwe, V. 2009, *"Land Redistribution in Zimbabwe,"* pp. 137-165, In Binswanger-Mkize, H. P. *Agricultural Land Redistribution: Towards a Greater Consensus,* Washington D C, World Bank.

Mukamuri, B. 1995. Making sense of forestry: A political and contextual study of forestry practices in south-central Zimbabwe, *Published PhD Thesis*, University of Tampere: Finland.

Naseem, S. B. 2000. Indigenous Knowledge and Agricultural Resources: Conflicts and Complementaries, pp. 139-143, In Sillitoe, P. (Ed) *Indigenous Knowledge Development in Bangladesh, Present and Future*, University Press Limited, Dakar.

Njie, N. and Muir-Leresche, K. 2000, *Overview of Important Issues for Sustainable Development in Sub-Saharan Africa"* Scandinavian Seminar College, Denmark.

Ntuli, P. 1999. The missing link between culture and education: Are we still chasing gods that are not our own? In Makgoba, M. W.

(Ed). *African renaissance*, Mafube-Tafelberg: Cape Town: South Africa.

Scoones, I. Marongwe, N. Mavedzenge, B. Mahenehene, J. Murimbarimba, F. And Sukume, C. 2010, Zimbabwe's Land Reform, Myths and Realities. Harare, Weaver Press.

Scoones, I. and Thompson, J. (ed) 2009, *Farmer First Revisited*, UK, Practical Action Publishing

Semali, L. M. and Kincheloe, J. L. 1999. Introduction: What is indigenous knowledge and why should we study it? In Semali, L. M. and Kincheloe, J. L. (Eds). *What is indigenous knowledge? Voices from the academy*, Falmer Press: New York.

Shizha, E. 2013. Reclaiming our indigenous voices: The problem with post-colonial sub-Saharan African School curriculum, *Journal of Indigenous Social Development* 2 (1): 1-18.

Sillitoe, P (ed) 2000. *Indigenous knowledge development in Bangladesh, present and future*, University Press Limited, Dakar.

Simpson, B. M. 1999. *The roots of change: Human behaviour and agricultural evolution in Mali*, Intermediate Technology Publications, UK.

Tatira, L. 2000. The role of Zviera in socialisation, In Chiwome, E., Mguni, Z., and Furusa, M. (Eds). *Indigenous knowledge and technology in African and Diasporan communities*, University of Zimbabwe, Harare, (pp. 146-151).

Turnball, D. 2000. *Masons, tricksters and cartographers: Comparative studies in the sociology of scientific and indigenous knowledge*, Routledge: London.

Warren, D. M. 1993. "Using Indigenous Knowledge for Agriculture and Rural Development: Current Issues". Indigenous Knowledge and Development Monitor 1 (1) 1-4.

Warren, D. M. Slikkerveer, L. Jan and Titilola, S. O (eds), 1999. *Indigenous Knowledge Systems: Implications for Agriculture and International Development*. Studies in Technology and Social Change, No. 11, U.S.A, Iowa State University.

Warren, D. M. 1993. "Using Indigenous Knowledge in Agricultural Development", World Bank Discussion Paper, Washington, D.C.

Wilson, K. 2013. *Zephania Phiri's book of life*, Muonde Trust and Friends.

Witoshynsky, M. 2000. *The water harvester: Episodes from the inspired life of Zephania Phiri*, Weaver Press: Harare, Zimbabwe.

World Bank, 1998. 'Indigenous knowledge for development: A framework for action', (Nov 4, 1998), Knowledge and learning centre-African Region, USA, Available at:

http://www.worldbank.org/afr/ik/ikrept.pdf (Accessed: 10 Jan 2015).

World Commission on Environment and Development (WCED), 1987. *Our common future*, Oxford University Press: Oxford.

Veitayaki, J. 2002. Taking advantage of indigenous knowledge: The Fiji case, *International Social Science Journal*, 54 (173): 395-402.

Chapter 13

Promoting Indigenous Knowledge for Sustainable Development in Africa: A Case Study of Ghana

Martin Quephie. Amlor

Introduction

In Africa's cultural and ecological diversities, a body of knowledge which have been depended on over the ages to tackle specific developmental and environmental problems is indigenous knowledge. Also referred to as traditional knowledge, it is embedded in the cultural milieu of all people, irrespective of race, colour or religion. According to Warren (1991:7):

> This knowledge system contrasts with the international knowledge system generated by universities, research institutions and private firms...and serves as the basis for local-level decision making in agriculture, health care, food preparation, education natural resource management, and a host of other activities in rural communities.

Zulu (2006:36), however, notes: "indigenous knowledge systems in Africa ironically remain dormant in slick misconceptions about African inferiority. African culture and knowledge that would otherwise educate the large population of the people on the continent remain hidden; unless a pro-active community of scholars rescue this situation and give it new meaning and significance".

Furthermore, (Maila and Loubser, (2003:276) jointly share the view that failure of indigenous knowledge, to contribute to improvement of the quality of human life can be attributed to the lower status accorded to this type of knowledge in societies which often, are assumed to lack the necessary social capital. On the contrary, the high attention accorded indigenous knowledge at present by academia, development institutions and international bodies such as the UN, UNESCO, and International Council for Science (ICSU, shows that it is a useful and indispensable social capital of the poor because it is their main asset, which helps them to struggle for survival, to produce food, provide shelter, and, as well, control their lives.

Inherited indigenous knowledge within a cultural setting is therefore crucial to the survival and development of a society that owns it. In the light of the above, it is worth understanding what the term, indigenous knowledge stands for.

Definition of Indigenous Knowledge

Noyoo (2007:167) explains indigenous knowledge as the complex set of knowledge, skills and technologies existing and developed around specific conditions of populations and communities indigenous to a particular geographical area. This knowledge, embedded in community practices and institutions, forms the basis for agriculture, food preparation, health care, education and training, environmental conservation and a host of other activities. Ntuli(1999) and Vilakari (1999) share similar views as they both see indigenous knowledge as a bona fide property of a people who are historically and culturally bound; and this knowledge system enables them to survive and sustain their communities. On the other hand, Eyong, (2007:121) draws our attention to the colonial racist view of indigenous knowledge:

> It is a monopoly of trials and error while western (modern) knowledge is science characterised by experimentation. Hence, while the former is presumed clogged, concrete, and inaccurate, the latter is painted as intangible, weighty, right and embedded with universal reasoning.

Odora-Hoppers (2008:142) views indigenous knowledge as that which is embedded in the cultural web and history of a people including their civilization and forms the backbone of their social, economic, scientific and technological identity.

According to the International Council for Science study group (ICSU, Vol.4, 2002:9): "traditional knowledge is accumulative body of knowledge, know-how, practices and representations maintained and developed by people with extended histories of interaction with the natural environment. These sophisticated sets of understandings, interpretations and meanings are part and parcel of a cultural complex that encompasses language, naming and classification systems, resource use, ritual practices, spirituality and worldview".

From my own perspective, indigenous knowledge is innate cultural values which enable people with a common cultural identity derive comfort and survival from local or natural resources they are endowed with. Approaches to the use of these resources are guided by patterned behaviours that are practised, preserved and transferred from the older to the younger generations to ensure continuous survival of the people and the society in which they live.

One can therefore deduce the fact that a continuous practice, preservation and transfer of indigenous knowledge over the years from one generation to the other without influence or obstruction, eventually leads to a sustainable development through progress and changes that are implemented in a given societal cultural setting.

What is Sustainable Development?

Sustainable development as defined by Brundtlandt Commission (1987:8), is "development that seeks to meet the needs and aspirations of the present generation without compromising the ability of future generations to meet theirs. In all activities, there is consideration of its impact on the future generation". Since it is an essential tool that enhances living standards of members of a society, efforts geared towards sustainable development can hardly ignore elements of culture. To corroborate the above statement, Noyoo (2007:167) adds:

Sustainable development is exemplified by on-going activities of self-sustenance by indigenous people, although at the same time, it is also a desired state that is not perilous to the livelihoods of those who are yet unborn. It is this kind of thinking that brings forth an understanding that sustainable development activities are both current as well as futuristic in form and foci.

Explaining sustainable development further, Onabajo (2005:93)states that it is the desire to improve or progress towards a lasting improvement in the quality of life of majority of the people in a given society or community. It is therefore, the condition in which people in a country have adequate job and food, fundamental and sustainable change through growth, social justice, equal opportunity for all citizens and equitable distribution of income.

Despite the fact that accumulated knowledge and traditional practices of indigenous African communities are powerful resources for the people, Semali (1999:309, 311), states that the promotion and implementation of indigenous knowledge of African societies are inundated with challenges.

The Study Site

Ghana, which is situated on the coast of West Africa, covers an area of 339,460 sq. km out of which 230,940 sq. km is land and 8,520 sq. of the land km is covered by water. The country shares boundaries with three Francophone countries: Togo to the East, Cote d'Ivoire to the West and Burkina Faso to the North. The Gulf of Guinea, borders the country to the south.

The country has about 539 kilometre low lying coastal line and its highest point is mountain Afadjato which rises to an altitude of 880 metres in the Volta Region which is one of the ten administrative regions of Ghana. The July 2010 census gives the population of the country as 24,339,838. Out of the ten administrative regions, Greater Accra in which the capital is located is the smallest but the most populated with the highest concentration of commercial and industrial activities. (http://www.ghanaweb.com).

Ghana, which has the Volta Lake as the largest artificial lake in the world, is a tropical country. While the south- eastern coast is warm and dry, the south-western area is hot and humid and her three northern regions are often hot and dry. Average annual rainfall in the coastal regions is about 83 cm. The country has natural resources that include minerals among which are gold, bauxite, and petroleum. The country has wildlife sanctuaries and a wide range of flora and fauna.

Challenges to the Promotion of IK for Sustainable Development

The promotion and practice of indigenous knowledge dating back to the colonial era, have been overshadowed and outpaced by western cultural dictates. The challenges to this unfortunate situation can be attributed to colonialism, forces of Westernization such as foreign religion, education, technology/mass media, and urbanisation.

Apart from foreign cultural impact, a major factor that continuously downplay the relevance, and practice of indigenous knowledge in Ghanaian traditional societies is lack of vision and knowledge by government leaders, policy makers/implementers to realise, the potentials of the country's indigenous knowledge systems and marshalling courage for promoting and using them to enhance the socio-economic life of the citizens. I shall examine each of these impeding factors in detail, and later discuss the way forward in promoting indigenous knowledge for sustainable development in Ghana.

Colonialism

Indigenous knowledge of societies in Ghana, like those of other societies in the West African sub-region, suffered protracted set-backs emanating from several strategies of Western ideologies. African Indigenous knowledge systems (IKS), suffered from disinformation rooted in western colonial and post-colonial education, religion, technology and often, misleading information on IK. One can therefore realise, that, what we know and understand about Africa, for that matter, Ghana, emerges from ideologically coloured lenses of 'prejudiced' colonial scholars who produced write-ups that described African cultures as raw, primitive, and uncivilised; acted this way to authenticate the genuineness of their Western knowledge and cultural values.

It can also be seen that Western colonialism in the Gold Coast aimed at changing the mind-set of the people and, thus, denying them their innate traditional values that store their history, culture and wealth. In order to boost European industrial exports, colonial rule largely hampered and deliberately undermined the indigenous societal technological and manufacturing competencies of African ancestors. In this direction, Boon and Eyong (2005:10) add: "hence, by a kind of perverted logic, colonialism turns to the past and values of the oppressed Africans and distorts, disfigures and destroys them". Colonial rule in the Gold Coast also came with an imposition of new legal systems based on European concept of law, which were often at variance with indigenous political system of the people. They set up courts that tried cases of libel and imposed subsequent fines and jail terms on the citizens. These types of punishment discouraged the practise of cultural values including indigenous musical types whose texts were full of satire, insults or reproach for negative societal conduct and attitudes.

Comprehensive reorganisation of indigenous societies in the Gold Coast and post-independence Ghana, in every aspect of life, continued to be dominated and tailored to suit colonial demands. The creation of artificial boundaries, which emerged in the 19th century and partitioned Africa, never took into account locations of cultural societies and institutions. European colonial powers including Britain, undertook systematic disintegration of settlements of indigenous societies with the same cultural identities and institutions in order to establish colonial rule as a form of concretising their legitimate ownership of the areas they controlled.

To date, Ghanaian traditional societies like the *Basare, Dagaaba, Ewe, Frafra, Kokoma* and *Krachi* among others, were split among the German, British and French colonial powers. As an initiative to annex these splinter groups that were formerly part of the then Trans-Volta Togoland, Dr. Kwame Nkrumah, prior to the attainment of independence for Ghana, held a referendum for these Ewe societies to decide between either joining Ghana or Togo. Though they chose to be part of Ghana, after parting from their relatives behind and across the artificial border of Togo, they are still glued to their neighbours not because of their newly acquired citizenship status, but the cultural communalism and identity they share in common as a people.

A major issue that also emerged from British colonial rule was a progressive integration of the Gold Coast into a capitalist system where the colony functioned primarily as a source of raw materials to feed Western industries. This move brought about a total re-structuring of the economic life of the natives through cash tie and imposition of taxes which forced most of the citizens into wage labour. Capitalism eventually reduced leisure time, stifled cultural performances and disrupted communal life of the people, which hitherto, formed the basis for collective societal activities including music making.

Effect of Colonial Economy on Ghanaian IK Systems

Boon and Eyong (2005:11) pointed out that introduction of monocultures took root during the colonial era. In the Gold Coast for example, vast portions of land with rich biodiversity were used for cultivating primary products and cash crops like cocoa, coffee, groundnut, palm oil and palm kernel oil. Small-scale farmers were lured into adopting western farming methods which were unsustainable and opposed to indigenous modes of mixed farming, bush fallowing and crop rotation that conserved the natural environment of the local people.

Examining colonial exploitation of Ghana's natural resources resulting into loss of biodiversity, Owusu and Kwarteng (2010:90) shed light on industrial need for palm oil, an indigenous food/crop that abounds in the forest belts of the West African sub-region:

> The industrial revolution in Great Britain, gave rise to a great need for lubricants in the 19th century. This led to the emergence of palm oil, a derivative of the oil palm, as an important technical oil that could be used for manufacturing soap and candles ... and the use of palm kernel oil for the production of margarine, chocolate, confectionary and pharmaceuticals. Cattle feed could also be obtained from the residue after kernel oil had been extracted. The high demand for

these cash crops for export to the European countries later brought about organized cultivation of oil palm on lands that the cultivators lay claim to. Hither to, there was neither organized cultivation of oil palm nor any individual or group ownership of this food/cash crop. Communal ownership of the oil palm before the advent of Europeans, ... embedded in Akan (a local language spoken by a large section of some Ghanaian ethnic groups) proverb states that *abɛbere a, woso fa, mesofa*; literally translated; when palm nuts are ripe, what you collect is yours and what I collect is mine.

They state further that European agricultural system did not yield the expected positive results envisaged by Ghanaians. For example, high yielding variety of seeds introduced as western promoted Green Revolution paradigm, lacked nutritional value. The objective of introducing the hybrid oil palm (dura and pisifera) to replace the local *abe* was only considered from the angle of selfish European economic gains in terms of the quantity of oil to extract to satisfy the production of their industrial goods and not how tasty and healthy it would be for human consumption (Owusu and Kwarteng, 2010:95).

The decline in oil palm production and export as a lucrative business later gave way to cocoa production. Clearing of forest belts for cocoa cultivation never came without problems. In this direction, Kwarteng (2010:120) further adds:

The rapid expansion of the cocoa industry in the forest belt of the country had drastic consequences on bio-diversity, particularly, the wildlife species ... and as such, an animal that suffered greatly from extensive cultivation of cocoa farms was the forest elephant (Loyodonta Africana Cyclotis). The implication of the acquisition of large tracts of forest lands for western influenced commercial agriculture was that the range or habitats of elephants were reduced to government constituted forest reserves ... and this became a hindrance to the free movement and survival of the elephants and other wildlife species.

The infringement on the habitat of the elephants made them to sporadically invade and destroy cocoa and food crop farms, settlements of farmers and, at times, killing some of the farmers. In their attempt at protecting their farms and property, the farmers also killed the invading elephants. Kwarteng observes that from the colonial period until 1989 when the African elephant was listed under the Convention on International Trade on Endangered Species of Wild Fauna and Flora (CITES), several thousands of them were killed together with other wildlife species.

From a recent visit I paid to local communities like Pampawie, Brewaniase and Nkwanta, which are all located in the forest belts of the northern Volta Region, Ghana, agricultural extension officers disclosed to me that the teak tree, a tropical hardwood (which is planted and sold by farmers for use as electric poles after they are chemically treated), have been found to be toxic to organisms responsible for soil fertility. Furthermore, application of chemicals such as fertilizer for increased food productivity, pesticides and weedicides like DDT and glyphocite for controlling weeds, have adverse effects on the local ecosystem and the people. Chemical applications and their negative effects on subsistence farmers in Ghana is similar to what the Andaman Chronicle (2013:1), reports about peasants of Andaman Island located off the Burmese coast in the Indian Ocean: "in applying chemicals for agricultural purposes, little quantities of these substances are retained in the tissues of vegetables and food crops and when consumed, the people suffer from serious health problems such as hypertension, kidney failure, bone diseases due to calcium deficiencies, and stone formation in the gall bladder and kidneys".

Colonial agricultural scientificism in post-colonial Ghana has transformed independent subsistence farmers to dependent consumers as a result of their drift from practising food crop to a fast falling cash crop economy and thus, giving rise to poverty, misery and diseases in the farming communities. The present state of food insecurity in the farming communities in Ghana is partly due to attempts made by the colonialists in flooding African markets with their home-made products which are eventually killing indigenous initiatives of the people. As rightly put, Eyong (2007:132), states:

Colonialists created captive markets that encouraged the dumping of goods. Supported by policies such as "the scrap iron policy" of Britain, African markets were flooded with cheap mass-produced textiles, glass and iron products. Among the first groups of artisans who felt the impact of the invaders' laws and activities were the metallurgists including blacksmiths who ... indigenous farmers largely depended on for their local farming implements.

Destruction of Ghana's Natural Environment

It is disheartening to note that at present, environmental conservation has been ignored because rural Ghanaian communities and their knowledge systems have become the target of western influenced exploitation. These rural dwellers, who are the producers of the food basket for the country through subsistence agriculture (food crop cultivation and raising livestock), face an ugly reality of deforestation as a result of vicious logging without effective tree-planting strategies to replace those that are felled. As a result, forest belts are gradually reducing to savannah lands and are almost at the verge of desertification.

Pastoral communities, in some of the regions of the country, have been turned into forest reserves and thus, evicting the rightful owners from their natural habitats. Similarly, Apusigah (2011:7) comments on the exploitation of lands that are purported to be rich in mineral deposits in the country:

Multi-national mining conglomerates, as well as local commercial miners backed by some traditional authorities in the communities in which they operate, have turned the earth's surface and beneath to exploit minerals. By this action, these companies have subjected water bodies (that are sources of drinking water) to high levels cyanide pollution and, as well, rendering them dirty, muddy, and unsuitable for human consumption.

Impact of Western-Generated Social Change on IK in Ghana

Social change, which has been precipitated by forces of Westernisation through Christian missionary activities, formal education, technology, the mass media and urbanisation has impacted both positively and negatively on the indigenous knowledge systems of traditional societies in Ghana.

Christian Missionary Activities

European missionary activities to a large extent influenced every cultural life of Ghanaians; most of them were converted to Christianity or Islam. Western religion has created a new type of an "educated" Christian, having European taste for clothing, food, drink and exposure to books, ideas and influences from outside the convert's cultural domain.

Despite some positive aspects of Christianity like formal education and total abandoning of some cultural practices such as human sacrifice, this foreign religion at the same time, undermined Ghanaian indigenous values by failing to express the Christian faith in African form and style. According to Hastings (1967:26):

The aim of the missionaries was to build mission stations, build churches, schools and hospitals; but most of them failed to understand Africans, their aspirations, hopes, their cultural values and civilisation. The teachings of the Christian church have been expressed in Western scholastic formulas.

Expressing his disgust at Western attempts at luring Africans from the practice of *Ifa,* a native religious worship among the Yoruba of Nigeria, to practising their values, Adedeji (2002:29), comments:

Many children and youth who were supposed to be priests(esses), to carry egungumaks and perform music of the traditional institutions, are today, either in the universities (in or outside the country), pursuing degrees or converted to Christianity and even ordained as priests or pastors. As a result, experienced practitioners of our indigenous values are reducing in number on daily basis.

Similarly, Darkwa (1974:79) also states that:

Christian converts in the Gold Coast were forbidden to practise their traditional values including music ... and urged converts to burn all traditional arts, paintings and handicrafts (repositories of indigenous historical data) and other things they termed 'pagan images' as proof of their sincere acceptance of the new religion.

AduBoahen (1962:122), further comments on this negative attitude of the European missionaries:

The missionaries looked down on everything African: African art, music, dancing; systems of marriage/naming ceremonies, and their converts had to renounce all these. The activities of the missionaries therefore created divisions in the (indigenous) African societies and retarded the development of African culture.

From investigations I personally conducted into activities of Christian converts during the colonial period in some northern and southern Ewe communities of the Volta Region of Ghana on Friday, October 31, 2014, information gathered was that in the past, customary practices like wailing, singing, drumming, dancing, pouring of libation and making sacrifices were not allowed at death and funeral ceremonies of deceased Christians. In addition, Christian converts who were later installed as chiefs or queen mothers in their communities, forfeited full membership of the churches to which they belonged.

By its entrenched position, Christian religion removed valuable forces that bound the people together and instead, isolated Christian converts from the larger indigenous community, and thus, undermining the concept of ontological continuity, where, families and clans by obligation, observe certain cultural values: care and respect for the elderly and those in authority as well as performing rituals to uphold their lineage and concretise community life as one people.

Sarpong (2005:4) explains the importance of being part and parcel of community life:

Before a person claims to be imbued with all the values that go into making a human being: the *sunsum* [spirit], *mogya* [blood], and *kra* [soul], are determined by the ancestral line from which the person comes. For this reason, it is binding on the person to live in the community, take part in societal activities, be involved in community rituals, enjoy his privileges and be committed to his responsibilities and....the character of the person's life must promote the peace and happiness of the community. In the traditional Ashanti communities of Ghana, a person whose behaviour distances him/her or contravenes laws that ensure good and stable community life, is regarded not only as a liability and a nuisance to the community but also, a trouble maker who reduces his/her self-image to the level of *aboa* [an animal].

Impact of Western Formal Education on IK in Ghana

One cannot doubt the fact that western culture has been the principal agent through which formal education emerged in Ghana. The coastal Fantes of Ghana first experienced contact with Europeans like the Portuguese in 1471, the Dutch in 1644, and the Danes in 1772. Alidza, (2010:120), therefore states:

The establishment of schools ushered into the Ghanaian community, foreign languages such as English and French and their related cultures and it was not until between 1800 and 1850 that western education began to admit ordinary Ghanaians since the earlier schools were mainly meant for immigrants from Europeans nations and children of merchants and wealthy Ghanaian businessmen.

Examining the merits of Western formal education, Maison (2010:63) indicates that it was started by the Portuguese in 1529 with an aim of Christianising the natives as well as teaching them to read and write. One can also acknowledge the fact that some Ghanaian citizens who have had Western education from the basic, through secondary to the tertiary levels, have taken up job opportunities in both government and private sectors.

Besides these positive measures, Maison (2010:65), further argues that Western missionaries focused on educational systems that served as vital nurseries for indoctrinating, processing and socialising children into Western cultural system and thereby, perpetuating colonial values and order which can be considered as forces for the destruction and alienation of Ghanaian indigenous knowledge systems. He concludes that:

> Understandably, Western school system was to ensure the maintenance of the colonial state, colonial social relations and colonial order and the state progressed according to the conditions of the hegemonic classes, erasing communal memories, traditions, indigenous languages and other forms of knowledge. This educational system promoted anti-African prejudices ... and as more people become educated, 'Eurocentric' consciousness metamorphosed and tagged 'progress or civilization'. This education served as the agency to replace the African mind with a European mind in order to replace Ghanaian indigenous education, religion, philosophical and psychological systems.

To date, the structure of formal education in Ghana has not totally departed from that of the Western model. For this reason, large population of students that pass out from the Technical, Vocational and Polytechnic institutions as well as the universities, lack the required knowledge and skills to meet challenges in the job market in the country. This situation has created a large population of unemployed secondary and graduate students who loiter about in the city and urban areas in search for non-existing white collar jobs

Another harm that Western formal education inflicted on IK in Ghana was the preference it accorded reading, writing and communication in English language at the expense of the Ghanaian types. Ghanaians, who speak English, see it as a form of civilisation worth passing on to their children at tender ages when they begin formal education at the crèche.

Western Technology and Mass Media

Social change, which affects IK in Ghanaian traditional societies today, are partly, due to the emergence of modern Western technology; print and electronic media. The people, especially the youth, now use audio-visual gadgets like tape recorders, computers, mobile phones, compact discs (CDs) and video cameras and largely enjoy recorded audio and live performances of assorted foreign music and films. Western radio and television broadcasts and programmes which are heard or watched in the urban and rural communities of the country, now urge on the youth to adopt and practise foreign cultural values to the detriment of their native types. The situation has now led to a cultural imperialism rather than cultural transformation of Ghanaians.   In examining African attitude and crave for Western cultural values at the expense of their indigenous types, Nzewi (1985:17) comments: "modern Africa has recklessly abandoned its human essence and cultural values while gobbling up with modern-publicity-hoisted glamorous allures of western thoughts and life styles".

Urbanisation

Urbanisation, simply defined, is the shift from a rural to an urban society, and involves an increase in the number of people in urban areas during a particular year. Urbanization therefore is the outcome of social, economic and political developments that lead to urban concentration and growth of large cities, changes in land use and transformation from rural to metropolitan pattern of organization and governance. (Nsiah-Gyabaah, 2003:4)

In a developing country, like Ghana, destruction of natural resources through logging, illegal mining, popularly termed galamsey, deforestation and bush fires have caused rural poverty and lack of basic infrastructure and services. These situations have driven most of the youth into the city in search of employment, food, shelter and education. "Even though city or urban areas offer

301

few jobs for the youth in many African countries, they are often attracted there by the amenities of urban life" (Tarver, 1996:95).

Why the neglect of IK in Ghana?

Western perception about African indigenous knowledge since the colonial era was that Africa was a tabula rasa (a clean slate), that is, a continent with no civilization, and for this reason, in Ghana, Western culture is perceived especially by the elite, as the only advanced wisdom that can best shape ideas, beliefs and general way of life of the citizens. In this way, Ghanaian IK was pushed by Western cultural dictates to almost its total neglect.

Lack of Vision and Leadership Qualities of Government Leaders

After over fifty-seven years of Ghana's independence, leaders in government still lack vision, good leadership qualities and the political will to change their western-inherited mind-set in order to re-direct their efforts at harnessing the country's socio-economic fortunes through the use of indigenous knowledge. Examining the ineptitude of government leadership in Ghana, (Amlor and Alidza (2011:22) comment:

> Leaders in authority either through inefficiency, fear, and lack of political will or in pursuance of selfish agenda, have woefully failed to address vital social, political and economic concerns of the masses in order to improve and raise their standard of living. In most cases, important virtues of governance are flouted and leaders cling to power after their tenure of office and display gross political misconduct.

The lack of political will of people in authority to correct or change Western contradictions and practices has resulted into unrealistic and unattainable socio-economic goals. Furthermore, the potentials of our indigenous knowledge system which should have been employed to mitigate social and economic hardships of Ghanaians were neglected. This neglect has eventually rendered the country economically unviable and bedevilled with unsurmountable problems among which are environmental degradation, poverty, food scarcity, poor education, joblessness, diseases and death resulting from hunger, poor sanitation and non-observance of good health habits.

The next factor that facilitated neglect for the use of IK, in Ghana is what I refer to as social change that came through agents of Westernisation, (Christian religion, education etc.), and attempted at totally eliminating some IK practices from the communities in which the missionaries settled and converted the indigenes to Christian faith. Other reasons which also accounted for the neglect of IK in the traditional societies in the country were: attitude(s) of Western trained Ghanaian elite, and the country's over dependence on foreign aid.

Attitude(s) of Ghanaian elite to IK

A class of Ghanaian citizens, whose attitudes and life styles have perpetuated the dictates of Western culture with its educational values, is the elite. The Ghanaian elite perceive Western formal education as a high intellectual ability that involves literacy and mastery of European languages, through reading, writing, and acquiring knowledge in mathematics, music and art as well as physical education as a foundation for what Maison (2010:23) describes as "acquiring tertiary knowledge to serve, eventually, the society as royal scribes, magistrates, priests, ministers, writers, and scholars".

To date, the perception and pride for going through the grill of Western education and training has made them distance themselves from Ghanaian cultural values. They neither see the need nor have the passion for re-directing their efforts at restructuring, promoting, or teaching indigenous knowledge to benefit their own people. (Alidza, 2010:119), complements the above statement:

African elite are lured by the attractions of Western culture, the rich folklore and indigenous knowledge system of the country remain largely untapped or totally relegated to the background. Not only has Ghana adopted the language of their colonial masters as their lingua franca, but also aid their elite citizens to look up to western tradition and culture as the panacea to the solution to all her internal problems.

In a statement of caution on negative Western educational approach to IK, in Africa, Broch Utne (2000: xxxii), in her response to World Bank "education for all" conference, held in Thailand, points out that:

> There is an intellectual re-colonisation present among many African nations south of the Sahara. Not only has Africa become dependent upon western aid, but also on western curricula, culture and languages. Western donors and part of the western educated African elite are involved in a re-colonisation process that benefits themselves to the detriment of African masses and therefore all the above robs the people of Africa of their indigenous knowledge and language, starves African higher education and subsequently perpetuates western domination.

Over Dependence on Foreign Aid

A long existing phenomenon that continuously shatters Ghana's development is over reliance on foreign aid which has led to complacency and apathy in seeking alternative sources of development from within Ghana's own geographical terrain. As a donee, she has been pampered over the years with financial aids, grants and loans from donor countries. In this way, the country has become addicted to seeking foreign assistance for any project she undertakes without assessing whether these aids meet her minimum national productivity targets or put our unmanageable fiscal policy in order. In this direction Leith (1996:66) states:

> Ghana still relies on international and foreign investors. By 2000, foreign debt totalled 160% of the Gross Domestic Product. After qualifying for International Monetary Fund's (IMF) Highly Indebted Poor Country (HIPC) initiative in 2002, the country received a reduction of external debt from $5 to $2.4 billion dollars. Despite this relief however, Ghana faces

significant challenges as vital economic resources contribute to servicing past loans instead of promoting internal infrastructural development. Ironically, as Britain continues to assume the role of the largest bilateral donor, British imperialism in Ghana has changed to an equally effective form of economic imperialism.

One can therefore realise that with her large foreign debt, the possibility for sustained long-term growth and development remains slim, because, important export revenue goes to pay off foreign debts at the expense of capital reinvestment.

According to Hutchful (2002:159), "though Ghana's financial reform has been superficially praised as a success; major infrastructural problems remain and continue to hinder long-term development. Ghana has continually failed to secure private long-term credit since it remains a risky environment for investors because of high rates.

Due to the above reasons, major Ghanaian-centred indigenous political, economic and social problems which confront citizens of the country still remain unattended to since the country's independence in 1957.

The Way forward

In finding solutions to challenges confronting the promotion of IK for sustainable development in Ghana, it is prudent to critically examine Semali's (1999:309) observations and critique which effectively highlights the call for Africans to "rethink education and schooling and begin a new path which departs from foreign interpretations of what is important at the local level".

Promoting IK for sustainable development in Ghana can therefore be achieved if the following concerns are addressed:

The need for African-Centred School Curriculum

Presently, there are many challenges confronting education in Ghana: lack of funds, teachers, classrooms, and learning materials. The use of suitably designed Ghanaian-centred school curricula, research/teaching methods and qualified teachers to step up teaching, learning and acquisition of indigenous knowledge from basic to the tertiary levels of education is virtually non-existent. A move in this direction would help the youth at these levels of education to understand and apply their indigenous knowledge systems to ensure their total well-being and those of the community members as well. This proposed new curricula, must be implemented in the ten administrative regions of the country to galvanise the citizens so as to maximise human resource potential to push forward our national development programmes.

There is the need also for leaders in government as well as education policy makers/implementers in Ghana to consider what Zulu (2006:44) terms "theory of African education that moves beyond problematic analysis to a constructive critique of internal and external forces that impede progressive social change", and see how this theory can be adopted and applied in Ghana's educational drive towards promoting, teaching and acquiring indigenous knowledge to solve social and economic challenges that confront the country. This would help create what Zulu terms as "an independent think tank that would be capable of addressing current and future educational and social needs of the country.

Empowering Pre-Tertiary Science Institutions

Though science education is struggling with dominating Western influences and almost killing prospects of developing educational curriculum with African cultural content, leaders in government, education policy makers/implementers should not relent and sit down unconcerned. At present, the Junior and Senior High Schools are challenged and hard put to studying science in schools due to lack of laboratories, equipment, textbooks and properly trained teachers. A solution to lack of books is access to the internet. According to Atta Sakyi (2012:1), "this is where we need to accelerate government programmes to provide internet access to all the nooks and crannies of Ghana; and this is only possible when the electrification exercise has reached 100% coverage. On the other hand, we may have to resort to alternative sources like solar power, bio fuels or biomass".

For our children to become renowned scientists, like Michael Faraday, Gugliomo Marconi or Bill Gates, their present knowledge base in science education should be firmly grounded. The motivation to study science and technology can open the avenue for them to combine their western acquired science education with their indigenous knowledge to make internationally accepted products with raw material acquired from their indigenous environments. Science students of our universities can also be given assignments on problems that confront the nation so that they apply their science-acquired knowledge in solving them.

Founding Centres for Scientific and IK Studies

Going by the calls of Zulu (2006) and Semali (1999), there is need for specific institutions of higher learning to be selected in the country to serve as centres where, a network of development workers, researchers, educators managers of local industries as well as respected members of the local communities should be brought together and tasked to design research methodologies. The methods should include how Ghanaian indigenous education and learning techniques can be tailored to suit modern social, economic and political realism.in the global world. In all, the role of high education, powered by academic educators in shaping the path towards a more culture-specific or culturally relevant curriculum, is quite critical.

These indigenous knowledge-centred educational institutions must be established in mostly, in the rural communities of Ghana to pool human resources drawn from the worldviews and energies of the local people and, as well, borrow from external technologies to enhance their socio-economic improvement and advance national and international development.

Since the study of indigenous knowledge depends on science and methods applied to understand humans as a way of improving their conditions of life, attention must be directed at the study of diverse Ghanaian cultures, beliefs, knowledge systems, indigenous technologies and practices of the people. In addition, human errors lead to abuse and disregard for societal values and thus create crises such as climatic, ecological, economic, and food scarcity. A study of Ghanaian cultures can help educate and bring about changes in human behaviour to re-shape the country's inter-cultural society and thereby, address challenges of poverty, hunger, joblessness, diseases, abuse of human rights which often bedevil the people.

To help co-ordinate and analyse research works from the centres in the country, a headquarters of Centre for Scientific and Indigenous Knowledge Studies should be established at the Kwame Nkrumah University of Science and Technology, an already existing institution for the study of science and technology in Ghana. The headquarters should also link scientific research with IK on natural resources including the use of medicinal plants. This must involve a holistic and multi-disciplinary approach involving both medical science educators and selected traditional medicine practitioners with long practicing experiences to not only produce drugs from our local plants to cure diseases but also, have knowledge of drugs produced protected, documented and modified to meet global health and development needs.

In considering the medium of instruction at the centres, emphasis must be placed on the use of major local languages of the communities in which they are located. Local teachers with in-depth knowledge and experience in IK must be recruited from within the local communities to approach the pedagogy and learning systems that would be consistent with the peoples' needs.

The Centre, must however, be subjected to continuous monitoring and appraisal to maintain an acceptably high value, relevance and quality of its products. In order to attain its goal, the University headquarters can establish close contacts with Companies, NGOs, UNESCO, friends in the Diaspora and philanthropists in and outside Ghana to support the Centre both in cash and kind to sustain its activities.

It is my avid hope that Ghana's current educational curricula for basic, Junior and Senior High Schools as well as tertiary institutions, would be refocused to produce a paradigm shift, away from theoretical education to one of practical application of foreign and local knowledge to solving our national problems. As the country at present continues to attract direct foreign investment because of our current oil find, there is the need to train more technicians than university graduates because in countries such as Germany, it is the technicians who work and drive industry.

In view of the above reasons, whereas we can produce few graduates to focus on research and development on the country's social, political and economic issues, more technical, vocational and polytechnic institutions should be built and resourced to turn out more vocational, technical and polytechnic graduates to acquire practical skills to meet the manpower needs of the country. This will automatically create job opportunities in future for the teeming population of the Ghanaian youth.

Controlling Environmental Degradation

Long before the advent of Europeans, many African cultures, had institutions which were built to conserve the earth and all what was within it through enforcement of customary laws, taboos and specific rituals. This accounts for why in some societies today, we see temporal ban on fishing prior to festival celebrations or abstinence from farming activities on specific days. To date, in some Ghanaian societies like the *Ga* and *Oguaa* societies occupied by the indigenous folks of Accra and Cape Coast respectively, a temporal ban is placed on drumming and fishing for some number of days preceding their respective *Homowɔ* and *Fetu Afahye* celebrations. For example at Cape Coast, a coastal Fante ethnic community and a former national capital of the Gold Coast, two weeks before the *Afahye* celebration, a temporary ban is placed on singing, drumming and dancing, funeral rites and fishing in the *Fosu* Lagoon located in the middle of the town and nearer to the sea.

The ban on music making, according to tradition, enables the *Omanhen* (paramount chief) and his *Beguafo* (members of his Council of Elders) a break from their courtly activities in order to meditate and concentrate on the impending celebration. It is also the opportune time for the court musicians and the different *Asafo* companies (traditional military groups) to repair all their musical instruments like drums, rattles, animal horns and bells that are used during the celebration.

Oral tradition of Cape Coast states that the ban on fishing "enables the parent tilapia and other species to lay eggs that are fertilized since during this period, they reach their reproductive stage. The ban therefore enforces aquatic agriculture as the fingerlings are given ample time to mature for harvest and consumption".

Knowledge about the environment in traditional societies rests primarily on two distinct factors: ecological curiosity and ecological concern. The former implies the desire for knowledge to explain facts about the environment. Ecological concern deals with commitment of self-feeling to conserve and enrich the environment. One can therefore not agree more with Mazrui and Wagaw (1985) when they admit that African indigenous knowledge leans towards the latter and not the former which European knowledge absolutely focuses on. This is why after many years of neglect following Ghana's colonial experience, it is sad to hear the description of indigenous knowledge about the environment as still "primitive and unscientific".

The Role of '*Sankofa*'

In re-claiming the natural environment from further forms of Western derogatory remarks and human degradation, firstly, there is the need to reconsider the Ghanaian *Akans* societal maxim; *sankofa* - which literally urges us to go back to our roots and pick up from where we have left off or abandoned our cultural heritage. It is obligatory for us as Ghanaians to go back and pick up our folklores from where we left or abandoned them. Before the advent of the Europeans, folklores, served as important cultural tools embedded with forest or environmental conservation principles. It is a universal acknowledgement in African cultures that traditional songs, dances, stories, proverbs, legends, myths, rituals, initiation rites, and artefacts constitute a data bank of indigenous knowledge that is used to satisfy specific needs and purposes of the people and conservation of natural resources for posterity is one of these needs. Owusu and Kwarteng's (op. cit) statement validates the conservation of the environment through folklore when they opine:

> In order to avert imminent danger, the local people devised strategies of conservation mostly shrouded in mystery ... essential environmental resources that were termed sacred lands/forests and groves (some which were sources of rivers) contributed to the sustainable growth of resources and engineered solutions to environmental challenges long before the coming of the whites. They put aside, portions of the land/forests and calling them *kyiridade,* (abhors iron tools), literally meaning no indigene of the community could ever dare

310

to enter that tract of land to harvest flora and fauna or clear a portion for farming or settlement because they believed them to be the abode of the gods and ancestors. A breach of this taboo incurred the wrath of the gods and such culprits were severely punished (p.93).

Indigenous societies in Ghana and elsewhere can also take clue from the Ewe and Akan concept of protecting the upper courses or the entire length of rivers which in most cases, are sources of drinking water to the rural folks. A notable feature about rivers in West Africa is that they swell and overflow their banks during the peak of rainy seasons and dry up during the harmattan season and in this way, prevent the people from using water for their domestic chores.

As a way of preventing rivers from drying up completely, clearing of vegetation along their banks is forbidden because the vegetation cover provides shade that helps to protect the rivers from the direct rays of the sun.

Tackling the Foreign Aid Dependency Syndrome

Delivering a paper on the topic "Overcoming Africa's addiction to foreign aid", Kwakye (2011), a senior economist at the Institute of Economic Affairs in Ghana notes that "aid had not done enough to spur development because most often, donors did not fulfil their pledges. Ghana's dependence on foreign aid comes with costs, and foreign aid resources have not matched the country's development needs particularly relating to building physical and human capital." With such high dependence on foreign aid and increase in annual debt, one cannot agree more with Nartey, (2004:1) who in a paper titled 'Stop the foreign aid dependency", states:

> For decades, foreign donor-countries and agencies pampered us with their financial aids, grants and loans without demanding that we meet our minimum national productivity targets or even put or disorderly fiscal policy in order. Thus, creating an addiction in us to the extent that we run out to seek foreign assistance for any project we embark on without

pausing for a moment to consider the outcome to our national image.

As a country endowed with lots of natural resources, it is high time we looked from within to survey and devise strong strategies for harnessing the country's resources properly to meet the economic demands of the people instead of jumping all the time from door to the door of international monetary institutions and foreign donors for assistance.

Attitudinal change by Leaders and Citizens

After close to six decades of self-rule in Ghana, the socio-economic situation in the country has grown no better. These years of self-rule is long a time enough to be able to turn things around. If successive ruling governments are unable to do so, then it is unjustifiable for them to continue passing the buck. (Amlor and Alidza, 2012:22).

It is high time policy makers/implementers, and indeed the entire citizenry of Ghana developed a change of attitude and look from within and devise African-focused social, political and economic strategies to solving problems instead of depending all the time on assistance from foreign donor countries.

Economic volatility seems to have become the norm in Ghana, and achieving inclusive growth is a big challenge that warrants sustained transformational leadership-targeted actions to generate policy solutions that can drive forward the economic growth of the country. Leaders should take bold economic reforms, aimed at sustaining growth and boosting human development. Policy-makers must be tasked to create diversified economies, (both foreign and local) that would be capable of generating employment and growth.

The Role of Good Governance

It is incumbent on leaders of ruling governments in the country and elsewhere in Africa to be aware of the fact that ensuring a sound socio-economic welfare of their citizens largely depends on the promotion and judicious use of indigenous knowledge and practices of the people through good governance. Good governance as analysed by United Nations Economic and Social

Commission for Asia and the Pacific (2014), is participatory, consensus oriented, accountable, transparent, responsive, effective and efficient, equitable and inclusive and follows the rule of law. It ensures that corruption is minimised, the views of the minority are taken into account and that the voices of the most vulnerable in society are heard in decision-making. Good governance is also responsive to the present and future needs of society.

In carrying out the above obligations, I also urge the government, private corporate bodies, companies, international bodies like the UN, UNESCO, FAO, UNESCO, Chiefs and their elders, Church leaders and NGOs as well as benevolent individuals, to jointly help in carrying out the following duties in order to promote, shape and transform our indigenous knowledge systems into a lasting socio-economic benefit to Ghanaians and their children yet unborn:

i. Modern ICT should be used for direct exchange of indigenous knowledge within and between communities.

ii Intellectual property rights of indigenous knowledge should be discussed by foreign companies and stake holders in the local communities so as to reach amicable and satisfactory agreements between the parties involved.

iii. Recording and documenting of information must include audio-visual technology, taped narrations or drawings.

iv. There should be transfer of indigenous knowledge to test its potency in new environments in terms of its economic and technical feasibility.

The Role of the Media

According to Voelker (1975:22), an important technological force that we can reckon with in our societies presently, is the power of the mass media (both print and electronic). They provide information, entertainment and, as well, have persuasive powers that are capable of effecting practical changes. For this reason, the role of the mass media in the promotion and development of the culture of a people cannot be underestimated.

When we talk about the media in promoting development, it simply refers to the steps that the media takes to encourage people to accept and practice changes in their attitudes and behaviours. To give adequate and meaningful promotion to our cultural heritage, the media must commit itself to carrying out the following responsibilities:

i.   To help promote indigenous knowledge by being culturally oriented in their programmes put out for public consumption. They should take note of the societies in which they are located and provide education on their culture, how it can be assimilated and at the same time, encourage them on the need to eschew negative or undesirable cultural practices that are inimical to the dictates of the societal values.

ii.   To encourage people through the power of radio or television, to participate intelligently and meaningfully in matters which affect their lives, culture and the environment.

iii. To help promote culture by accentuating indigenous values that continuously unite or bind us together as one people and as much as possible, avoiding unsavoury statements that can brew hatred and division and break the society apart.

Conclusion

Ghanaians generally acknowledge the fact that the greatest wrong which the departing colonialists inflicted on them, perhaps, and which they now continue to inflict on themselves is their inability to see the merits and use of their indigenous knowledge systems which have been ignored and maligned by Europeans. After attainment of independence, fifty-seven years back, successive governments in Ghana have fallen prey to this derisive behaviour and in this way, put the country into an economically unviable state with no possibility of real development.

What also accounts for this bizarre state of the economy culminating into poor standard of living of majority of Ghanaians is the leadership style of those in authority. Either through inefficiency, fear or lack of political will or pursuing their own selfish agenda, they have woefully failed to address the concerns of the people. There is the need now for a paradigm shift away from those colonial-influenced mentalities to a more pragmatic action to be embarked upon by the government and the entire Ghanaian citizenry to realise the potentials of IK, and use it for sustainable development policies and projects to enhance their socio-economic well-being.

This chapter therefore proposes that, workable modalities for operationalizing IK systems in Ghana's development, in a sustainable manner should be initiated by government and supported by development agents like Corporate Body Organizations, NGOs, donors, academic educators, local leaders, and private sector initiatives to constantly interact with Ghanaian local communities to recognize, and value the worth of this knowledge. In this regard, the role of higher education and intellectuals in influencing the direction towards a more culture-specific or culturally related school curriculum is very critical. I, therefore, agree with Vilakari (1999:206) when he argues that "Africa needs to formulate and implement policies which would ....initiate agricultural revolution, to adequately feed her millions of people and lay a foundation for industrialization and modernization".

To realise this goal as partners in pursuit of harnessing knowledge potentials of IK for sustainable development of Ghana, perhaps, we should ponder over Flavier et al.'s (1999:482) Credo of Rural Reconstruction which states: "Go to the people, live among the people, learn from the people, plan with the people, work with the people, start with what the people know, build on what the people have, teach by showing and learn by doing".

References

Adedeji, S.O. 2002. Effect of acculturation on traditional African music: Ifa music of the Yoruba as a case study. In *Asia Journal of Theology*, 16(1) 29-35.

Alidza, M.Q. 2010. The repository of indigenous knowledge: Re-focusing scholarship on African Cultural Practices in D.D. Kuupole and D. Botchway (ed.) *Polishing the Pearls of Ancient Wisdom*. University of Cape Coast Printing Press, Cape Coast.

Amlor, M.Q. and Alidza, M.Q. 2012.Searching and picking the rotten grain from within: Conflicts as barriers of Africa's development. In *World Scholars' International Journal of DevelopingSocieties, Vol.1, No. 1 pp. 20-26.*

Andaman Chronicle, 2013.Hazardous health effects of chemical fertilisers and pesticides. Available at<http://www.andamanchronicle.net>(Retrieved: 13November 2014).

Apusigah, A.A 2011.Indigenous knowledge, cultural values and sustainable development. In Africa. Paper Delivered at the 2nd Annual Ibadan Sustainable Development Summit in Nigeria.

Boahen, A1962.*Topics in West African history.* London: Longmans.

Boon, E.K. and Eyong, C.T. 2005. History and civilisations: Impacts on sustainable development in Africa in *Regional Sustainable Development Review: Africa,* Oxford: EolssPublishers.Available   at <http://www.eolss.net>(Retrieved: 20 October 2014).

Brock Untne 2000.*Whose education for all? Recolonisation of the African mind.* New York. Falber Press.

Brundlandt Commission,1987.*Our common future*: The World Commission on Environment and Development. Oxford: Oxford University Press.

Darkwa, A. 1974. Musical traditions in Ghana, Unpublished PhD Dissertation, Wesleyan University, Middletown, Connecticut.

Flavier, J.M, De Jesus, A, and Mavarro, S. 1999. Regional programme for the promotion of indigenous knowledge in Asia in: D.M. Warren, L.J Slikkeveer, and D Brokensha, (eds.) *The Cultural Dimension of Development: Indigenous Knowledge Systems.* London: SRP, Exeter.

Ghana Web, n.d. 'The country of Ghana'. Available at: http://www.ghanaweb.com/Ghana   Home Page/country_information. Retrieved: 14 November, 2014.

Hutchful, E. 2002.*Ghana's adjustment experience: The paradox of reform.* Accra: Woeli Publishing Services. Accra.

ICSU, 2002. Science and traditional knowledge, Report from ICSU Study Group. Available at http://www.icsu.org/science - traditional knowledge.(Retrieved: 6November, 2914).

Kwakye, K. 2011.Overcoming Africa's addiction to foreign aid.Available   at

http:/www.ghanaweb.com/GhanaHomePage/NewsArchive.
Retrieved: 27September2014)

Kwarteng, K.O. 2009. The Gold Coast ivory exports during the colonial era, 1875-1932. In
Drumspeak, International Journal of Research in Humanities, Vol. 2(2), pp. 120, Cape Coast University. Press, Cape Coast.

Leith, J.C. 1996.*Ghana structural adjustment experience.*ICS Publication.

Maison, K.B. 2010. The re-emergence of ananse: Re-inventing African Universities through indigenous knowledge systems. In D.D. Kuupole and D. Botchway (ed.) *Polishing the pearls of ancient wisdom.* University of Cape Coast Printing Press. Cape Coast.

Maila, M.W. and Loubser, C.P.2003. Emancipatory indigenous knowledge systems: Implications for environmental education in South Africa. In *South African Journal of Education, Vol.* 23(4)276-280.

Mazrui, A.A. and Wagaw, T. 1985. Towards decolonising modernity: Education and culture conflict in eastern Africa. *The Educational Process and Historiography in Africa,* France: UNESCO.

Nartey, R. 2004.Stop the foreign aid dependency: It's hurting our image abroad. Available at http://www.modernghana.com. (Retrieved: 5 October 2014)

Noyoo, N. 2007. Indigenous knowledge systems and their relevance for sustainable development: A case study of Southern Africa. In *Journal of Tribes and Tribals, Vol. 1, (167-172).*

Nsiah-Gyabaah, K. 2003.Urbanization, environmental degradation and food security in Africa. Paper prepared for poster presentation at the Open Meeting of the Global Environmental Change Research Community, Montreal, Canada. Available at http//sedac.ciesin.columbia.edu/ openmtg/docs/Nsiah-Gyabaah.pdf. (Retrieved:5October 2014).

Ntuli, P. 1999. The missing link between culture and education: Are we still chasing gods that are not our own? In M.W Makgoba. (ed.) 1999. *African Renaissance.* Cape Town, Mafube-Tafelberg.

Nzewi, M.1985.Features of musical practice in Nigerian societies. In E. Ihekweazu (ed.) 1985. *Traditional and modern culture: Readings in African humanities.* Fourth Dimension Publishers Ltd. Enugu.

Onabajo, F. 2005. Promoting indigenous culture and community life through the mass media. In *Journal of Studies of Tribes Tribals, 3(2): 93-98*, ISSN 0972-639X. Kamla-Raj Enterprises.

Odora-Hoppers, C. A. 2008.Culture, indigenous knowledge systems and sustainable development: A critical view of education in an African context. In *International Journal of Educational Development. Vol 29(2)140-148.*

Owusu, A.S. and Kwarteng, K.O. 2010. The despirados: A study of local knowledge and forest culture in development agenda of Ghana. In D.D. Kuupole and D. Botchway (ed.) *Polishing the Pearls of Ancient Wisdom.* University of Cape Coast Printing Press. Cape Coast.

Polikanov, D and Abranova, I.2003. Africa and ICTs: A chance for breakthrough? In *Information, Communication and Society, Vol. 6(1).*

Sakyi, K.A. 2012.Role of science and technology in development in Ghana. Available at http://www.ghanaweb.com. (Retrieved: 6November 2014).

Sarpong, P.K 2005. Cultural values and discipline: Character formation. Paper presented a National conference on culture & education, Elmina Beach Hotel, Central Region, Ghana.

Semali, L. 1999. Community as a classroom: Dilemmas of valuing African indigenous literacy education. In *International Review of Education*, 45 (3-4), 305-319.

United Nations Economic and Social Commission for Asia and Pacific, 2014.Available at http://www.unescap.org.(Retrieved: 8November 2014)

Vilakari, H.W 1999. The problem of African universities in W.W Makgoba (ed.) *African Renaissance.* Cape Town Mafube - Tafalberg.

Warren, D.M. 1991. Using indigenous knowledge in agricultural development. World Bank Discussion Paper No. 127. Washington D.C. The World Bank.

World Bank, 1997.Knowledge and skills for the information age.1st Meeting of the Mediterranean Development Forum; Mediterranean Development Forum.

Zulu, I.M. 2006.Critical indigenous African education and knowledge. In *The Journal of Pan African Studies, Vol. 1(3).*